Prophet al-Khiḍr

Prophet al-Khiḍr

Between the Qur'anic Text and Islamic Contexts

Irfan A. Omar

LEXINGTON BOOKS
Lanham • Boulder • New York • London

Published by Lexington Books
An imprint of The Rowman & Littlefield Publishing Group, Inc.
4501 Forbes Boulevard, Suite 200, Lanham, Maryland 20706
www.rowman.com

86-90 Paul Street, London EC2A 4NE

British Library Cataloguing in Publication information available

Library of Congress Cataloging-in-Publication Data available

ISBN 9781498595919 (hardcover) | ISBN 9781498595933 (paper) | ISBN 9781498595919 (epub)

In memory of my parents,
Najma & Anis
اللهم احفظهما تحت ظل عرشك
Allāhumma aḥfiẓhumā taḥt ẓill-i ʻarshik
For
Chen Xue Zhu
aka Farah

Contents

Preface ix

Acknowledgments xi

Note on Transliteration xiii

Introduction 1

Chapter 1: The Origins and Meanings of the Khiḍr Story 15

Chapter 2: Khiḍr in Muslim Sources and Traditions of Piety 35

Chapter 3: Khiḍr in Sufism 57

Chapter 4: Khiḍr in Folklore 79

Chapter 5: Khiḍr in Muḥammad Iqbāl's Poetry 103

Conclusion 117

Works Cited 123

Index 135

About the Author 141

Preface

This book has been in the making for some years, and it is offered here in its complete form. Some portions of this final version draw upon my previous work published in French as *El-Khaḍir/El-Khiḍr: Le Prophète-Sage dans la tradition musulmane*.[1] The present work contains significantly developed and elaborated argument in favor of recognizing the breadth of the Khiḍr narrative while debating some of the methodological issues not addressed in the French account. It includes analysis of and new discussion on (1) the theological and cultural connections between Khiḍr and older pre-Islamic legends, (2) the presence and impact of the Khiḍr story beyond West and South Asia, and (3) the location and placement of Khiḍr narrative within the "Islamic" as opposed to the Islamicate frame of reference. In effect, this is a different book even though it follows a similar thematic order of presentation as the French.

NOTE

1. Translated by Jean-Pierre Lafouge (Casablanca: La Croisée des Chemins, 2021), 202 pages.

Acknowledgments

The idea to study Khiḍr initially came from Dr. Mahmoud Ayoub as I sat in his graduate seminar on the Qur'ān at the Hartford Seminary. After that first "encounter" with Khiḍr, I continued to pursue the subject for personal interest. I was aided in my understanding by Professors Ibrahim Abu Rabi,' Willem Bijlefeld and David Kerr, also at the Seminary. Since then, I have learned much from other scholars' writings on this topic and some of that learning is reflected in the pages that follow.

I am grateful to Rick Hansen and Daniel Mueller for reading parts of an earlier draft of the book and for providing valuable feedback. I should also like to thank Carolyn Sperl, Veronica Yapriadi, Jakob Rinderknecht, and Jenn Marra for their help with research at various stages of this project. Jean-Pierre Lafouge assisted me in locating and unpacking some of the more difficult-to-grasp sources in French. I am indebted to him for the many conversations we have had over the years on topics of common interest.

Many friends and colleagues contributed in important ways to help me complete this book. I want to especially mention Phillip Naylor, Enaya Othman, and Richard Taylor, my dialogue partners and collaborators at Marquette for a number of years. By being in conversation with them, I have learned to see the study of Islam through a wider, interdisciplinary lens. Others who have been tremendously supportive over the years include Rahim Acar, Mehdi Aminrazavi, Etin Anwar, Gretchen Baumgardt, Deirdre Dempsey, Amir Hussain, Shalahudin Kafrawi, Conor Kelly, Patrick Kennelly, Rajiv Mallikarjun, Robert Masson, Danielle Nussberger, John Renard, Philip Rossi, S.J., Zeki Saritoprak, Jame Schaefer, and John & Bobbie Schmitt. I gratefully acknowledge their help.

I would like to thank Jeanne Hossenlopp, Vice President for Research and Innovation at Marquette for her unwavering support of faculty research. The numerous Faculty Development Awards I received through her office made it possible for me to share my research with scholars at conferences in the United States as well as internationally. I would be remiss if I did not acknowledge the 2015 Summer Faculty Fellowship from Marquette University which provided the impetus for me to resume working on the manuscript after a considerable gap.

At Lexington Books, I was treated most hospitably, first by Michael Gibson and later his colleague Trevor Crowell. Without their timely guidance this book would have taken far longer to appear in print. I must also thank the anonymous reviewers who offered valuable suggestions to clarify and, in some cases, to expand on issues that helped enhance the arguments and proposals presented here. All remaining mistakes are my own.

Finally, I am pleased to dedicate this work to Farah, whose patience during the time I worked on this book remained far more stable than mine.

Note on Transliteration

Foreign terms transliterated into Roman script from Arabic, Urdu, and Farsi are equipped with proper diacritical marks to represent their approximate phonetic representation. This includes words such as the Qur'ān and the *ḥadīth*, however an exception is made for terms commonly used in English and/or those which are anglicized forms of their original such as "quranic," "Sufi," and "Sufism"—these are left without diacritics.

Names of persons and places in Western language publications are presented just as they appear in the original. Similarly, titles and author names in Roman letters are noted as in the original. Those in non-English works have been written with diacritical marks to facilitate a more accurate pronunciation. Hence an author's name may appear differently depending on the language of the publication.

In placing diacritical marks, I have followed the system of Arabic transliteration used by the *Muslim World* journal. For Urdu words I am guided by the style found on Columbia University site, "Urdu Letters, Names and Transliteration," which is accessible at http://www.columbia.edu/~mk2580/urdu_section/handouts/alphabet.pdf

There are some exceptions to the rules noted in the sources above. For example:

- word-final *h* is used regardless of whether it is pronounced, such as in Sūrah. If it is followed by another word as in Sūrat al-Kahf, *h* is replaced with *t.*
- *iẓāfah* is suggested by adding -e (for Farsi) and -i (for Urdu) to the first word in the compound, e.g., *baḥr-e kashtī* and *jām-i zindagī* respectively.
- English rules for capitalization are followed for titles of books in Urdu, Arabic, and Farsi, but only for the first word in the title, e.g., *Bāng-i dara.*

Introduction

Al-Khiḍr is the name given to the legendary figure mentioned in the Qur'ān in Sūrat al-Kahf (18:60–82) only as a "servant of God." These verses are primarily concerned with an allegorical story about Moses' journey in search for a mysterious spiritual person. The reasons offered for Moses' effort vary according to tradition, raising questions concerning genealogy, hierarchy, status, and knowability. The spiritual person is identified in the tradition as al-Khiḍr, "the Green One." Although Moses was not seeking a spiritual master in the traditional Sufi sense, as we have come to know it, he nevertheless expressed an interest in a figure who—according to the master narrative—is known for imparting wisdom. This story is significant for a variety of reasons not least because of the appearance of Moses who is recognized as an influential and important prophet in the Qur'ān. His sudden need to consult and converse with this spiritual figure is out of the ordinary. Interestingly, Moses, as instrumental as he is in implementing divine will in society and upholding the Covenant, is not the main hero in this particular story. Rather, the figure of Moses is being used to point to even higher truths pertaining to the spiritual dimensions of faith. By a wide consensus among scholars, practitioners, and mystics, the Khiḍr story symbolizes these truths by providing a perspective on the tension that exists between materiality and spirituality, the *ẓāhir* (exoteric) and the *bāṭin* (esoteric), and between human and divine forms of knowledge.

The Muslim figure of Khiḍr can be studied from a variety of methodological and analytical perspectives. Indeed, many scholars and believers have looked into the story in search of meanings hidden beneath the metaphors and symbolic references.[1] The quranic story ("Khiḍr—Moses episode") that gives rise to the Khiḍr narrative, and various other textual sources in Muslim tradition where he is mentioned, provide a rich field of study for understanding and interpreting Khiḍr's role and his legendary status. In fact, the quranic story and the attendant exegetical literature have been utilized in the weaving of multiple narratives where Khiḍr plays a major, if not always a central, role. These narratives vary depending on how he is viewed in each of the spheres and disciplines (e.g., Sufistic/spiritual descriptions, symbolic folk storytelling, scriptural exegetical accounts, etc.).

The Khiḍr story is firmly rooted in the textual sources of Islam: namely, the Qur'ān (see the relevant verses quoted below) and the *tafsīr* literature (quranic exegesis or commentary) as well as the *ḥadīth* (the prophetic traditions). Khiḍr appears abundantly in the *Qiṣaṣ al-'anbiyā'*[2] (stories of the prophets) and in Sufi literature. Within the *tafsīr* literature and stories of prophets, Khiḍr acquired a status by virtue of the need to elucidate certain unexplained notions within the quranic passages concerning his meeting with Moses. For example, the Qur'ān speaks of the mysterious person whom Moses seeks as "one of [God's] servants." The Qur'ān does not name this servant which may be providential in that leaving him unnamed sparked the creative imagination of early quranic commentators (*mufassirūn*). For them it became essential to find the most plausible explanation for who this "servant" of God might be, and, since the servant is also said to have received knowledge from God, how he might possibly fit within the prophetology of Islam. Most Qur'ān commentators state that the mysterious person mentioned in Sūrat al-Kahf (chapter 18) verse 65 is none other than Khiḍr. They named him "the Green One" or "the evergreen" (al-Khiḍr) and in doing so affirmed and preserved "his unnamable, unhistorical or suprahistorical, archetypal or folkloristic essence."[3] For Sufis, Khiḍr became a symbol of the higher dimensions of faith and truth, remain hidden from most people. These dimensions are manifest only to the elect (*khāṣṣa*), who by their spiritual excellence and striving (*jihād*) are given a glimpse of these truths.

The idea of Khiḍr is embedded in the Qur'ān where he is referred to as God's "servant" while the name given to him appears in the *tafsīr* literature. Thus in quranic commentaries we find a good deal of discussion concerning Khiḍr's identity while in Sufism he has acquired a multivalent personality. In folk traditions and popular piety, Khiḍr became a household name in many Muslim societies and routinely figures in their cultural and customary practices. Khiḍr is known in every Muslim culture in one way or another; he is part of religious, mystical, and folk traditions of West Asia (the Middle East), South and Southeast Asia, Northern and Sub-Saharan Africa, and many Central Asian countries. Variations in spelling and pronunciations of his name exist such as: al-Khaḍir, al-Khoḍr, Khizr, Khizir, Khizar, Hizir, and Hilir, among others. Although he has many names, one of the earliest pronunciations appears to be "al-Khaḍr" which is perhaps an indication that he was first thought of as having a distinctive quality of making things green. Khiḍr's regenerative qualities connect him with pre-Islamic myths, some of which are assimilated in later stories and legends associated with him. Khiḍr is also seen as a figure who inspires beliefs that put him at the intersection between Islam and other religious traditions. In fact, the Khiḍr phenomenon and its associated traditions have taken up such a huge space within the Islamicate traditions[4] and cultures that it is impossible to do justice to this topic in a single book. What follows is a brief account of some of the literary, religio-cultural, and symbolic aspects concerning the person of Khiḍr. The main questions I address in this book can be located within the religious and spiritual disciplines as well as in the associated sub-disciplines related to myths and what has been described in Sufi studies as "the imaginal world" (*'ālam al-khayāl*). Here I am not interested in historical accounting of the Khiḍr legend or a detailed discussion of hagiographical narratives of Khiḍr circulating among specific groups and sects. Although these are part of the book, they are not central to my examination of the figure of Khiḍr. Instead, the aim is simply to provide an overview of the legacy of the quranic Khiḍr; the expanding roles he assumed as his story[5] became intertwined with other legends; and to showcase a variety of symbolic representations emanating from key characteristics Khiḍr is said to possess.

METHODOLOGY

Analyzing the sacred has not been an easy task. Whenever canonical boundaries are challenged or appear to be violated, the orthodox everywhere feel threatened. The Muslim "mainstream"—also a fluid category in itself—has tolerated, even embraced as we shall see in the pages below, subjective expressions of piety and claims of experiences of the sacred. It would be hard to argue against inexplicable spiritual realities within the context of religious beliefs since the latter belong in that very category. The key problem, as many Sufis themselves have argued, is not that experience of the sacred is impossible or "blasphemous" even, but rather any attempts to describe or explain such to others leads one to that threshold. After all, how else would the sacred manifest if not through the numinous experience, however overwhelming and irrational it may appear to others.[6]

Shahab Ahmed in his ground-breaking work *What Is Islam?* discussed six examples or "expressions" of Islam from Muslim history; expressions that he believes are "quite contrary"[7] to each other. Each of these expressions were/are seen as "normative" by some segment/s of Muslims in one or more places where Muslims have lived. For most of Muslim history many of these expressions have co-existed and even thrived in proximity to each other. This work does not seek to privilege a particular understanding of Islam. Instead, it assumes that there are connections between these various understandings and expressions that have placed them within shared spaces across time and space. The most obvious connection between all the various expressions of Islam is that they are anchored in the text of the Qur'ān and agree on much of the *ḥadīth*. Here we enter into the realm of what Shahab Ahmed calls "meaning-making" process which is largely determined by one's focus and context. In my attempt to unpack the personage and role of Khiḍr, I have sought to examine sources from a variety of vantage points and perspectives. Nevertheless, given that Khiḍr is extensively discussed most notably in fields related to mysticism and popular piety, sources that speak to these areas are examined in greater proportion than the ones dealing with scripture commentaries and with orthodox-leaning, outward (*ẓāhirī*) aspects of faith and tradition. It is tempting to consider what bridges and unites these very different Muslim perspectives, but as I noted above, that task falls outside of the scope of the present work. Still, I have organized my comments below as an attempt to—what Shahab Ahmed calls—"conceptualize and categorize" Khiḍr "*in terms of inclusion [not elimination] of difference*"[8] for Khiḍr is indeed a figure who connects Muslims *through* their differences, vast as they may be.[9]

Religious practice is multi-dimensional and involves "*embodiment, materiality, emotion, aesthetics, moral judgment* " and spirituality.[10] These dimensions intersect in hundred different ways and are situation dependent. The narratives included in this study are a testament to this multi-dimensionality and intersectionality. They show how a figure like Khiḍr has been utilized by Muslims in various ways depending on their own context and location. While Khiḍr is used as a lens to view Islam by many, believers' context and location also determines their view of Islam hence generating countless ways of receiving Khiḍr despite the unifying narratives centered on the quranic story. Indeed, Khiḍr story resonates with all of the dimensions noted above. He raises moral and legal questions by his actions and generates passion and emotion; he is the reason for numerous aesthetic and material representations of faith sometimes blurring religious boundaries as in the case of the shared Christian and Muslim views of Saint George and Khiḍr. In short, Khiḍr symbolizes cultural commonalities, interreligious irregularities, and spiritual possibilities. Khiḍr liberates even as attempts are continually made to constrict him historically, culturally, and exegetically.

PRIMARY TEXTUAL SOURCES: QUR'ĀN 18:60–82 AND RELEVANT *AḤĀDĪTH*

For Muslims, the Qur'ān and the Prophetic traditions, known as the *ḥadīth* are centrally important. Together they form the foundation for the vast and complex tradition that encompasses every aspect of life, and which can help explain Muslims' religio-cultural practices and the dynamics of continuity and change through history. The Qur'ān in the original Arabic is believed by Muslims to be the divine word communicated to the rest of humanity through Prophet Muḥammad. It is translated in almost every language and the translations are used as an aid for understanding the meanings of the original Arabic. The Qur'ān in Arabic supplies the liturgy used in five daily prayers as well as in formal ritual recitation. If the Qur'ān is central to the faith of a Muslim, the *ḥadīth*, which is next to it in importance, provides keys to the first layer of understanding the Qur'ān. *Ḥadīth* is important to Muslims in determining the meanings of quranic verses. The *ḥadīth* contains the words of Prophet Muḥammad as he explained to his followers what the Qur'ān meant, as well as his actions which for Muslims were aimed at putting the teachings of the Qur'ān into practice so Muslims around him could "experience" the Qur'ān. The Qur'ān and the *ḥadīth* are two of the foundational sources for the *sharī'ah*, also known as "Islamic law" or more appropriately, the guidelines for the practice of faith.

The Qur'ān and the *ḥadīth*—as Muslim scriptures—mediated the construction and development of Islam in history. They, along with numerous interpretations, translations, explanations, and manuals, continue to facilitate how a Muslim's faith is animated and expressed. Thus, one may argue that mediation and facilitation are terms that we must contend with if we are to understand the line that connects divine will expressed in the pages of scriptures with the end product, i.e., actual expressions of faith through prayer, supplication, fasting, empathizing, and everything in between. Indeed, the subjects covered in this book particularly demand such a consideration. Both the Qur'ān and the *ḥadīth* have been utilized to support Sufistic beliefs and in establishing Sufi practices and those related to the veneration of saints. *Ḥadīth* literature provides ample justification of the value of saints (*awliyā'*) and thus also validates the veneration that takes place in their name. A divine saying (*ḥadīth qudsī*) relates the qualities among saints that are to be extolled: *poverty* (which represents freedom from materiality), *prayer* (which represents communication with the divine), and *service to God* (which signifies their involvement in helping individuals find meaning).[11]

Before going any further, it might be fitting to consider the scriptural passages that are foundational for the topic of this book. As already mentioned, the Khiḍr story originates in Sūrat al-Kahf (chapter 18 of the Qur'ān) verses 60–82, apparently as a spiritual lesson on divine mysteries and in order to grasp the limitations of human understanding. This Sūrah includes three other stories that equally lend themselves to mystical and "mythical" interpretations. According to Arkoun as an interpreter, one feels the greatest need for *ijtihād* (intellectual reasoning) and of *ta'wīl* (mystical approach to exegesis) when encountering the stories in this chapter.[12] The first of these stories is about *asḥāb al-kahf* or "people of the cave" who were a group of believers who went into hiding in a cave to escape persecution. The story has a happy ending as the group awoke from a three-hundred-year-long sleep only to find that the city dwellers had turned believers. The second story is that of two men with different fortunes and it ends with the rich man losing his wealth due to his material pride. The third story is that of Moses (Mūsa) and Khiḍr and the fourth that of Dhu'l Qarnayn, a pious king who was blessed with material means to promote righteous justice on earth who taught that humility is the greatest resource one can have in this life. Each story is a parable about temptations and trials and how best to face them. Since the focus here is on Khiḍr, I have reproduced the verses in question below before discussing the various ways of receiving them and the "meaning-making" process among Muslims.

Sūrat al-Kahf, 18:60–82: Moses' Journey in Search of a Servant of God

18:60. Moses said to his attendant: "I will not rest until I reach the place where the two seas meet, even if it takes me years!"

61. But when they reached the place where the two seas meet, they had forgotten all about their fish, which made its way into the sea and swam away.

62. They journeyed on, and then Moses said to his attendant: "Give us our meal! This journey of ours is very tiring."

63. And [the attendant] said: "Remember when we were resting by the rock? I forgot [about] the fish—Satan made me forget to pay attention to it—and it [must have] made its way into the sea.' 'How strange!"

64. Moses said: "That was the place we were seeking." So the two turned back, retraced their footsteps.

65. And [they] found one of Our servants—a man to whom We had granted Our mercy and whom We had given knowledge of Our own [presence].

66. Moses said to him: "May I follow you so that you can teach me some of the right guidance [or higher truths] you have been taught?"

67. The man said: "You will not be able to bear with me patiently."

68. "How could you be patient in matters beyond your comprehension?"

69. Moses said: "God willing, you will find me patient. I will not disobey you in the slightest."

70. The man said: "If you follow me then, do not ask me questions about anything I do until I mention it to you myself."

71. They traveled on. Then, when they got into a boat, and the man made a hole in it, Moses said: "How could you make a hole in it? Do you want to drown its passengers? What a strange thing to do!"

72. He replied: "Did I not tell you that you would not be able to bear with me patiently?"

73. Moses said: "Forgive me for forgetting. Do not make it too hard for me to follow you."
74. And so they travelled on. Then, when they met a young boy, and the man killed him, Moses said: "How could you kill an innocent person? He has not killed anyone! What a terrible thing to do!"
75. He replied: "Did I not tell you that you would not be able to bear with me patiently?"
76. Moses said: "From now on, if I ask you about anything you do, banish me from your company—you have tolerated enough from me."
77. And so they journeyed on. Then, when they came to a town and asked the inhabitants for food but were refused hospitality, they saw a wall there that was on the point of falling down and the man repaired it. Moses said: "But if you had wished you could have taken payment for doing that."
78. He said: "This is where you and I part company. I will [now] tell you the meaning of the things about which you were impatient."
79. "[As for] the boat [it] belonged to some needy people who made their living from the sea and I damaged it because I knew that coming after them was a king who was seizing every [serviceable] boat by force."
80. "[As for] the young boy [he] had parents who were people of faith, and so, fearing he would trouble them through wickedness and disbelief."
81. "We desired that in his place their Lord should give them another child—better in purity and in compassion."
82. "[As for] the wall [it] belonged to two young orphans in the town and there was a buried treasure beneath it belonging to them. Their father had been a righteous man, so your Lord intended them to reach maturity and then dig up their treasure as a mercy from your Lord. I did not do [these things] of my own accord: these are the explanations for those things about which you were impatient."[13]

Relevant *Aḥādīth* (pl. of *ḥadīth*)

Apart from the apparent meaning of these quranic passages it is important to consider how these verses were understood by many early Muslims. The Muslim interpreters' understanding of the Qur'ān was primarily aided by the narrations of the *ḥadīth* (the reports of what Prophet Muḥammad said) which elaborated on the meaning of the verses in question. In conjunction with the *ḥadīth* another literary genre was deemed essential in the process of exegesis, known as the occasion of revelation (*asbāb al-nuzūl*) which described in some detail when and where did each particular verse (or set of verses) was revealed; what was Prophet Muḥammad—the recipient of the revelation—was doing at the time; and what were his responses to the message therein.[14]

Here is a key *ḥadīth* related to the quranic passages on the encounter between Moses and Khiḍr.

> Ubayy ibn Ka'b [said] that the Prophet, peace be upon him, said: "Once Moses stood up and addressed Banū Isra'īl. He was asked who was the most learned man in the world. He said: 'I am.' God admonished him . . . [and] said to him: 'Yes, at the junction of the two seas there is a worshipper of mine who is more learned than you.' Moses said: 'O my Lord! How can I meet him?' God said: 'Take a fish and put it in a large basket and you will find him at the place where will lose the fish.' Moses took a fish and put it in a basket and proceeded along with his attendant, Yūsha bin Nūn, till they reached the rock where they laid down. Moses slept, and the fish moving out of the basket, fell into the sea. It took its way in the sea straight as in a tunnel. . . . They travelled through the night and the next day Moses said to his attendant: 'Give us our food, for we have suffered much fatigue due to our journey.' The attendant replied: Do you know that when we rested near the rock, I forgot [to tell you] about the fish, and none but Shaytān [Satan] made me forget, and the fish found its way into the sea in some wonderous way." So there was a path [visible] for the fish which astounded them. Moses said: "That was exactly what we were seeking." So both of them retraced their steps till the they reached the rock. There they saw a man lying and covered with a garment.[15]

This *ḥadīth* provides background information regarding the events that led up to the meeting. Moses' attendant (Q. 18:60) is identified in the *ḥadīth* as Yūsha' bin Nūn (Joshua). He plays an important role in providing a framework for weaving the story. It is Joshua and not Moses who is fitted with the tasks of forgetting and losing the fish. Moses as a prophet of rank could not be tempted by Satan hence the use of the attendant. Interestingly, Nūn could mean "fish" while fish signifies knowledge, suggesting that Moses as a prophet had the potential of spiritual knowledge that he was to seek out from Khiḍr once they met. There are other apparently insignificant motifs such as divine admonishing, water of life, dying and coming alive of the fish (Q. 18:61), forgetting, amazement, the rock (Q. 18:63), retracing steps back on the path (Q. 18:64), etc., however, each of these play a role in meaning making. I will return to some of these in the pages that follow. A second, related account addresses the most important part of the story—the dialogue between Moses and Khiḍr:

> Moses greeted [Khiḍr] . . . [and] said: "I am Moses." [Khiḍr] asked: "Moses of Banī Isrā'īl?" Moses said: "yes, I have come to you so you may teach me from those things that God has taught you." [Khiḍr] said: "O Moses! I have some of the knowledge of God which God has taught me and which you do not know, you have some of the knowledge of God that God has taught you and which I do not know." Moses asked: "May I follow you?" [Khiḍr] said: "But you will not

> be able to remain patient with me, for how can you be patient concerning things that you will not be able to understand?" Moses said: "You will find me . . . absolutely patient and I will not disobey you."
>
> So they both set out and walked along the shoreline. A boat passed by and they asked if the crew would take them on board. The crew recognized Khiḍr and they took them on board free of charge. When they were on the boat, a bird came and sat on the edge of the boat and dipped its beak once or twice into the sea. Khidr said to Moses: "O Moses! My knowledge and your knowledge combined does not take away from God's knowledge except as much as this bird has decreased the water of the sea with its beak." Then suddenly Khiḍr took an axe and pulled one of the planks. Moses did not notice this until later. Moses said to him: "What have you done? They took us on board without charge and yet you have intentionally made a hole in their boat. Surely, you have done a terrible thing." Khiḍr replied: "Did I not tell you that you would not be able to remain patient with me?" Moses replied: "Do not blame me for my forgetting, and do not be harsh on me for this mistake." The first excuse of Moses was that he had forgotten the promise he made.
>
> When they had left the sea, they passed by a boy playing with his friends. Khiḍr took a hold of the boy's head and plucked it with his fingers as if he were plucking some fruit. Moses said to him: "Have you killed an innocent person who has not killed any? You have really done a horrible thing." Khiḍr said: "Did I not tell you that you could not remain patient with me?" Moses said: "If I ask you about anything after this, do not accompany me."

This—second of the three events—appears to be a bit more intense, legally speaking, as it involved taking life of an innocent person. Understandably this must have been the most difficult one for Moses to accept given his reputation as a "lawgiver." The themes emerging here include knowledge of God being given to some human beings and yet the comparative minuteness of that knowledge in relation to divine knowledge, the boat, discipleship, intentionality, apology, and taking of life and the response to it based in religious law. As the narrative continues in the next passage it highlights the theme of patience and that there are different forms of knowledge thus a true seeker's journey never ends:

> Then both of them went on till they saw some people in a village and they asked if they can have some food but the villagers refused to entertain them as guests. Then they saw a wall which was about to collapse and Khiḍr repaired it just by touching it with his hands. Moses said: "These are the people who did not give us food, nor entertained us as guests, yet you have repaired their wall. If you had wished, you could have taken wages for it." Khiḍr said: "This is the parting between you and me and I shall tell you the explanation of those things about which you could not remain patient." The Prophet, peace be upon him, added:

> "We wish that Moses could have remained patient by virtue of which God might have told us more about their story."[16]

These passages, constituting as primary sources for the Muslim tradition, provide several insights into the quranic and the Orthodox Muslim worldviews; they offer teachable moments about knowledge, knowability, and the unknown. As I hope it will become evident in the discussion that follows, Khiḍr's story speaks to many dimensions of the human condition. It highlights the limitations of human knowledge; underscores the need for patience and of being inquisitive; it offers a variety of understandings of divine providence and of the esoteric dimensions of faith. It reveals the dynamics of master-disciple relationships and suggests new ways of understanding divine justice and divine presence. The Khiḍr story is particularly relevant in that it sheds light on the important role of interpretation which is instrumental in how we receive and entertain notions such as "truth" and "reality."

This book aims to provide an account of Khiḍr's role and symbolism from a wider perspective than to merely lay out a theological explanation based on Qur'ān commentaries. It seeks to locate Khiḍr within the textual and historical context of Islam but does not stop there. The person of Khiḍr is said to have impacted innumerable lives and has enriched a whole host of genres in a variety of disciplines spanning several centuries. The chapters that follow are an attempt to study Khiḍr from this wider view and consider the role, meaning, and symbolism that he represents. It is important to study Khiḍr from all these various viewpoints so as to understand his significance and meaning for this moment, because while "[m]eaning is context-bound . . . context is boundless."[17]

CHAPTER OUTLINES

Chapter 1 provides an overview of the sources for the study of Khiḍr and contextualizes the various narratives associated with this figure. Based on the stories emanating from the primary sources (referenced above), I offer an analysis of the quranic story in light of the narratives from traditional Muslim as well as Western sources. Here I elaborate on the need for studying Khiḍr from a religious studies perspective and discuss relevant methodological tools employed in this work. I also consider the significance of Khiḍr for a critical understanding of Islamic cultures across time and space. This chapter outlines the historical dimension of the legend associated with Khiḍr. I utilized several early writings on Khiḍr that link the origins of the story with ancient legends such as the Alexander Romance and the Epic of Gilgamesh. These studies also aided in formulating a theoretical framework to understand how these earlier legends were "Islamized" in medieval Islam and were integrated to make Khiḍr a household name.

Chapter 2 goes deeper into the Muslim sources to unpack the symbolic representations of Khiḍr. Based on the quranic text, some clarity is sought as to whether Khiḍr is a prophet, a saint or both. The classical reading of theological sources suggests that many scholars were fairly amenable to the idea of recognizing the prophetic status of Khiḍr all the while distinguishing him from the somewhat superior status held by Moses; the latter being a prophet (*nabī*) *and* a messenger (*rasūl*). In trying to reconcile the relationship between Moses and Khiḍr while maintaining Khiḍr's special role in the divine plan, many early Muslim scholars employed creative solutions as will be seen below.

Chapter 3 is concerned with Khiḍr's role in Sufism. It includes an analysis of how Khiḍr as a symbol of sainthood and prophetic wisdom informed organized Sufism since the rise of Sufi orders in the 8th and 9th centuries. While Sufi literature is filled with accounts of Sufis' encounters with Khiḍr, there is very little scholarship on Khiḍr himself. Khiḍr thrives in the writings and practices belonging to organized mystical orders. He appears in the serious literature as well as in popular mythic traditions as a person who is indispensable for seekers and accomplished mystics alike. Khiḍr is often seen as an initiator of individuals into mystical orders and helping their journey on the path. The chapter summarizes some of the celebrated accounts of encounters with Khiḍr and their lasting transformative impact on the individual. Khiḍr is a teacher of many, and the etiquette of master-disciple relationships are important and are often observed with rigor and ritual formalism. Khiḍr, the master-teacher, is often seen as a conduit for divine light (*al-nūr*). Following Khiḍr and being initiated by him may enable the seeker to attain the illumination of the soul allowing the knowledge of the divine to enter one's heart. This chapter offers a glimpse of the process of sacralization of place and person through the appropriation of tropes associated with the person of Khiḍr.

Chapter 4 examines Khiḍr's designation as being a "shared saint" known through many names and appellations. Here I present symbolic meanings of the story of Khiḍr as they are received in mythical and folk traditions. In parts of the world, he is revered by both Muslim and Christian practitioners although thought of and invoked by different names. This is particularly true among Palestinian Christian and Muslim communities who often see the figures of al-Khiḍr and Mar Jiryis (Saint George) as one and the same. The sharing of saints, shrines, and in some cases even festivals and forms of "worship," associated with these figures has been, historically speaking, a major factor in preserving neighborly relations and peaceful co-existence of Muslims and Christians in many parts of the Middle East and Turkey. Similarly, Khiḍr has been remembered in South Asia by fishermen and sailors as their guardian angel, as it were. He appears to be immortal by virtue of his heroic powers enshrined in folk traditions and literary works alike. Like in the stories originating in the Arab Middle East, Khiḍr's religio-mystical persona is sometimes exaggerated in non-Arab cultures projecting him as a kind of superhero capable of magical feats beyond human capabilities. This chapter includes a variety of manifestations of the Khiḍr legend in select South and Southeast Asian Muslim cultures.

Chapter 5 is a study of Khiḍr as seen through the eyes of the poet-philosopher, Muḥammad Iqbāl. If the mythic images of Khiḍr in folk literature attest to his immortality, the poetic descriptions help to seal that impression. Khiḍr appears in the collections by major poets and mystics such as Rūmī and Ḥāfiz and is often depicted as an exemplary spiritual actor with supernatural qualities. In Iqbāl, Khiḍr is a pre-eminent guide who helps anyone in need. Khiḍr imagery is richly laden with symbolism and communicates the idea of divine help for those who strive on the path, which in Iqbāl leads to self-actualization or self-hood (*khudī*) in the world, rather than spiritual resignation. This chapter presents the various ways in which Khiḍr is situated in Iqbāl's thought as an immortal guide, a faithful servant of God, and most importantly, as an embodiment of action for the common good.

Khiḍr's story touches many lives and is multifaceted. It has roots in the Qur'ān and the *ḥadīth*, but its branches spread across traditions, cultures, religious beliefs, and time and space. He is as relevant today as he was in the 8th century and all through in between. Insofar as what Khiḍr represents—versatility, empathy, ethical centeredness, and the ever readiness to help others—he is indeed a model for many to emulate. His is a teaching story for anyone who is willing to learn, whether with or without affiliation to faith or a belief system.

NOTES

1. For a brief overview see John Renard, "Khaḍir/Khiḍr," in *Encyclopaedia of the Qur'ān*, ed. Jane Dammen McAuliffe (Washington, DC: Georgetown University), http://dx.doi.org/10.1163/1875-3922_q3_EQSIM_00248, and Irfan A. Omar, "Khiḍr in the Islamic Tradition," *The Muslim World* 83 (July–October 1993): 279–94. For Khiḍr in the Qur'ān and *tafsīr* literature see the following: 'Ala al-Dīn 'Alī ibn Muḥammad al-Khāzin al-Baghdādī, *Tafsīr al-Khāzin: al-musamma' lubāb al-ta'wīl fī ma'ānī al-tanzīl* (Bayrūt: Dār al-Ma'rifah, n.d.); Sultān Ḥasan, *'Irfān al-Qur'ān* (Agra: Maktaba 'Irfān, n.d.); Abū'l Qāsim Maḥmūd al-Zamakhsharī, *Al-Kashshāf 'an ḥaqā'iq ghwāmiḍ al-tanzīl wa 'uyūn al-aqāwīl fī wujūh al-ta'wīl* (Beirut: Dār al-Kutub al-'Ilmīyah, 1995) and other Qur'ān commentaries from classical and modern periods. For religio-cultural aspects of the Khiḍr story see Françoise

Aubaile-Sallenave, "Al-Khiḍr, 'L'homme au manteau vert' en pays musulmans: ses fonctions, ses caractères, sa diffusion," *Res Orientales* 14 (2002): 11–35.

2. *Qiṣaṣ al-'anbiyā'* refers to a popular genre in Islamic literature and contains stories and hagiographical accounts of the prophets' lives and teachings. It is closely linked with the tradition of writing commentaries of Qur'ān. Since the quranic commentaries necessitated expounding on the notions and topics noted in the Qur'ān, the exegete often relied on the *hadīth* as well as on Jewish and Christian sources at their disposal. See Isḥāq ibn Ibrāhīm al-Nishabūrī, *Qeṣaṣ ol-anbiyā'*, ed. Ḥabīb Yaghmāyī (Tehran: Intishārāt-e Bungāh-e-Tarjumah va Nashr-e Kitāb, 1961); and Wheeler M. Thackston, trans., *The Tales of the Prophets of al-Kisā'ī*. (Boston: Twayne Publishers, 1978). This genre developed in the Muslim world between the ninth and eleventh centuries as a helpful resource for elaborating on the brief quranic mentions of or references to various prophets and messengers common to all three Abrahamic religions. Its sources are said to include pre-Islamic Jewish and Christian literature on themes and figures that appear in the Qur'ān. See David Sidersky, *Les Origines des Legends Musulmanes dans le Coran et dans les vies des Prophetes* (Paris: P. Geuthner, 1933); and William Brinner, "Prophets and Prophecy in the Islamic and Jewish Traditions," in *Studies in Islamic and Judaic Traditions II*, ed. William M. Brinner and Stephen D. Ricks (Atlanta: Scholars Press, 1989).

3. Norman Brown, "The Apocalypse of Islam," in *The Apocalypse and/or Metamorphosis* (Berkeley: University of California Press, 1991), 82.

4. Islamicate is a comprehensive term that embraces the variety and richness of Islam and Muslim civilizations generated since the rise of Muslim empires in the 8th century. The term was first introduced by the noted scholar of Islam Marshall Hodgson. He viewed it as something referring not only to the religion of Islam but also and perhaps more importantly "to the social and cultural complex historically associated with Islam and the Muslims, both among Muslims themselves and even when found among non-Muslims." Marshall G. S. Hodgson, *The Venture of Islam: Conscience and History in World Civilization* (Chicago: University of Chicago Press, 1974), 1:59. Shahab Ahmed has argued against Hodgson's logic making the case that all such phenomena should simply be referred to as "Islamic." See his *What is Islam? The Importance of Being Islamic* (Princeton: Princeton University Press, 2015), 157 and 444–49 especially note 89.

5. There are various ways to refer to the story of Khiḍr: "Khiḍr-Moses episode" refers to the basic quranic narrative. "Khiḍr story" and "Khiḍr legend" (sometimes used interchangeably) are terms that describe how the narrative was later developed by exegetes, interpreters, hagiographers, biographers, and (literally) storytellers in various Muslim cultures. "Story" is arguably a better word than "legend" to refer to the quranic narrative although some scholars do not see the difference. If the story of Khiḍr as told by the earliest Qur'ān interpreters uses extracanonical sources (mainly belonging to the Christian and Jewish traditions) the legends followed no singular pattern and were often embellished using folk traditions from various cultures.

6. Mircea Eliade, *The Sacred and the Profane: The Nature of Religion*, trans. Willard R. Trask (New York: Harcourt 1959), 99.

7. Shahab Ahmed, *What is Islam?*, 102.

8. Ibid., 302.

9. Ibid. Ahmed seems to suggest that internal differences do not necessarily imply plurality of "islams" but rather the dynamism of Islam allows for contradictions to co-exist and still be considered a "*single thing*." Ahmed cites Clifford Geertz (*Islam Observed: Religious Development in Morocco and Indonesia* [New Haven: Yale University Press, 1968], 55) as evidence for the idea of such unity despite the differences.

10. Nancy Tatom Ammerman, *Studying Lived Religion: Contexts and Practices* (New York: New York University Press, 2021), 8.

11. This *ḥadīth* is part of al-Tirmidhi, cited in Albertus Bagus Laksana, *Muslim and Catholic Pilgrimage Practices: Explorations Through Java* (Burlington: Ashgate, 2014), 16.

12.Mohammed Arkoun, *Lectures du Coran* (Paris: Albin Michel, 2016), chap. 4, 143–70.

13. English translation by M.A.S. Abdel Haleem, *The Qur'an* (New York: Oxford University Press, 2004), slightly modified.

14. For more on this see Ahmad von Denffer, *'Ulūm al-Qur'ān: An Introduction to the Sciences of the Qur'ān* (Markfield, UK: The Islamic Foundation, 1994), 68–78.

15. Abū al-Fidā' Ismā'īl Ibn Kathīr al-Damishqī, *Qiṣaṣ al-'anbiyā': Qur'ān-o ahādith-i ṣaḥiḥa kī roshnī mēṅ*, extracted from *al-Bidāya wa-l nihāya*, ed. and trans. 'Aṭāullah Sājid (Lahore: Dār al-Salām, n. d.), 539–40.

16. Ibid.

17. Jonathan Culler, *Literary Theory: A Very Short Introduction* (Oxford: Oxford University Press, 2011), 68.

Chapter 1

The Origins and Meanings of the Khiḍr Story

The passages from the Qur'ān and the *ḥadīth* (noted in the Introduction) that inspired the story of Khiḍr try to communicate an allegorical story about Moses—an influential and important prophet in the Qur'ān—and his meeting with a mysterious spiritual person, later identified as al-Khiḍr "the Green one."[1] Islamic normative tradition offers an explanation for this meeting. God wanted to prove to Moses that there is someone more knowledgeable than him (Moses) in the world[2] in order for Moses to gain some perspective. This is one way it has been explained in the exegetical (*tafsīr*) literature. The quranic narrative includes—among other things—Moses witnessing three acts by Khiḍr which the former finds reprehensible in that they seem to violate the law. It all began when Moses sought out Khiḍr and eventually found him at "the meeting place of the two oceans" (*majma'al-baḥrayn*). In some accounts, embellished no doubt to fill the curiosity gap, when Moses and his companion first came upon Khiḍr, they found him lying on a green cloth on the surface of the ocean.[3] Moses greeted Khiḍr and expressed his wish to accompany him. The journey takes them through three distinct situations. In each, Khiḍr's actions seemed to contradict the ethical norms subscribed to by Moses. Khiḍr's first such act was to damage the very boat which carried them across a body of water. It would appear that instead of being grateful to the owner he was being unkind. The second act was apparently even more egregious: Khiḍr killed a young boy who had apparently done nothing wrong. Similarly, the third act was equally bewildering to the law-conscious Moses; it involved Khiḍr taking the time to repair a crumbling wall in a village even though the villagers had been rather inhospitable to them. To Moses these acts violated ethical, religious, and customary practices and he questioned Khiḍr about these after each incident. On the third occasion, Khiḍr said to Moses that since, despite several promises, Moses was not able to keep to his word and remain patient, he no longer may travel alongside Khiḍr. But before parting, Khiḍr shared his reasons for the three seemingly unlawful actions. The quranic story is clear in stating that Khiḍr begins by saying that these actions of his were based on direct instructions from God.[4] The boat was about to be unjustly seized by the cruel ruler of the region but because of the damage it would be spared, and the owner will only have to repair it to make it fully functioning again. The second action was in a class by itself. The boy whom Khiḍr killed was going to make life miserable for his pious parents and God wished to spare them the pain and suffering. In other words, the benefits of that boy being dead were greater than him being alive. The act of killing, according to Ibn Kathīr, is not permissible without a highest level of religious authority and that is the authority of a prophet who receives *waḥy* or revelation from God.[5] The third act was about securing the rights of defenseless children against an avaricious group of people. It was driven by compassion and forgiveness: compassion for the orphans who were vulnerable, and forgiveness for the villagers who were unkind to the travelers. If the wall fell prematurely, the treasure, meant as inheritance for the orphans, would have been usurped by the corrupt villagers. In fact, all three acts of Khiḍr can be seen as symbolic of the availability of divine help for those who are vulnerable to harm at the hands of unjust people. The meeting and the experience turned out to be instructive for Moses but not before revealing the rupture that exists between esoteric and exoteric knowledge.

The main thrust of the quranic story is that the scope of knowledge is so vast that no mortal may lay claim to be truly knowledgeable. Surely, there are individuals who possess some knowledge and to whom God has granted a portion; among them are the prophets (*anbiyā,*' sing. *nabī*) and messengers (sing. *rasūl*) such as Moses, Jesus and Muḥammad. God also gives from his knowledge to those who have traversed the spiritual path (*ṭarīqah*)—these are the so-called "friends of God" (*awliyā,*' sing. *walī*) or the saints,[6] who have attained *ma'rifah* (knowledge of God, or of the spiritual, "hidden" world, *al-"ālam al-ghayb*). They have received this knowledge because of their exceptional rigor in the path of God and their piety, and because God grants knowledge and wisdom "to whomever He will" (Q. 2:269a). Khiḍr is indeed such a person known in the Qur'ān only as "one of Our [i.e., God's] servants—a man to whom [God] had granted [divine] Mercy and whom [God] had given knowledge" (Q. 18:65). In fact, Moses' objections were predicted by Khiḍr even at the beginning of the narrative when the former asks permission to accompany him. Khiḍr said to Moses "how could you be patient with me when you have no knowledge of the things I would do." Moses was confident he would be able to stay calm, but as the quranic story reveals, that was not the case. Thus, Khiḍr was compelled to explain the hidden meanings or mystery behind each act which when seen in their entirety do not seem objectionable. The object of the story seems to be to convey the mysteries and forms of knowledge and the various ways of knowing. While Moses was given the *sharī'ah* or the law (exoteric knowledge), Khiḍr was endowed with *'ilm ladunnī* or the knowledge of the unseen world (esoteric knowledge). This story is sometimes presented as evidence of Khiḍr's role as an initiator of Moses into the realm of esoteric knowledge[7] thus being a strong indicator of Khiḍr's status as a prophet.[8]

The main message and symbolism of the Moses-Khiḍr encounter is that divine knowledge may be received in the form of "law" or revelation (as Moses did) or as mystical, intuitive knowledge (as was given to Khiḍr). These two forms of knowledge are complementary, and neither is above the other. This is stated to be the reason for Moses' journey in search of the mysterious servant of God (Khiḍr) in order for Moses to learn something in addition to the knowledge he already received from God as a prophet.[9] For Sufis, this is not a difficult concept. As Shahzad Bashir notes, "[m]astery and discipleship are roles that could be occupied by the same person, depending on who he or she was confronting: great masters remained disciples in front of their own masters no matter how many others saw them as masters."[10] However, not all exegetes and scholars are convinced that Khiḍr and Moses are substantially equal in rank and status. Some Muslim theologians have argued that Moses is higher in rank for the simple reason that he received a "law" and a message from the divine both of which are tangible and applicable, while Khiḍr's knowledge, even though it is from God, is not implementable. Below, I will elaborate on these claims in the light of the arguments from scholars belonging to different schools of thought.

The name "al-Khiḍr" emerges in the writings of early interpreters of the Qur'ān (*mufassirūn*) who thought of him as a person who by his very presence revives, regenerates, and makes things green, hence the Arabic, al-Khiḍr, "the Green One." Although this quality of "greening" or making things come "alive" remains at the center of his identity, in different parts of the Islamic world, Khiḍr came to be known as Khwājā Khizir, Pīr Badar, Rājā Kidar, Abū'l Abbās, among others. These names reflect Khiḍr's multiple roles as a guide, teacher, and even as a "savior" of sorts who has been venerated by many as a saint. Some of these names are attempts to link Khiḍr with a particular era and place; others such as "khwājā," "pīr," and "rājā" are honorific titles that show an elevated status in spiritual and mythical receptions of Khiḍr. He was always seen as someone who could not be contained within a single tradition or be confined to a single region especially with respect to his popular manifestations. In the flowering of the Islamic(ate) civilization Khiḍr quite literally became part of many cultures and traditions simultaneously. He is by profession and by job description — a wanderer, and much like Elijah (or Ilyās, as he is known in Muslim sources), always on the move, looking out for those in distress and those in need of spiritual guidance and advice.[11]

Seeking help and advice from Khiḍr takes on many different forms as will become clear in subsequent chapters. For some he is a folk hero who mediates between the supernatural and ordinary beings whose services range from deliverance from physical ailment to a relief from mundane earthly problem. For others, including many Sufis, Khiḍr is master-teacher for life who guides the seeker in pursuit of knowledge of the divine.

NARRATIVES ABOUT KHIḌR

Khiḍr is said to appear in "green" or in some accounts, a "white" cloak. In *ḥadīth* we find an explanation: "Al-Khiḍr was named so because he sat over a barren . . . land, [and] it turned green with plantation."[12] The greening of a patch of barren land (*farwa*) referred to by several early Muslim scholars implies making the land fertile and in its allegorical sense may also mean rejuvenation of the human spirit, something which Khiḍr came to be identified with in later traditions. In the present context one might ask, "what nationality does Khiḍr belong to?" or "what is his ethnic identity?" and "where does he live?" "does he still exist," and so on. However, these are questions that cannot be dealt with in any literal sense, because Khiḍr belongs to that category of Islamic/religious literature which is known as the "imaginal" or that which pertains to the world of images (*mundus imaginalis*).[13] The world of images (*'ālam al-amthāl*) plays an important role in connecting the other two worlds—the spiritual and the material (*'ālam al-rūḥ* and *'ālam al-khalq*)—in that it allows ordinary yet pious human beings to possess the ability (by leave of God) to perform or witness miraculous things. Those who are advanced in their journey on the spiritual path (*ṭarīqah*), God may enable them to have such powers. Stories of meeting with Khiḍr and other "miraculous acts" are generally explained to have been taking place in the imaginal realm—or *'ālam al-khayāl*—the world of images. This is sometimes compared to "dream imagery." An example of one such claim is made by Ibn 'Arabī, who experienced several miraculous appearances of Khiḍr.[14] Among the hundreds of other, even earlier than 12th century, reports of meetings with Khiḍr is that of Ibrāhīm ibn Adham, who reportedly said: "In that wilderness I lived for four years. God gave me my eating without any toil of mine. Khiḍr the Green Ancient was my companion during that time—he taught me the Great Name of God."[15] While verification of such stories may not be feasible, asking questions may help us understand some of the mystery and curiosity regarding Khiḍr. Stories about him are found throughout the Muslim world and they appear to give meaning to those who hold them as truths. Khiḍr has no particular nationality or ethnicity; he is neither old nor young. In a post-modern sense, we can even say that he continues to "exist"—irrational as it may sound—because countless people claim to have "known" him and have had some form of "interaction" with him.[16]

The mythic dimension notwithstanding, early *tafsīr* (exegetical literature) provides a variety of answers to the kinds of questions raised above. An enormous wealth of details pertaining to his name, genealogy, appearances, origins and status is found there. The fourteenth century Qur'ān scholar Khazin al-Baghdādī (d. 1324) reports that Khiḍr's real name was Baliya bin Malkān, while the *ḥadīth* scholar Imam Nawāwī (d. 1277) refers to him as Abū'l Abbās which he says was his nick name.[17] According to Tha'labī (d. 1035), he lives on an island from which he protects sailors; he is the guardian of the sea, etc.[18] Others have suggested places such as the Nile delta where two bodies of water converge (*majma' al-baḥrayn*). Besides the hagiographical literature known as the *Qiṣaṣ al-'anbiyā,'* information about Khiḍr is found in works of *tafsīr* and in Sufi writings, especially Sufi biographies which are often filled with reports of meetings and encounters with Khiḍr; and, finally in folk literature where Khiḍr takes on a super-human persona. Most of these material representations of Khiḍr's multivalent personality take their cue from earlier, foundational works such as the one by Abū Ja'far Muḥammad Ibn Jarīr al-Ṭabarī (d. 935), whose *al-Tārīkh* sets the frame for later Muslim writings on and about Khiḍr. The figure of Khiḍr from the start became an object of fascination for mystics and orthodox theologians. He could not be dismissed by the orthodox scholars simply because primary narratives attributed to him are anchored in the Qur'ān and the *ḥadīth*, and he could not be ignored by the Sufis because he offered so much in the way of mystery which often lends itself to the mystical. Between the orthodox and Sufi scholars there is the cultural dimension where Khiḍr seemed to have filled the deepest need for seeing the dynamic link between the divine and human spheres.[19] Contemporary orthodox religious understandings of Khiḍr seldom venture beyond the literal interpretation of the quranic verses in question. In contrast, the mystical and popular views of Khiḍr are often embellished by allegorical and metaphorical interpretations. One might say the former is primarily concerned with an "Islamic" view of Khiḍr, while the latter would most certainly fall under the purview of the Islamicate tradition. In practicing the latter there is often an attempt to stretch the interpretation by exercising what has been termed as "interreligious hermeneutics" by making use of extracanonical texts (in particular those belonging to other religious traditions) to derive (or some would say "impose") a meaning purportedly emanating from the quranic text. Therefore, when it is noted that Khiḍr from the start seemed a larger-than-life figure who could not be contained within one religious tradition, it also alludes to the fact that before assuming an Islamicate persona, some aspects of the character which embodies Khiḍr existed in different forms and were known by different names. Similarly, because of Islam's influence, other pre-Islamic legends adopted variations of his name, substituting it with existing figures in those legends. As Khiḍr's quranic narrative Islamizes some pre-Islamic ideas these same ideas were recycled in older legends adding newer elements to them. For example, in some Indian legends the patron of sailors is known as "Khwājā Khizr," even though these legends had existed long before Islam arrived in South Asia. The name, "Khwājā Khizr," suggests that he was a later substitute for an earlier figure that fulfilled the role of a guide and protector deity for the sailors of that region.[20]

Many Western scholarly discussions of Khiḍr trace the quranic narrative to three sources: the Alexander Romance, the Epic of Gligamesh, and the story of the wandering Elijah. Since its development in the Islamicate tradition, the Khiḍr legend has grown into a global phenomenon. The story of Khiḍr has played a particularly important role in folklore and popular mysticism in Muslim societies.[21] As a mystical figure, Khiḍr has had an enormous impact on various dimensions of Sufi thought and practice. Among some prominent Sufis he is regarded as the spiritual teacher who continues to guide those who do not have an earthly teacher.[22] Despite the topic's scholarly significance, until recently few studies focused solely on the figure of Khiḍr. The importance of this topic is clearly evident if we consider the role Khiḍr has played in the Islamicate tradition bringing disparate stories under a single umbrella narrative. Upon close examination, it appears that through his different facets, Khiḍr has served as a bridge between religions, cultures, and communities for many centuries. Some of the early studies on Khiḍr originated either within the context of Orientalist attempts to "unpack" and "explain" Islam or as part of the hagiographical (in service of making human beings look magical and superhuman) understandings of Islam.[23] European Orientalist scholars such as Vollers and others sought to map out the workings of the Khiḍr legend to explain its connections with biblical and Greco-Roman literature including the attendant myths and folklore. This exercise was common among Orientalists who wished to treat Islamic ideas and texts in the same manner as Christian texts. Thus, they applied the historical-critical approach to examine the Qur'ān and *ḥadīth*. Their primary aim was to understand the origins of ideas and pre-Islamic sources of the scriptural passages of the Qur'ān and the *ḥadīth*. No doubt, some of these scholars also wished to explain Islam's rise in a manner suited to their goal of discrediting historical (and confessional) claims made by Muslims.

STUDYING KHIḌR: SOURCES AND MEANINGS

Within the Muslim tradition al-Khiḍr was developed and pursued from a different vantage point. Khiḍr appears in numerous works of prose and poetry, fiction and non-fiction. He figures as a hero in stories and legends and is frequently referred to in hagiographies and travel accounts. He was made into an indispensable figure within the world of Sufism where master-disciple relationships play an important role. Khiḍr is everywhere in Muslim literature, religious or otherwise; ideas about him inform beliefs and practices in many Muslim cultures, and yet it is intriguing to note that:

> Considering that a singular motif plausibly links multiple doctrines, al-Khiḍr is highly undertheorized. His characterization as enigmatic and mysterious may factor in this neglect, but if posited links hold up to more discerning scrutiny it is plausible that he foundationally connects several of the world's great traditions in ways hitherto unexhausted.[24]

This assessment is enormously important because so much focus has been placed on the pre-Islamic origins of the Khidr story by Orientalists that the interreligious connections engendered by Khidr story remained unexplored. As already noted, until recently there were no serious studies that focused on Khiḍr as a main subject of inquiry. The two important works that approach the subject from a phenomenological lens are Patrick Franke's *Begegnung mit Khidr: Quellenstudien zum Imaginären im traditionellen Islam* and Hugh Talat Halman's *Where the Two Seas Meet: The Qur'ānic Story of al-Khiḍr and Moses in Sufi Commentaries as a Model of Spiritual Guidance*, both of which are groundbreaking in different respects. Franke's work remains the most detailed and covers both the textual analysis and spiritual manifestations of the narrative as well as its wider adaptions in popular folklore. It is thorough and exhaustive and includes photographic and other evidence of the legend's global presence in the form of shrines and memorials. Halman's work is rooted in Sufism's emphasis on the master-disciple relationship and how the Khiḍr narrative opens new pathways to understand the dynamics of that system.[25]

Additionally, I came across several works in Arabic and a few in Bahasa Indonesia that may be mentioned for their contribution to the Muslim view of Khiḍr and for their symbolic value of addressing the thirst for stories featuring figures like Khiḍr.[26] There are also several shorter article-length studies on various aspects of Khiḍr that have appeared more recently as the interest in Khiḍr's enigmatic role continues to grow. These contributions are a welcome addition to the growing literature on the subject.[27] The present work on al-Khiḍr takes a different path. Here I do not seek to discuss or analyze the Orientalist findings on the supposed origins of the Khiḍr narrative or to its connections with specific pre-Islamic legends. Nor do I attempt to authenticate the hagiographical perceptions of Khiḍr in Islamic mystical and popular traditions. Rather, my aim is simply to consider the story of Khiḍr from a wider frame of understanding that includes textual and literary representations as well as symbolic and legendary perspectives. I have tried to show key intersectional ties between the Khiḍr story and other savior-sage type legends (e.g., Saint George, Elijah, Saint Behnam) noting the symbiotic as well as synergetic connections as much as they are visible to our mind's eye. Some such connections may have existed in the original formulations of the story and others were developed later as the process of adaptation of the Khiḍr's story continued in various Muslim and Islamicate cultural domains. One of the main points to note here is that Khiḍr's Islamic story is not purely Islamic; it is Islamicate in that it intersects with stories from other traditions, including the Jewish and Christian traditions, and that this cross-border exchange happened at various stages of its development resulting in a metamorphosis as well as in an amalgamated view of the figure of Khiḍr.[28]

Reading the early exegetical works, we find some of the first set of questions raised by the interpreters of the Qur'ān: 1) Is Khiḍr a name or does it represent a title? 2) Is Khiḍr a messenger and/or a prophet, or simply a saint (*walī*)? and 3) what does it mean for Khiḍr to be immortal as claimed by hagiographical accounts? These are foundational questions which occupied the minds of scholars in order to make sense of this mysterious figure in the larger exegetical narrative. Within this scope the questions most pertinent to this inquiry deal with three different aspects of Khiḍr: his identity; status, and relevance. Below I will try to address these in the light of the primary sources, the Qur'ān and the *ḥadīth*, aided by the secondary sources that particularly speak to Khiḍr's relevance in the Islamic and Islamicate worldviews including the story's symbolic and allegorical understandings.

Khiḍr is said to be the name which symbolizes agency on his part. As noted, the name is given by the first set of *mufassirūn* (interpreters of the Qur'ān) and is elaborated upon in the *qiṣaṣ* literature for its symbolic meanings. However, many of the interpreters, theologically speaking, sought to limit Khiḍr's agency by laboring on his obedience to the divine will; acting exactly as he was told in the three actions narrated in the quranic story. This view limits Khiḍr's agency but does not deny it altogether as all his efforts are framed as divine acts, done through him but not of his own volition. When we look at the Khiḍr legend where he is often a larger-than-life figure, a superhuman, a savior with a charge from on high, it seems Khiḍr's agency is accentuated. There are also questions that are not considered in this work. While the precluded or "missing" questions may not be fully warranted they nevertheless need to be stated[29] as they are related to the question of agency. So, for example, when Khiḍr damaged the boat which carried them across the river free of charge, what kinds of reactions did it elicit from the people witnessing that act? What did the owner say or ask? Most commentators appear to be silent on such matters, and perhaps rightly so, since they do not add anything of relevance to the overall moral of the story. It is clear that Moses was uneasy about Khiḍr's actions. From the outset, it would seem Khiḍr was asserting his agency when he did not readily reveal the reason for his actions, only sharing these with Moses at the end of their journey and primarily to allay his concerns about the legalistic implications of the acts. It might be safe to say that Khiḍr is one of those figures who strides along the path where human and divine agency "meet" or have a shared border. This would be perfectly in line with him being a prophet. Theological grounding demands Khiḍr's absolute reliance on divine agency, while Sufistic and popular religio-cultural traditions long for the master/teacher/savior to be connected to the divine will and yet be acting with his/her own agency.

Ibn Jarīr al-Ṭabarī, the great Muslim historian, used as a title "The History of Prophets and Kings" for his encyclopedic classic *Oeuvre* in order to emphasize that Islamic history has a prophetic quality. In Ṭabarī's view, history has been suffused with prophecy to the extent that it is impossible to extricate the sacred from the profane. Looking at it from a historical-critical perspective, Islamic history revolves around a great many legends and historical events that cannot be proven by modern science. Nevertheless, the great dynamics of Islamic history, in the view of Ṭabarī and other Muslim historians, revolved around the event of revelation of the Qur'an and its interpretation.[30] The goal of "existence" from an Islamic perspective is to follow prophetic model. Although prophets were not sinless, they represent the "perfect" human effort, and embody the ultimate human achievement in God's eyes. Because of their role as standard bearers of the divine-human and human-human relationships, prophets became the special focus in human history. Thus, the impact of prophets, saints and other kinds of heroes is clearly noticeable in Islamic history for having shaped the religio-cultural ethos in Muslim societies. Khiḍr is certainly one such figure whose contribution to Muslim cultural traditions is deep and long-lasting. In Muslim literature of all eras and belonging to various genres, references to Khiḍr are as numerous as they are varied. Depending on the genre, Khiḍr takes on different roles and personas always retaining his original and central role of being a savior of the dispossessed. Among the scholars of the Qur'ān and the *ḥadīth*, speculation and intrigue ruled the day. Some said Khiḍr is a title, others surmised that it is an epithet.[31] For the storytellers and the hagiographers, Khiḍr was equated with Saint George,[32] identified as the Muslim "version of Elijah"[33] and has been called the "eternal wanderer."[34] As already mentioned, a great many scholars consider him a saint, or a prophet-saint; and, remaining close to the quranic portrait from Sūrat al-Kahf, Khiḍr was also regarded as the mysterious prophet-guide. The name al-Khiḍr is not mentioned in the Qur'ān, however, the commentators are generally in agreement on this, relying as they do on the information found in the *ḥadīth*.[35] For many Sufis and spiritual thinkers, Khiḍr symbolizes much more than an ordinary prophet; he is not just any guide but someone who represents "the utmost depth of mystic insight accessible to man."[36]

Khiḍr is one of the four prophets whom the Islamic tradition recognizes as being "alive" or "immortal,"[37] the other three being *Idrīs* (Enoch), *Ilyās* (Elijah), and *'Īsā* (Jesus).[38] These prophets are known to have not tasted earthly death. It is immortality through divine intervention which, however, does not imply attribution of divinity or any magical powers on the part of these prophets who from the Islamic point of view are human beings.[39] From the very beginning Khiḍr was seen as someone who could not be contained within a single tradition or be confined to a single region in terms of his popular manifestations. In the flowering of the Islamic civilization, he quite literally became part of many cultures and traditions simultaneously.

One of the earlier studies in Western scholarship, that of Rodwell's, stated that perhaps the name Khiḍr is "formed from Jethro," the father-in-law of Moses.[40] However, Rodwell could not find any specific connection between the two.[41] The Khiḍr narrative is said to have some common elements with ancient legends, notably, the Epic of Gilgamesh and the Alexander Romance.[42] According to Wensinck these legends provided the background for the original story of Khiḍr's encounter with Moses.[43] George Sale, another early Orientalist scholar of the Qur'ān, has noted that the Muslim tradition confounds Khiḍr with Phineas, Elias, and Saint George as if to say that "his [Khiḍr's] soul passed by a metempsychosis successively through all three."[44] Recent scholarship has shown a different, more nuanced view of the connections between Khiḍr narrative and earlier, pre-Islamic sources.[45] Brannon Wheeler has written about the similarities between the quranic narrative and the pre-Islamic legends. He questions the view of the Orientalist Arent Jan Wensinck who believed that the quranic narrative (or at least significant parts of it) depends on or "borrowed" from earlier narratives of ancient legends.[46] For Wensinck, the quranic Khiḍr story was "derived from the 'Jewish' story of Rabbi Joshua b. Levi and Elijah . . . which describes how Rabbi Joshua b. Levi meets Elijah and asks to follow and observe his actions."[47] As the story continues, one finds parallels with the Moses' encounter with the person who is later identified with Khiḍr. Wensinck assumed that the parallels imply borrowing with a change in names substituting Moses and Khiḍr for Joshua b. Levi and Elijah. However, as Wheeler noted Joshua b. Levi and Elijah story is a "Hebrew paraphrase of an earlier Arabic work attributed to the eleventh century Nissim b. Shāhīn of Qayrawān."[48]

Similar to Wensinck, Julian Obermann contended that the Qur'ān "'as a rule' is dependent upon earlier Jewish and Christian sources."[49] Scholars like Wensinck, Rodwell, and Obermann were interested in finding links to the quranic story that reflected direct and perhaps exclusive reliance on earlier stories and traditions.[50] Wheeler rejects these assumptions and concurs (to an extent) with Haim Schwarzbaum that "there is no earlier Jewish or Christian story that parallels" the quranic Khiḍr story, even though there are certain elements in it that may resonate with pre-Islamic stories. Wheeler goes further and rejects the notion that "parallels represent borrowings, or that an earlier context explains the use of the motif or story in another context."[51] He argues that such similarities are mainly due to the shared sources. Historically speaking, the Khiḍr narrative contains many familiar aspects from earlier stories and traditions,[52] however, the Islamic components of the story are authenticated by a closer examination of the sources involved.[53] Further, with centuries of integration the "familiar" pre-Islamic elements in Khiḍr's story have long been thoroughly Islamized. For Wheeler, early Muslim exegetes apparently intentionally incorporated familiar elements of pre-Islamic legends to demonstrate the continuity of the Islamic narrative. Intertextual connections between the truths of the Qur'ān and those found in previous cultures and civilizations strengthen the case for the authenticity of Muḥammad's prophetic claims.[54]

Later, Khiḍr's story itself would influence many (post-7th century) versions of these (and other) legends. Apparently, there are "various recensions of the Alexander Romance, which include stories of Khiḍr, [that] can be found in Ethiopia, Iran, Central Asia, France, Russia, and Iceland."[55] This is not surprising because from the 8th century onwards, Khiḍr had become an important figure and a repository of roles that pertained to the notion of a supernatural hero and a savior of sorts. In its mythic dimensions, Khiḍr's narrative is connected to notions of "immortality" and "water of life" as reflected in the Alexander Romance[56] which relates, among other things, to stories that ascribed supernatural powers to Alexander of Macedonia. Those stories are believed to have been influenced by the Epic of Gilgamesh in which the protagonist is known for his lifelong struggle in search of the water of life. In the end, the "warrior-hero" Gilgamesh who conquers all is defeated by death. He was powerful beyond belief yet he could not attain eternal life.[57] One of the early German studies on Khiḍr, influenced as it was by the work of the medieval author Zakarīyah al-Qazwīnī (d. 1283), noted that some of the Alexander elements in the Khiḍr narrative may be traced back to Persian Alexander (Iskandar) legends.[58] Persian literary masterpieces, such as the *Shāhnāma* of Firdawsī, contained references to ideas such as the immortality of the soul which could be achieved by drinking the "water of life." The *Shāhnāma* goes further in claiming that whoever bathes in it will be free of sin.[59] In the Alexander Romance, the story of Alexander and his cook bears similarities with elements in the Khiḍr story where Moses and Yūsha' bin Nūn (Joshua)[60]—who is sometimes described as his "cook" or "servant"—embark on their search for the water of life. It is possible that these two may be connected due to a shared source where Moses is substituted for Alexander.[61] Over time, it is argued, the Khiḍr narrative expanded to combine the Alexander story with that of Elijah and his companion Joshua bin Levi[62] and as a result Moses represents Gilgamesh and Alexander in the first part (search for the water of life) of the story and Elijah in the second (having a companion-cook).[63]

The figure of Khiḍr is sometimes conflated with Hermes who in the Islamic tradition is known as Idrīs (Enoch) who is recognized in the Qur'ān for his "civilizing" role. Particular anecdotes about him are related to the angelic figures and he is known for his celestial connections. Like Hermes, Idrīs is seen as a source of wisdom.[64] In fact Hermes has been claimed as having other parallel connections. René Guénon compares him with the figure of the Buddha on the basis of a similarity between the name of the mother of Hermes (Maia) and Siddhartha Gautama's mother who is known in the Buddhist tradition as Maya Devi.[65] Hermes was regarded as the "link between the corporeal and spiritual worlds and the interpreter of the realities of the higher plane of existence" for those seeking his guidance on earth.[66] This prophetic intermediary quality of Hermes/ Idris (Enoch) links him/them with Khiḍr in his role as a "ruler" of the place where the two oceans meet (*majma' al-baḥrayn*), a possible reference to the twin sources of knowledge—that of heaven and of earth. According to Seyyed Hossein Nasr, apart from this connection that both Enoch/Idrīs/Hermes and Khiḍr are considered "immortal" the two figures are quite distinct from one another.[67]

As the story developed simultaneously in various regions and in differing contexts, it began to assume the shape of a legend and took on the characteristics of parallel mythical figures.[68] One modern Muslim commentator has this to say about the historical links of Khiḍr: "The nearest equivalent figure in the literature of the People of the Book is Melchizedek. . . . In Gen. xiv. 18–20, he appears as king of Salem, priest of the Most High God."[69] It would appear that some of the early Muslim accounts of Khiḍr's origins acknowledged more similarities with biblical figures. Attempts to equate Khiḍr with Elijah (Ilyās) were made by both the Sufis and the quranic scholars who saw in Khiḍr a person with similar qualities of being invincible and indispensable. They were often seen together; Elijah (Ilyās) was associated with land as he was the "custodian of the desert" whereas Khiḍr's abode is the sea since he was reported to have been found at the confluence of the two seas (*majma' al-baḥrayn*). In this way the two important prophetic figures from two competing traditions can be seen to be on the same side, having divided their territorial charge between them.[70] There are several opinions as to the historical identity of Khiḍr in Muslim writings. Historical identity here does not mean determining the actual person of Khiḍr in history but as it is related in the "divergent sources" such as "prophetology, folklore," etc.[71] As I noted earlier, in quranic commentaries there is much detail pertaining to his name, genealogy, appearance, origin and status. Muslim commentators and historians since the beginning of Islamic scholarship have tried to explain Khiḍr and his pre-Islamic connections within the context of Islam.[72] Most of this literature is connected to the commentary for Sūrat al-Kahf or is linked with the genre of stories of heroes and prophets (*qiṣaṣ al-'anbiyā'*). If the former is characterized as theological the latter may be classified as folkloristic in nature. Ibn Ḥajar al-'Asqalānī (d. 1449) relates that there are about fifteen or so traditions which attempt to describe Khiḍr's lineage. They include a diversity of opinions; e.g., one tradition holds that he is a direct son of Adam; another claims that he is son of the daughters of Pharaoh;[73] that his father was a Persian and mother Roman.[74]

Some scholars explain Khiḍr's multiple belongings by suggesting that because he has different nick names such as Baliyā bin Malkān, Abū'l 'Abbās, and others, he must have lived in different communities at various times.[75] Ṭabarī notes in his famous *Tārīkh* that Khiḍr lived in the reign of King Afridūn.[76] There are aspects of Khiḍr's original story that connect it to classical Babylonian myths. However, within a century after Muḥammad's death in 632, Khiḍr became a larger-than-life figure, larger even than the ancient figures with whom he was originally linked. Khiḍr developed a distinct identity and in Muslim folk literature he became an important trope as a savior figure. In the following chapters I will explore Khiḍr's various qualities as a divine emissary who is tasked with helping the faithful and seekers of truth and peace regardless of time or place, rank or religion.

As is evident from the foregoing, there are plausible connections between the Khiḍr's quranic story and its various motifs with other legends and pre-Islamic narratives. Even though these concerns are not central to this study, I have cited works by Orientalists and other scholars whose focus has been to find such connections in order to provide a bit of context. It should be noted that many quranic exegetes were also interested in connections and links between the Qur'ān and earlier Jewish and Christian "truths." Brannon Wheeler writes that the Qur'ān's inclusivity and acknowledgement of "earlier stories and revelations," enabled the exegetes to "build intertextual links" in explaining the overall message of the Qur'ān.[77] In fact, the Qur'ān is fully conscious of its context so as to be able to claim continuity. Perhaps this is nowhere more evident than in the quranic story of Khiḍr, who is from the outset seen as a "boundary-crossing character."[78] Khiḍr is known for crossing between worlds; he navigates time and space unlike any other; thus, it is fitting that he is known for crossing religious boundaries as well. Perhaps this aspect of multiple belonging is what makes him an enduring figure.

NOTES

1. As noted earlier, Khiḍr is spelled in several ways: al-Khaḍir, Khezr, Khizr, Hizir and so on. In this book, I will refer to him simply as Khiḍr.

2. Arkoun, *Lectures du Coran*, 162.

3. Ibn Kathīr al-Damishqī, *Qiṣaṣ al-'anbiyā'*, 535. Other accounts of the first encounter with Moses with Khiḍr portray him (Khiḍr) as standing on his prayer mat hovering over the ocean.

4. The emphasis on making clear that Khiḍr was not acting on his own volition is important as it bears heavily on later disagreements between those who argued for Khiḍr's superior status based on his knowledge of the unseen and thus claiming for him a degree of spiritual charism compared with believers, and those who see these powers of Khiḍr as nothing but divine action channeled through an ordinary human being who plays no significant role in the matter.

5. Ibn Kathīr al-Damishqī, *Qiṣaṣ al-anbiyā'*, 536.

6. Although this is the common English rendering for *walī, pīr* and other related Islamic terms, it, nevertheless, "obscures the considerable diversity underlying these terms." The word "saint," if unqualified, does not convey the hierarchy reflected in Arabic, Farsi, and Urdu terms. See P. M. Currie, *The Shrine and Cult of Mu'īn al-dīn Chishtī of Ajmer* (Delhi: Oxford University Press, 1989), 1.

7. Henri Corbin, *Histoire de la philosophie islamique* (Paris: Gallimard, 1964).

8. Ibn Kathīr al-Damishqī, *Qiṣaṣ al-anbiyā,'* 537.

9. Hāshim Fayyād Ḥusaynī, *Ḥayāt al-Khiḍr: 'ard wa-dirāsah*, 1st ed. ([Iran]: Dār al-Kitāb al-Islāmī, 2004), 33–34. Ḥusaynī's work is one of the most thoroughly researched presentations of the subject in Arabic. It is also one of the few that includes Shi'ī sources including Majlisi's *Biḥār al-anwār* to substantiate its claims.

10. Shahzad Bashir, *Sufi Bodies: Religion and Society in Medieval Islam* (New York: Columbia University Press, 2013), 79.

11. There appears to be a consensus that Khiḍr is not the same person as Elijah and that it is not a conflation of two distinct albeit mythic figures. However, in folk traditions of the Middle East, the two are sometimes venerated at the same sanctuary. Ernst Küry, "Monothéisme abrahamique et tradition primordiale." *Etudes Traditionnelles* 84, no. 481 (1983): 109.

12. *Ḥadīth* no. 1423 in Muḥammad bin Ismā'īl al-Bukhārī's, "The Book of the Stories of the Prophets," *Mukhtaṣar ṣaḥīḥ al-Bukhārī* (Riyādh: Maktabah Dār al-Salām, 1994), 674. See also Aubaile-Sallenave, "Al-Khiḍr," 14.

13. In Sufi cosmology it is believed that there is a "world of images" (*'ālam al-amthāl*) which (like the isthmus, or *barzakh*) lies in between the other two spheres of "existence" as it were, the "world of spirits" (*'ālam al-rūḥ*) and the "world of matter" (*'ālam al-khalq*). Henry Corbin, *En Islam iranien: Aspects spirituels et philosophiques* (Paris: Gallimard, 1972), 4:108.

14. Muḥyīddīn Ibn 'Arabī, *Al-Futūḥāt al-makkīyah* (Beirut: Dār Ṣadir, 1968), 1:86.

15. Sufi Ibrāhīm ibn Adham quoted in Cyril Glasse, *The Concise Encyclopedia of Islam* (San Francisco: Harper and Row, Publishers, 1989), s.v. "Khidr," 224–25.

16. Siti Chamamah Soeratno, "Khidlir est Proche, Dieu est Loin," *Archipel* 15 (1978): 87. Many Sufis have claimed to have met Khiḍr; thus, meeting or an "encounter" with Khiḍr became an important motif in Sufi theology of moral progression. For more on this see Patrick Franke, *Begegnung mit Khidr: Quellenstudien zum Imaginären im Traditionellen Islam* (Beirut and Stuttgart: Franz Steiner Verlag, 2000).

17. Al-Baghdādī, *Tafsīr al-Khāzin*, 205; Shihāb al-Dīn Aḥmad bin 'Alī Ibn Ḥajar al-'Asqalānī, *Al-Zahr al-naḍir fī nabā' al-Khaḍir* (Beirut: Dār al-Kutub al 'Ilmīyyah, 1988), 25.

18. Abū Iṣḥāq Aḥmad ibn Muḥammad al-Tha'labī, *Qiṣaṣ al-'anbiyā' al-musammā 'Arā'is al-majālis* (Beirut: al-Matba'ah al-Thaqāfīyah, n.d.), 197; cf. al-Nishabūrī, *Qeṣaṣ ol-anbiyā'*.

19. Hassan Elboudrari, "Entre le symbolique et l'historique Khadir im-mémorial," *Studia Islamica* 76 (1992): 36–37.

20. A. K. Coomaraswamy, "Khwājā Khadir and the Fountain of Life in the Tradition of Persian and Mughal Art," in *Ars Islamica* 1, no. 2 (1934): 173.

21. See chapter 4.

22. Central Asian Sufi group known as the Uwaysīs who were named after a contemporary of Prophet Muhammad do not always have an earthly teacher. Uways converted to Islam without ever meeting the Prophet, thus establishing a model of following a teacher who is either distant or invisible or both, and yet present and available to the seeker. Uwaysīs regard Khiḍr as their guide and as a "hidden" master. Annemarie Schimmel, *And Muhammad is His Messenger: The Veneration of the Prophet in Islamic Piety* (Chapel Hill: The University of North Carolina Press, 1985), 22.

23. Karl Dyroff, "Wer is Chadir?" *Zeitschrift für Assyriologie* 7 (1892): 319–27; Gustav Zart, *Chidher in Sage und Dichtung* (Hamburg: Verlagsanstalt und Druckerei A.G., 1897); and K. Vollers, "Chidher," in *Archiv für Religionswissenschaft* 12 (1909): 234–50.

24. Jibril Latif, "The Green Man: What Reading Al-Khiḍr as Trickster Evinces about the Canon." *Ilahiyat Studies* 11, no. 1 (2020): 14. Latif's excellent but brief study mentions the connection made by the Muslim scholar Shahrastānī (d. 1153) between Khiḍr and the Buddha. He also explores similar connections made by other contemporary scholars between on account of the fact that these two figures appear to connect past and present, religion and personal experience, historical and "supra-historical . . . radically transcending human modes of comprehension, and even 'normal' modes of prophetic guidance." Hamza Yusuf, "Buddha in the Qur'ān?," in *Common Ground between Islam & Buddhism*, ed. Reza Shah-Kazemi (Louisville: Fons Vitae, 2010), 110–13, cited in Latif, "The Green Man," 15.

25.Talat Halman, *Where the Two Seas Meet: Al-Khidr and Moses, The Qur'anic Story of al-Khidr and Moses in Sufi Commentaries as a Model for Spiritual Guidance* (Louisville: Fons Vitae 2013). This may be the first book-length study in English apart from two other substantial, yet unpublished, works: Wheeler M. Thackston, "The Khidr Legend in the Islamic Tradition" (A. B. thesis, Princeton University, 1967); and James Paul Jarvis, "Al-Khaḍir: Origins and Interpretations, A Phenomenological Study" (M.A. thesis, McGill University, 1993).

26. In Arabic, besides Ḥusaynī's *Ḥayāt al-Khiḍr*, which I already noted, there are a few other works that have contributed to Khiḍr studies. These include: Muḥammad Khayr Ramaḍān Yūsuf, *Al-Khiḍr baynā al-wāqi' wa'l-tahwīl* (Damascus: Dār al-Mushaf, 1984); 'Alī bin Sulṭān Muḥammad al-Qārī al-Harawī, *Al-Ḥadhar fī 'amr al-Khaḍir* (Damascus: Dār al-Qalam, 1991); and Maḥmūd al-Marākibī, *Musā wa'l-Khiḍr: 'ilmī al-ẓāhir wa'l-bāṭin* (Cairo: Dār al-Ṭibā'a wa'l Nashr wa'l Islāmīyah, 1996). In Bahasa Indonesia there are a few, but the only one worth mentioning on account of it being attentive to scholarly norms is by M. Fathor Rios, *Menyimak Kisah Dan Hikmah Kehidupan Nabi Khidir* (Jakarta: Zaman, 2015).

27. Select studies that advance the conversation on the subject are as follows: Barbara Annan, "Subjectivity and the Other: Khidr and Transformation in Liminal Encounters," in *Ethics and Subjectivity in Literary and Cultural Studies* (New York: Peter Lang, Bern, 2002), 101–15; Stephen Hirtenstein, "The Mantle of Khadir: Mystery, Myth and Meaning," in *Symbolisme et herméneutique dans la pensée d'Ibn 'Arabī*, ed. Bakri Aladdin (Damascus: Institut Français du Proche-Orient, 2007), 83–97; Josef W. Meri, "Re-Appropriating Sacred Space: Medieval Jews and Muslims Seeking Elijah and Al-Khaḍir," *Medieval Encounters* 5, no. 3 (1999): 237–64; David Emmanuel Singh, "Qur'ānic Moses and his Mysterious Companion: Developmental Revelation as an Approach to Christian Discourse with Muslims?," *Transformation* 22, no. 4 (2005): 210–24; Shawkat Toorawa, "The Modern Literary (After)Lives of al-Khiḍr," *Journal of Qur'anic Studies* 16 (2014): 174–95; Ethel Sara Wolper, "Khiḍr and the Changing Frontiers of the Medieval World," *Medieval Encounters* 17, nos. 1–2 (2011): 120–46; Ethel Sara Wolper, "Khiḍr and the Politics of Place: Creating Landscapes of Continuity," in *Muslims and Others in Sacred Space*, ed. Margaret Cormack (New York: Oxford University Press, 2013), 147–63; and Jibril Latif, "The Green Man," cited above. One of the most insightful analyses of Sufi views of the quranic story is found in Kristin Zahra Sands, *Ṣūfī Commentaries on the Qur'ān in Classical Islam* (Abingdon: Routledge, 2006), chap. 7, 79–96.

28. This is contested by Shahab Ahmed in *What is Islam?*. See my discussion below in chapter 4.

29. I am grateful to Ibtisam Abujad for a fruitful conversation on the issue of the "missing" questions.

30. Cf. Mahmoud Ayoub, *Islam: Faith and Practice* (Markham, Ontario: The Open Press Limited, 1989), 33–34.

31. Muhammad Asad, *The Message of The Qur'ān* (Gibraltar: Dār al-Andalus, 1980), 449, note 73; See also, Arent Jan Wensinck, "al-Khaḍir" in *The Encyclopaedia of Islam,* new ed. (Leiden: E.J. Brill, 1973), 4:902.

32. A. Augustinovic, *"El-Khadr" and the Prophet Elijah* (Jerusalem: Francescan Printing Press, 1972). This study is devoted to comparative analysis of shared identity between Khiḍr, Elijah, and Saint George.

33. "Muslim version of Elijah" is mentioned by George K. Anderson, *The Legend of the Wandering Jew* (Providence: Brown University Press, 1965), 409. Khiḍr's resemblance to Elijah is also discussed in Israel Friedlaender, "Khidr," in *Encyclopaedia of Religion and Ethics* (New York: Charles Scribner's Sons, 1915), 7:693–95.

34. Extensive references to Khiḍr are found in Haim Schwarzbaum's *Biblical and Extra-Biblical Legends in Islamic Folk-Literature* (Waldorf-Hessen: Verlag fur Orientkunde, 1982), 17–18.

35. See the *ḥadīth* quoted from Ibn Kathīr's *Qiṣaṣ* in the Introduction.

36. Asad, *The Message of the Qur'ān*, 449.

37. Giacomo Arnaboldi, "Élie Le Verdoyant," *Aurora*, Supplement aux *Cahiers d'Orient et d'Occident*, no. 3, (n.d.): 2.

38. Annemarie Schimmel, *Mystical Dimensions of Islam* (Chapel Hill: The University of North Carolina Press, 1975), 202.

39. The Muslim views of these prophets also parallel biblical references, e.g., Elijah is said to have gone up to heaven as he walked with Elisha (Ar. al-Yasa‘) in 2 Kings 2:11 ("As they continued walking and talking, a chariot of fire and horses of fire separated the two of them, and Elijah ascended . . . into heaven." NSRV). Similarly, Enoch is said not to have seen death (Hebrews 11:5) and is said to have been taken by God (Genesis 5:24). It is believed that Ilyās / Élie was raised mysteriously without death. The Qur'ān speaks of Jesus (Īsā) being raised unto God at the time of his crucifixion. Apparently pious individuals being raised up to God without experiencing physical death is a recurrent theme in Abrahamic traditions.

40. Note 16 of Sura 18 in J. M. Rodwell's translation of the Qur'ān (*The Koran* [London: J.M. Dent Everyman, 1994], 461). In the Bible, Jethro is also noted as the priest of Midian. In the Muslim tradition he is identified as Shu‘ayb. See Brinner, "Prophets and Prophecy in the Islamic and Jewish Traditions," 66–67; and Thackston, *The Tales of the Prophets of al-Kīsā'ī*, xxiv.

41. Rodwell, *The Koran*, 461, note 15.

42. Wensinck, "al-Khaḍir," 902; cf. Augustinovic, "*El-Khadr*" *and the Prophet Elijah*, 10.

43. Wensinck, "al-Khadir," 902–3.

44. George Sale, *The Koran* (London: William Tegg, 1961), 244. See also F. W. Hasluck, *Christianity and Islam Under the Sultans* (Oxford: Clarendon Press, 1929).

45. Kevin van Bladel, "The *Alexander Legend* in the Qur'ān 18:83–102," in *The Qur'ān and its Historical Context*, ed. Gabriel Said Reynolds (London & New York: Routledge, 2008), 175–203, and Gabriel Said Reynolds, *The Qur'ān and the Bible: Text and Commentary* (New Haven: Yale University Press, 2018).

46. Brannon M. Wheeler, *Moses in the Quran and Islamic Exegesis* (Abingdon: Routledge, 2002), 10.

47. Ibid., 19.

48. Ibid., 20.

49. Ibid., 21.

50. Wensinck and Rodwell are mentioned above; for Obermann's assumptions about the quranic Khiḍr story, see Julian Obermann, "Two Elijah Stories in Judeo-Arabic Transmission." *Hebrew Union College Annual* 23 (1950–1951): 387–404.

51. Wheeler, *Moses in the Quran and Islamic Exegesis,* 22

52. Augustinovic, *"El-Khadr" and the Prophet Elijah*, 10.

53. Ismail Albayrak, "The Classical Exegetes' Analysis of the Qur'ānic Narrative 18: 60–82." *Islamic Studies* 42, no. 2 (Summer 2003): 289–315. Albayrak offers a

good summary of the discussion from various classical exegeses. His study begins with Wheeler's critique of Obermann and Wensinck's theory that the Khiḍr's quranic story is almost identical to a pre-Islamic Jewish story. Wheeler shows otherwise, saying that the quranic story has no Jewish antecedents. Wheeler, *Moses in the Quran and Islamic Exegesis*, 21.

54. Wheeler, *Moses in the Quran and Islamic Exegesis*, 6.

55. Scott B. Noegel and Brannon M. Wheeler, *The A to Z of Prophets in Islam and Judaism* (Lanham, MD: Scarecrow Press, 2002), xliii.

56. Some Muslim commentators have also utilized the figure of *Dhu-l-Qarnayn* (Sūrat al-Kahf, verses 83–98) and portrayed Khiḍr as a *vizier* in his army.

57. The Khiḍr story became particularly popular because it "improved" on the outcomes portrayed in that ancient legend of Gilgamesh. The hero Gilgamesh was mortal despite his greatness and heroism. Khiḍr is also mortal as necessitated by Islamic theology, and yet he is believed to be ever present to help those sincere believers no matter where they may be.

58. Armand Abel, *Le roman d'Alexandre: légendaire médiéval* (Bruxelles: Office de Publicité, 1955). Abel's work has shown that the figure of Alexander gradually became known for all kinds of traditions and stories projecting him as the hero. Uplifting and superhuman elements of Alexander stories were naturally selected for inclusion in the legend of Khiḍr as the latter spread throughout the Muslim world during the medieval period.

59. Zart, *Chidher in Sage und Dichtung*, 12. Zart's work heavily draws on Zakarīyāh Qazwīnī's *Ajā'ib al-makhlūqāt wa-gharā'ib al-mawjūdāt* (*Marvellous Things of Creation and Wonderous Things of Existence*) a German translation of which was published in 1868. Zart's work is an attempt to address the question of origins of the Khiḍr legend. He also speculates about the location of the "meeting of the two seas" and of the well that supposedly contained the "water of life." Zart rightly noted that the Khiḍr legend became one of the most impactful stories spanning centuries and found in numerous cultures around the world.

60. He is not mentioned in the Qur'ān by name and is believed to be the biblical prophet, but Muslim tradition gives a different account of him than the biblical one. Bernhard Heller, "Yūsha' bin Nūn," *The Encyclopaedia of Islam* (Leiden: E.J. Brill, 1933), 4.2:1177.

61. Gordon D. Newby, *The Making of the Last Prophet: A Reconstruction of the Earliest Biography of Muhammad*, (Columbia: University of South Carolina Press, 1989), 114.

62. In Jewish version of Elijah, where he is known as an "eternal wanderer," Joshua bin Levi appears as his companion.

63. Newby, *The Making of the Last Prophet*, 114.

64. Pierre Lory, "Hermès/Idris, prophète et sage dans la tradition islamique," in *Présence d'Hermès Trismégiste*, ed. A. Faivre (Paris: Albin Michel, 1988), 103–4.

65. René Guénon, *Traditional Forms and Cosmic Cycles*, trans. Henry D. Fohr (Hillsdale, NY: Sophia Perennis, 2003), 81, note 6; see also Seyyed H. Nasr, "Hermes and Hermetic Writings in the Islamic World," in *Islamic Life and Thought* (London: Routledge, 1981), 113, note 9. There are other attempts to present Khiḍr as a

Siddhartha-like figure by suggesting that he escaped his rich father's kingdom, who wanted him to live a life of luxury, only to choose an ascetic life instead. Patrick Franke, *Begegnung mit Khidr*, 58.

66. Nasr, "Hermes and Hermetic Writings," in *Islamic Life and Thought*, 104.

67. Ibid., 105ff.

68. Cf. Augustinovic, *"El-Khadr" and the Prophet Elijah*, 10.

69. 'Abdullah Yūsuf 'Alī, *The Holy Qur'ān: Text, Translation and Commentary*, (Lahore: Shaikh Muhammad Ashraf, n.d.), 1:748, note 2411.

70. Ibn Ḥajar al-Asqalānī narrates a *ḥadīth* in support of this claim. See his *al-Zahr al-naḍir fī nabā' al-Khaḍir*, 36–7; cf. Augustinovic, *"El-Khadr" and the Prophet Elijah*, 61.

71. Henry Corbin, *Creative Imagination in the Sufism of Ibn 'Arabi*, tr. Ralph Manheim (Princeton, NJ: Princeton University Press, 1969), 55.

72. See Wensinck, "al-Khaḍir," 902–5.

73. Ibn Ḥajar al-'Asqalānī, *al-Zahr al-naḍir fī nabā' al-Khaḍir*, 17.

74. Ibn Asākīr, the historian quoted in Ibn Ḥajar al-'Asqalānī, *al-Zahr al-naḍir fī nabā' al-Khaḍir*, 23. It could be taken as a reference to the legend's composite character; or it may simply be a reference to the meeting place where the Persian and Roman seas meet. For more on this see al-Zamakhsharī, *Al-Kashshāf*, 2:395.

75. Al-Baghdādī, *Tafsīr al-Khāzin*, 205; Wahbah al-Zuhaylī, *Tafsīr al-munīr*, vols. 15 & 16 (Beirut: Dār al-Fikr al-Mu'āsir, 1991), 288; Ibn Ḥajar al-'Asqalānī, *al-Zahr al-naḍir fī nabā' al-Khaḍir*, 25.

76. Quoted in al-Zamakhsharī, *Al-Kashshāf*, 2:395; also Ibn Ḥajar al-'Asqalānī, *al-Zahr al-naḍir fī nabā' al-Khaḍir*, 27.

77. Brannon M. Wheeler, "Moses," in *Blackwell Companion to the Qur'ān*, ed. Andrew Rippin (Oxford: Blackwell, 2006), 262.

78. Latif, "The Green Man," 10. The term "boundary-crossing" is also used by others to describe Khiḍr. See for example, Su Fang Ng, *Alexander the Great from Britain to Southeast Asia: Peripheral Empires in the Global Renaissance* (Oxford: Oxford University Press, 2019), 84.

Chapter 2

Khiḍr in Muslim Sources and Traditions of Piety

As mentioned earlier Khiḍr is identified with the unnamed figure mentioned in the Qur'ān in Sūrat al-Kahf (18:60–82). The background to Khiḍr's Islamic story is provided for in the *ḥadīth* and the literature called the *qiṣaṣ al-'anbiyā'*. It starts with Moses' declaration to his companion ("fatah")[1] that "I will not give up till I reach the confluence of two oceans."[2] Moses and this young attendant, Joshua (Yūsha' bin Nūn) had begun to search for "a servant of God" from whom Moses was to learn the "secret knowledge" given to this mysterious servant by God. And Moses said: "I will continue to seek for years to come."[3] Going back to the origin of the story we find a different set of arguments emerging from the rationale behind Moses' search for, and subsequent meeting with, Khiḍr. It begins with Moses making a claim about being the most learned person in the world.[4]

> [Due to this belief] . . . he no longer tried to acquire more knowledge. So God sought for an occasion to stimulate him to obtain more knowledge . . . [and one day after his address to his people] one of them asked him: "Can there be found anybody more learned than you?" He replied: "No, such a man I never met." Then God revealed: "Yes, such a man does exist. Our servant Khiḍr is more learned than you are."[5]

Al-Baghdādī includes a similar *ḥadīth* related by Ubayy ibn Ka'b that describes Moses giving a speech where he claims to be the "most learned" person in the world. God was apparently not pleased, hence the journey Moses undertook leading to the encounter between Moses and Khiḍr.[6] Moses, by holding such a view, created a necessity of being instructed by someone who surpassed him in knowledge. Although one may argue that the reason for this "instruction" was the mannerism in which he proclaimed it,[7] and not necessarily due to his lack of knowledge. The narrative assumes that Moses was indeed the most knowledgeable person in the sense of having received divine revelation and for being an important prophet. Yet there was this tone of voice Moses projected which appeared to lack humility, something prophets are expected to possess. Thus God willed his meeting with Khiḍr.[8] As the encounter takes place, Moses asks Khiḍr to "teach" him some secrets of divine knowledge (*ma'rifah*) he has received from God. Khiḍr's reply to him was that "you may not be patient with me because I was granted knowledge you were not, and you were granted knowledge that I do not have."[9] But Moses insists and Khiḍr agrees after explaining terms of this arrangement. Khiḍr then performs "three acts of mercy" which apparently defy the law (*sharī'ah*) that Moses represents. Therefore, Moses questions Khiḍr about them thus being impatient as anticipated by Khiḍr. Moses is impatient with Khiḍr because the *ẓāhir* of his knowledge did not agree with the *bāṭin*[10] of Khiḍr's knowledge.[11] Hence there is a tension between the two "poles," or pillars of faith, as it were, which is exacerbated when Moses at first "fails" to comprehend the providence behind Khiḍr's three actions. It should be noted, however, that as a recipient of God's law, Moses' primary responsibility was to judge those actions in light of the *sharī'ah*.[12]

The quranic commentators have related different opinions with regard to Khiḍr's status. Some say he is one of the prophets;[13] others refer to him simply as an angel who functions as a guide to those who seek God.[14] And there are yet others who argue for his being a perfect *walī* meaning the one whom God has taken as a friend.[15] Generally speaking, in Muslim literature, Khiḍr is seen as *walī*, (saint) as well as a *nabī* (prophet), although there is some difference of opinion about this. Many exegetes in Muslim history regarded Khiḍr as prophet since he seemed to fulfill the criteria for being one; that is, he is said to have received knowledge from God and has been referred to as a "mercy" from God. Others questioned whether the modality of knowledge and its purpose can be considered equivalent to that given to Prophet Moses as he (Moses) in addition to being a prophet (*nabī*) is also a messenger (*rasūl*) and bearer of divine law.[16] The scholars holding this view are more comfortable accepting Khiḍr as an important saint but not as a prophet even though overwhelming number of exegetes noted that the "servant" mentioned in the verse in question refers to Khiḍr and he is later identified in the *ḥadīth* as much more than a saint. Some modern Qur'ān interpreters have a very different assessment of the verse in question. Sayyid Qutb, for example, argued that the "servant" mentioned in 18:65 should not be identified as Khiḍr in the first place since there is no clear quranic evidence.[17] Others with similar views are Ibrāhīm ibn Fathī 'Abd al-Muqtadar, and Maḥmūd Marākibī, both of whom also appear to be critical of Sufi-leaning ideas.[18] Marākibī cites a few well-known classical scholars to support his position which is based on the method described for the reception of knowledge. He notes that there is a considerable difference between Moses and Khiḍr because of the way they received their knowledge and which for him determines their individual status. For Moses it was *waḥy* but for Khiḍr it was *ilhām* (inspiration) which is received without the mediation of an angel (as in the case of *waḥy*). Saintly inspiration takes the shape of finding within oneself knowledge not previously possessed. The lack of a mediator is what differentiates between a prophet and a saint.[19] A solution proposed by Reynold Nicholson, which may not be acceptable to everyone, tries to accommodate Khiḍr's important role without placing him above in rank to Moses. He argues that the nature of Khiḍr's prophecy was different from that of Moses: Khiḍr was given a prophecy of "saintship" (*nubuwwatu'l wilāyah*) whereas Moses' charge was what is called a prophecy of "institution" or "law" (*nubuwwatu'l tashrī'*) respecting Moses' status as a lawgiver.[20] Although Nicholson is not a quranic commentator, his nuance is helpful in resolving the difference of status (i.e. Moses' apparent superiority due to his role as a messenger of God versus Khiḍr's obscurity in the quranic text). From this perspective Khiḍr is fully accorded the status of prophethood but without taking away the importance of the role Moses is given by the Qur'ān and thus, they can be considered differently equal. Some quranic commentators prefer to see Khiḍr simply as an "angel" who functions as a guide to those who seek God.[21] Below I will discuss the apparent role Khiḍr is cast in the quranic weltanschauung. Here I am interested in exploring a different question, namely, "how does Khiḍr's 'presence' constitute an act of mercy (*raḥmah*) on the part of God?" In chapter 3, I will ask the follow up question: what does this presence and his being a symbol of divine compassion say about the characteristics endowed within the figure of Khiḍr with respect to the motif of light and spiritual illumination?

KHIḌR AS AN EMBODIMENT OF DIVINE MERCY

Many Qur'ān commentators, who have thought of Khiḍr as a prophet, have based their argument on the quranic reference to him as a symbol of God's *raḥmah*.[22] What does *raḥmah* mean in its quranic context? As related above, the Q. 18:65 says that Khiḍr is one of those "whom We had blessed" (*ātaynāhu raḥmatan min 'indinā*). This characterization usually applies to the prophets.[23] *Raḥmah* comes from the root RḤM meaning "womb." From *raḥimah/yarḥamo*, comes the *maṣdar* "*raḥmah*," which is understood to mean "mercy." Other translations of 18:65a include: "And there they found a devotee among Our devotees. We had blessed him with Our grace."[24] George Sale renders it as: "they found one of our servants unto whom we had granted mercy from us."[25] Similarly in Sūrat al-Zukhruf, 43:32, the Qur'ān, while expounding one of the characteristics of God's prophets, declares them as "the ones who dispense the favour of your Lord" as against those who are seemingly "wealthy" and hold important positions (chiefs) in this world. Here the Qur'ān argues for the Prophet as the one who embodies God's *raḥmah* due to God's will alone and not due to any worldly title or position which he did or did not have. The quranic usage of *raḥmah* here is the same as in Q.18:65. It deals with the quality of being *Al-Raḥīm*—the "ever-merciful"—the superlative degree of which is applied to God alone. Thus, God being *Al-Raḥīm* sends messengers (and prophets) as symbols of divine *raḥmah.* And as a result, they become a channel through which God's *raḥmah* is dispensed in the world. Towards the end of Sūrat al-'Anbiyā', where in reference to Prophet Muḥammad, the Qur'ān (21:107) says, "We have sent you as a [*raḥmah*] to the inhabitants of the world," using again the word *raḥmah* as denoting the sending of the Prophet as "the mercy" from God. Other verses which bear similar association between the prophets and *raḥmah* are found in Sūrah Hūd, Q. 11:28 and 63 where Nūh (Noah) and Ṣāliḥ[26] respectively speak of God's "grace" and "blessings." In the second part of the verse, i.e., Q. 18:65b, we read, "and [Khiḍr has been] given knowledge from Us" (*wa 'allamnāhu min ladunnā 'ilman*). Sale continues the translation of this verse as, "and whom we had taught wisdom from before us." Amir-Ali translates it as "and endowed him with knowledge from Ourself." There is apparent clarity in the Qur'ān to argue that the notion that Khiḍr is a "mercy" from God is because he has been given knowledge from God. The knowledge is of and from God, hence it is the intuitive knowledge (*ma'rifah*)[27]—the knowledge which is immediately attained as opposed to the discursive knowledge. Here it seems plausible to argue that these qualities certainly allude to his elevated status. To possess divine knowledge (*ma'rifah*) is a quality of saints, but Khiḍr is evidently more than a saint, since he symbolizes God's "mercy" (*raḥmah*) which in the quranic sense clearly refers to prophecy (*nubūwwah*). The exegetes are more or less in agreement that the status of Moses is certainly higher than that of Khiḍr, since he (Moses) is not only a messenger (*rasūl*) but also a prophet (*nabī*),[28] bearer of the divine revelation and provisions of the law. Khiḍr, on the other hand, does not hold these titles, although the Qur'an calls him a "Servant" of God. Ibn 'Arabī's account of the encounter between Moses and Khiḍr also sheds some light on the nature of their relationship. Netton, interpreting Ibn 'Arabī, states that there is an "overwhelming emphasis on rank and knowledge . . . For al-Khadir is aware that Moses holds the exalted rank of Messenger (rasul), which he, al-Khadir, does not."[29] The following verse in Sūrat al-Kahf, verse 66 (*hal attabi'uka 'alā an tu'allimanī mimmā 'ullimta rushdan*), deals with Moses' request to be instructed by Khiḍr, which, seemingly at least, puts Khiḍr at a higher position than that of Moses. This further confirms the status of Khiḍr as a prophet, as mentioned in the previous verse. The emphasis here is on two key words which perhaps determine the overall meaning of the verse, *attabi'oka* and *tu'allimanī*—which may have direct bearing upon the status of Khiḍr. Ahmed Ali translates the verse as: "May I *attend upon you* that you may *instruct* me in the knowledge you have been taught of the right way?" (emphasis added). Amir-Ali has translated the key words as: "May I *follow thee* so that thou mayst *teach* me something of thy wisdom?" (emphasis added).

According to the Qur'ān, therefore, Moses requests Khiḍr to be his guide (translation of *tu'allimanī* is "instruct me" or "teach me") and asks him to instruct him (Moses) "in the knowledge . . . of the right way" (Q. 18:66b). Seeking knowledge from a non-prophet would not befit the status Moses held, especially spiritual knowledge and wisdom. If Moses had been seeking worldly knowledge of some kind, technical or trade-related, that would be a different matter. But a prophet of distinction, who is a recipient of divine revelation and who represents *raḥma* from God, seeking wisdom from an unknown "Servant" of God is going a bit too far. Thus, it may be said that it would not be feasible for Khiḍr, firstly, to have knowledge from God, and, secondly, to "instruct" Moses in that knowledge he is given by God, without being a prophet and *raḥmah*, himself. It would be absurd to believe that Moses of all God's messengers was less in spiritual knowledge than a non-prophet.[30]

A contemporary scholar has argued for a third reason why Khiḍr should be seen as a prophet. It lies in one of Khiḍr's actions when he was with Moses; the killing of the young boy. It is argued that if Khiḍr was not a prophet, he would not have been able to take such a drastic action in front of Moses who is the messenger (*rasūl*) as well as the prophet (*nabī*).[31] Sufis on the other hand speak of distinct forms of knowledge: exoteric and esoteric, revelatory and inspirational, this worldly and other worldly, and so on. If Moses was the recipient of one form of divine knowledge, Khiḍr received another form of divine knowledge through a different medium (not revelatory but "direct") as the quranic narrative seems to suggest.[32] Classical Muslim scholars tried to accommodate by saying that Khiḍr's knowledge should be classified as *ilhām* (inspiration) which is a "kind of revelation (*waḥy*) . . . not restricted to prophets."[33] Yet there is apparent tension between these two major figures as Moses at first fails to comprehend the providence behind Khiḍr's three actions. If Khiḍr is not a *nabī,* as is argued by some,[34] then is it conceivable that Moses, with whom Khiḍr's meeting takes place, is not the (biblical) Moses of Banū Isra'īl? Those who state this point provide a *ḥadith*, (albeit weak, *mawḍū'*) in support of their claim, which is refuted by others on the authority of the report by a reliable early Muslim scholar 'Abdallah ibn 'Abbās.[35]

One of the earliest opinions on this matter is found in Ibn Ishaq's *Kitāb al-mubtadā* which also does not regard the *ḥadīth* to be a reliable source, especially in the absence of any quranic evidence that there was more than one person named Moses who could be relevant to the story.[36] It is safe to say that a majority of Qur'ān commentators regard Khiḍr as a prophet. The quranic concept of *raḥmah* analyzed above suggests as much. Moses and Khiḍr both possess divine knowledge however each received a different kind of knowledge.[37] Khiḍr symbolizes divine mercy (*raḥmah*) here on earth which is dispensed through his presence and actions. The Qur'ān describes Khiḍr as one of God's special servants to whom God had given from his mercy and from his knowledge.[38] Khiḍr is thus a "repository" of divine knowledge on earth, which also makes him a "mediator" between God and human beings who are on the path and seek divine proximity (*qurb*). Khiḍr is a symbol of God's mercy because he is a recipient of God's knowledge; here mercy and knowledge are (in a sense) synonymous. Both God's mercy and God's knowledge are meant for all servants of God, in essence for all members of God's creation. Khiḍr here becomes integral to how divine mercy (*raḥmah*) reaches a worshipper (especially those in need) and seekers of *qurb*.

According to 'Abd al-Razzāq Qāshānī, God has made some "a manifestation of the Harmful—like Satan and his followers, and others a manifestation of the Beneficial—like Khiḍr, and those who have affinity with him."[39] The notion of *raḥmah* appears many times in the Qur'ān. The quranic passage in 43:32 (Sūrat al-Zukhruf) speaks of God's prophets as those who "distribute" (*yaqsimūna*) God's Mercy to protect the vulnerable from the wealthy and powerful who might be more inclined to misuse their power to maintain their wealth. The role of the prophets is deemed to be that of being "protectors" of the masses and in full accordance with the will of God for humanity. The prophets dispense mercy because God has granted them certain spiritual powers, personal charism, as well as other resources to do so. In this worldview all prophets and messengers are treated as symbols of God's mercy; they are guides to the path to God; they are also known to announce warning of the impending wrath of God for those who cause *fitna* (anarchy and social unrest). Being the bearers of knowledge of and from God, they represent God's concern for the creation. God is most often invoked as "most merciful" (*Al-Raḥmān*) and "most compassionate" (*Al-Raḥīm*). The quranic usage of the term *raḥma* referring to Khiḍr's knowledge, as granted by God, resonates with other appearances of that term in the Qur'ān. In addition to Q. 43:32 we should consider Q. 21:107 (Sūrat al-'Anbiyā'), where the Qur'ān, while referring to Prophet Muḥammad says, "It was only as a mercy that We sent you [Muḥammad] to all people" (*raḥmat al-l-il 'ālamīn*).[40] Here again the usage of the term *raḥmah* denotes the sending of prophets as "mercy" from God. The Q. 18:65b suggests that this symbol of mercy, i.e., Khiḍr, is as such because he is given certain knowledge from God. These two ideas converge in this verse enabling one to deduce that Khiḍr has an elevated status in the Qur'ān: that of being a prophet who, by virtue of being endowed with divine knowledge, is a representative of the mercy of God. To possess divine knowledge is a quality which is often also claimed by spiritual masters and saints (*awliyā'*). Khiḍr is thus both a prophet and a saint. This dual identity is confirmed by scholars, mystics, Qur'ān interpreters as well as numerous persons who have claimed to have had an "encounter" with Khiḍr.

From the preceding, it may be argued that Khiḍr is an embodiment of God's mercy because of the knowledge he has been given by God. This is how he is received in terms of his role and function in Muslim piety as well as by the scholars and commentators of the Qur'ān. Khiḍr's prophetic status and his dealings with Moses are foundational to his charism in carrying out his divine mandate. He is known to perform "miraculous" and "magical" acts of healing the sick and providing guidance to those who have lost their way. It is these acts or the believability of Khiḍr's ability to perform such acts which have transformed him into a popular figure among the masses and made him a sought-after and much-remembered teacher among the Sufis and the like. Khiḍr's role as a repository of divine knowledge makes him a person who reflects divine light (*al-nūr*) in the metaphoric sense where light can be the source of spiritual countenance (*jalāl* or *tajallī*). This way of seeing Khiḍr is primarily found in Sufism, the mystical dimension of Islam, where he lends himself to a host of allegorical understandings. Below I will address some of the textual and historical connections that may be considered in support of this assertion.

On the one hand Moses is placed above Khiḍr in rank as a messenger and on the other, it is argued that they both possess different sets of knowledge, so in a way they are equals. This latter position represents the views of Ibn 'Arabī, perhaps in order to promote the idea that esoteric knowledge is relevant and valuable and, more importantly, equal in status to exoteric knowledge. Ibn 'Arabī appears to go even further in saying that the gnosis is important because it "perceives not only the necessity for and validity of [the] Law, but also the inescapable validity and necessity of those aspects of cosmic becoming that elude the Law."[41] Ibn Ḥajar al-'Asqalānī notes that if Moses was given knowledge of the *sharī'ah*, knowledge given to Khiḍr was related to the end of *sharī'ah*; if Moses' knowledge was of the substance (of the text), Khiḍr's was of its purpose.[42] These ideas are not welcomed by all Muslims, especially those who view Sufism with suspicion. The idea that Khiḍr can do things that even Moses would not do suggest that Khiḍr operates differently than other human beings and other prophets. Besides the semantics used to try and fit Khiḍr in the hierarchy of saints and prophets, there is the question of tenure with regard to extraordinary feats. The miraculous powers granted by God to Khiḍr (as a saint) are said to be temporary while those which Moses was endowed with are permanent. In fact, some notable Sufis have commented on the apparent errancy of elevating Khiḍr above Moses in rank.

In *Friends of God*, John Renard discusses the views of Abū Nasr al-Sarrāj noting that *wilāyah* (sainthood) can never be seen as higher than *nubūwwah* (prophecy) and that such ideas emanate from "inappropriate exegesis" of the quranic story regarding Moses and Khiḍr. He elaborates:

> One must take care not to misinterpret the scripture's references to the divine origin of Khidr's knowledge. Though Khidr's knowledge might appear to be superior to that of Moses, one must remember that a saint's prerogatives always reflect the higher status of the principal prophet of the age. Sarrāj identifies Khidr as a Friend of God, rather than as a prophet as some traditions do. He insists that but for the illumination of Moses, Khidr would have had no light to reflect. Friends of God enjoy only ad hoc divine knowledge, whereas prophets continually receive divine inspiration. Though Khidr may appear to be leading Moses in the Qur'ānic story, the two men's essential roles are actually the reverse.[43]

Even when Khiḍr is seen to be both a prophet (*nabī*) and a saint (*walī*), it does not diminish the importance of Moses,[44] who is seen as a messenger (*rasūl*). Each messenger is by definition also a *nabī* a *walī,* and a *mu'min*—a prophet, a saint and a believer.[45] Moses and Khiḍr both possess divine knowledge but due to their specific mission each is given a different form of knowledge. In the spiritual realm Khiḍr is both *quṭb al-ghawth* (pole of invocation for help for the believers) and *quṭb al-ḥaqīqah* (pole of the Truth).[46] Therefore, Khiḍr acts in the prophetic as well as the mystic spirit since he is given both *raḥmah* and *'ilm ladunnī* from God.[47]

Notwithstanding Sarrāj's reservations noted above, Khiḍr's status as a prophet is widely recognized but with an understanding that his prophecy was different from that of Moses. The quranic concept of *raḥmah* is closely linked with divine "guidance" either in the form of revelation given to the prophets or simply by their mere presence and witness unto humankind.[48] Therefore Khiḍr indeed fulfills the requirements of being a prophet and yet he is also seen to be much more. In the next chapter on Sufism, I will follow up on the connection made by Nicholson with respect to Khiḍr holding a "prophecy of saintship" (*nubūwwatu'l-wilāyāh*) as opposed to the "prophecy of institution" (*nubūwwatu'l-tashrī'*) which characterized the status held by Moses.[49]

SYMBOLIC REPRESENTATIONS OF KHIḌR

Symbolism is a way or a means to express higher realities. It is a way to express the metaphysical principles which are the origins of all outward or lesser realities. The Khiḍr-Moses story is an allegory; it has symbolic meanings because it represents higher truths that may only be expressed by figurative, non-literal means.

Symbolism of Being "Green"

Khiḍr means "the Green One," representing freshness of spirit and eternal liveliness; green symbolizing the freshness of knowledge "drawn out of the living sources of life."[50] The name implies regeneration,[51] exoterically understood, it is the regeneration of the physical space; but a Sufi may also draw esoteric meaning to suggest regeneration of the spirit. The color green may also be related to how the story is related of Khiḍr's disappearing into the "green landscape" after he and Moses split up.[52] It is a sort of "becoming green," or by way of vanishing and teaching a lesson, making knowledge "afresh" for those who need it. It is "afresh" because it is "drawn from Allah's own Presence."[53] The title "al-Khiḍr" is explained in various ways. In the *ḥadīth* he is called Khiḍr because after sitting on a dried-up patch of grass, when he got up the place became lush green (*khaḍrā'*).[54] In another version he is known as Khiḍr "because on one occasion when he sat on a white pelt, it shook beneath him and became green."[55] The name could also be taken to imply the connection with the wilderness, fields, and the like, where Khiḍr is most likely to meet the lost and troubled whence he could guide them. Ibn Kathīr notes that when Moses arrived at the "meeting place of the two oceans" (*majma'al-baḥrayn*), he and his companion saw Khiḍr lying on a green cloth which was laid out on the surface of the ocean.[56] Whatever the source for this green may be, it has come to symbolize the benign presence of divine wisdom as imparted by God to Khiḍr and to Prophet Muḥammad. This also might explain the inseparable association between expressions of prophetic love (*'ishq al-rasūl*) such as chanting praises of Muḥammad in pious Muslim religious ceremonies and the color green which is sufficiently represented on such occasions.[57] Similarly, the cloak of the Prophet is often depicted as green.[58] Interestingly, however, not all accounts of Khiḍr's appearance describe him in green. Nicholson reported that Abū Sa'īd ibn Abī'l-Khayr would often go into self-imposed exile and "would flee to mountains and wilderness, where he was sometimes seen roaming with a venerable old man clad in white raiment . . . [who as] he declared [later] was the prophet Khadir."[59] There is yet another account of Khiḍr seen in white in a *ḥadīth* which relates that Anas and Huzayfa, two of the companions of Prophet Muḥammad, saw Ilyās or Khiḍr (confusing between the two) wearing a white garment.[60] Khiḍr roams the world of the unseen; he sees the physical world but those who live in the physical world do not see him, except Moses because God made it possible for him. This is the reason why Khiḍr could perform the three seemingly unlawful things when he was with Moses.

To the other human beings who witnessed the three events, those were acts of providence; they were not aware that Khiḍr was actively involved.[61]

Symbolism of Fish and Water

Besides the symbolism surrounding Khiḍr's name, the story has other rich elements that may best be interpreted allegorically. First, there is the mention of the fish which is a symbol of knowledge in many cultures.[62] In Sufi thought, the "fish are symbols of the mystic swimming in the ocean of God's unity."[63] Then, there is the water motif, a symbol of life, as well as the sea, which signifies the limitlessness and the vastness of the phenomenon, in this case, of knowledge, especially esoteric knowledge. The imagery can be extended further if we consider that element in the story where the fish disappears at the confluence of the sea (Q. 18:61). If the sea is like a reservoir of knowledge, the meeting of the two seas suggests coming together of different forms or domains of knowledge. These may represent the esoteric and the exoteric forms of knowledge. According to the story, this fish (symbol of knowledge but even more so as Renard noted, an act of immersion in mystical knowledge or discipleship), was to be Moses' breakfast, which is precisely what Moses needed before he "understood" the subtlety of the events which occurred while he was with Khiḍr in the role of a disciple. The fish, however, was dead when it was with Moses and Joshua, only to become alive soon after, thus suggesting the need for them to follow it (strive) to discover the "way" to knowledge. The reason why Joshua (he is noted in the *ḥadīth* as being the son of Nūn, which is taken to mean "fish") may have forgotten to tell Moses about the disappearance of the fish is yet another event that signals that the meeting between Moses and Khiḍr was by design; it was divine intervention. It would appear that even the seemingly insignificant things in the story have a role to play in the final outcome. If Nūn could mean "fish" while fish signifies knowledge, it may suggest that the idea of the attendant is just a stand-in for the potential, always present in Moses who is a prophet after all, for recognizing spiritual knowledge that he was to seek out from Khiḍr once they met. According to Muḥammad Shafī', Joshua may also be homesick which made him forget about the fish's disappearance, as his thoughts wandered away thinking about his homeland.[64] Yūsuf Alī suggests "inertia" as the cause of forgetting. "In [Johsua's] case the 'forgetting' was more than forgetting. Inertia had made him refrain from telling the important news. In such matters inertia is almost as bad as active spite, the suggestion of Satan. So new knowledge or spiritual knowledge is not only passed by in ignorance, but sometimes by culpable negligence."[65]

Another explanation is that the "*fatā*" (the young attendant) was made to forget by God so as to force them to make the journey back at the appointed time and place where they were expected to find Khiḍr.[66] Whatever may be the reason for Joshua's forgetfulness it certainly seems to contain yet another moral for the reader of the story. The link between the symbolism of the fish (knowledge and immersion in it) which is being carried during travel (*jihad*, striving is required in acquiring knowledge) in order to arrive at (understand) the "meeting of the two oceans" (perfect knowledge). The two oceans, once again, are parallel to the two kinds of knowledge, the exoteric (like that of Moses) and the esoteric (like that of Khiḍr) and the "perfect knowledge" is the coming together of the two.[67] The concept of the "meeting of the two oceans" is mentioned in the Qur'ān more than once. On the one hand, it contains a rich analogy to the two domains of knowledge which come to a point of meeting ("*majma' al-baḥrayn*" as in Q. 18:60); on the other, it is taken "as an allusion to the World of Light and the World of Darkness,"[68] where they (the two oceans) are "let loose" and even though "they pass through each other, [they] remain distinct . . . with their distinct functions" ("*maraja al-baḥrayn*" as in Q. 25:53).[69] Two oceans or two distinct kinds of knowledge perform distinct functions in the world but are instituted for a single divine purpose: the knowledge that leads one to the Source of all knowledge or God. The meeting of Moses and Khiḍr was made necessary by God so as to signify their "unity of purpose," and the parting of the two was to emphasize their "distinction in method." It is evident here, however, that the two are not mutually exclusive; instead, they complement each other.

Symbolism of Travel (*riḥla*)

Khiḍr and Elijah (Ilyās) are said to meet every year during the time of pilgrimage at Mecca, not only to perform the *ḥajj* themselves but also to meet the needs, as it were, of hundreds of other travelers to the holy cities of Islam. The conception of Khiḍr as the protector of travelers is derived from Khiḍr's own travels as related in the tradition. Travel being full of hardships and dangers, travelers have a special need of a protector in a dire necessity. The significance of their (Khiḍr and Ilyās') meeting at the time of pilgrimage, therefore, cannot be underestimated as it may be understood to be symbolic of the fact that God's help comes to those who strive in God's way whether through journeying for pilgrimage (*ḥajj*), emigrating for intellectual gain (*riḥla*) or simply to visit the shrines of *awliyā'* and other places of reverence (*ziyārah*) in other lands. In effect, they all constitute striving (jihad) in the path of God for which God's help (*naṣr Allāh*) is granted-sometimes through Khiḍr. Thus, Khiḍr in some cultures is known as a patron-saint of travelers. Travel and journeying to new places are considered acts of piety (*īmān*) and striving (jihad) as they inspire learning and increase one's chances of attaining wisdom through new experiences. The motif of being a patron-saint of traveler elevates Khiḍr as an exemplar of piety and wisdom. Those who follow in his footsteps and journey to new lands are praised.[70] Travel is "preeminently an act of imagination"[71] or as in this case, religious imagination. Travel inspires imagination and allows one to visualize a different place with better economic prospects. It motivates a person to find avenues for growth even if it means upsetting one's present comforts in the hope of attaining that different experience. Travel in all its forms, but especially as *hijrah* (migration), involves both physical and psychological change; it can be undertaken for any reason: for seeking peace, livelihood, or for education and learning. In effect, it is a "movement of the soul from a state of corruption to one of purity,"[72] and by extension, from a state of ignorance to a state of knowledge, from failure to success, and from stagnation to dynamism in whatever form it may be imagined. Travel and migration are also regarded as noble means to attain knowledge. Since knowledge in Islam encompasses all knowledge—both divine and worldly—it is inevitably linked with the attainment of divine wisdom. Moses and his companion *traveled* to seek "the secret of divine knowledge," where they met Khiḍr. Similarly, travelers by making a *hijrah* seek divine guidance through God's servant Khiḍr.

Symbolism of Immortality

Ibn Ḥajar al-'Asqalānī relates a *ḥadīth* where the Prophet is reported to have said that Khiḍr lives in the sea and Ilyās is in- charge of the land; they are both alive and they come together every year for pilgrimage.[73] Ḥasan al-Basrī (d. 728) believed that both Ilyās and Khiḍr will live until the first blow of the trumpet on the day of Judgement.[74] In the opinion of Mullā 'Alī Qārī they are brothers,[75] however, there is some difference of opinion regarding whether Khiḍr is still "alive" or has moved on to another plane of existence. According to Imām Abū Zakariyyā al-Nawawī (d. 1277), Khiḍr is alive and present among us so he can continue to help those in need. He will die at the precise time when the Qur'ān will be "lifted up to heaven."[76] Said Nursi (d. 1960) in his *Mektubat* noted that Khiḍr is alive but at a level different from other human beings who are alive only for a duration. According to Nursi,

> There are five degrees of life. . . . The first level is that of our life, which is very restricted. The second level is that of the lives of Khidr and Ilyas, which is free to an extent. That is to say, they can be present in numerous places at the same time. They are not permanently restricted by the requirements of humanity like we are. . . . The third level is that of Idris and Jesus . . . , which is removed from the requirements of humanity, and is an angelic level of life. . . . The Fourth level of life is that of the martyrs . . . [and the fifth] is that of the spirits of the dead in their graves.[77]

Each of the above views seek to explain something that is inexplicable. Scholars who are more receptive to the idea of an "imaginal" or "hidden" world (the *bāṭin*) appear to readily believe that Khiḍr is alive while others remain skeptical. The famous North African Sufi al-Shādhilī is reported to have hated two things: one of which is that some *fuqahā'* insist that Khiḍr is no longer alive.[78] However, as the contemporary scholar Ṣalāḥ al-Khālidī has noted, although many of the *"ulamā"* have acknowledged some evidence of Khiḍr being "alive" in the sense of being available to a sincere seeker, one should not take that to mean literally. Many of the *ḥadīths* cited in support of such claims are found to be either *ḍa'īf* (weak) or *mawḍu'* (fabricated).[79] Ibn Kathīr in his *Tārīkh* mentions some sources that speak of Khiḍr being alive while acknowledging that these cannot be authenticated. There are other scholars who did not consider Khiḍr to be "alive"; these include Imām Bukhārī (d. 870) and 'Abd al-Raḥmān Abū'l Farash Ibn al-Jawzī (d. 1201). Their argument is that we should consider the quranic principle noted in Sūrat al-Anbiyā' (Q. 34: 21) "*wa mā ja'alnā libasharin min qablika al-khuld*, i.e., no human being can be said to be immortal" before making claims such as these.[80]

Another argument against Khiḍr being alive today lies in the fact that were he living, he would have been helping Muslims in assisting in Muḥammad's mission in a more prominent way instead of being hidden from most people. In Islamic prophetology, Khiḍr as a prophet of lower rank than Muḥammad would be obligated to assist in the latter's mission. Ibn al-Jawzī contends that it is likely that Khiḍr lived before the time of Muḥammad.[81] Beyond the issue of death, there is a question whether figures like Khiḍr are to be understood as real persons at all. It has been suggested that Khiḍr and Ilyās are symbols rather than real persons, where Khiḍr is the symbol of *basṭ* (expansion) and Ilyās symbolizes *qabd* (contraction).[82] If Khiḍr is not divine (as this would immediately place him outside the fold of Islam) and he is not immortal (since no human being can be such), how does one explain the experiences of thousands of Muslims who speak of him as if he is real? Perhaps we should consider what René Guénon calls "effective immortality" as opposed to "virtual immortality" where Khiḍr may be seen to be spiritually "present," regardless of whether he is physically alive.[83]

According to Abu'l Fath Qushayrī, Khiḍr may have existed in history, but he is not a living person any longer. Rather, the name Khiḍr is a rank which those righteous people who walk in his footsteps inherit.[84] Thus "Khiḍr" is a *state of being* whereby individuals become special instruments of God in order to carry out divine guidance in accordance with the will of God. It is said that there would be a Khiḍr in every age,[85] thus the immortality of Khiḍr lies in the continuation of his work beyond any one era. However, the traditionalist belief persists regarding the four prophets who have not tasted death as of yet and Khiḍr is one of them. By virtue of being ever-present and for his role in straightening out Moses' difficulties with paradoxes, he is revered in the Muslim tradition and looked upon by the Sufis in great veneration. But Sufis have used Khiḍr as a symbol in multiple ways. Farīd al-Dīn 'Aṭṭār, in his long allegorical poem *Manṭiq al-ṭayr*, presents him as the opposite of what a Sufi may desire. In a dialogue between Khiḍr and a dervish—a "fool of God,"[86] Khiḍrian lifestyle is shown to be antithetical to the spiritual path: Khiḍr asks the dervish, "O perfect man, will you be my friend?" And the reply from the one in the way of God is: "You and I are not compatible, for you have drunk long draughts of the water of immortality so that you will always exist, and I wish to give up my life."[87]

Despite the various receptions of Khiḍr among Muslims, the story is a good reminder that in the end humility is the true measure of piety and that one should never cease to strive for knowledge of God despite one's spiritual accomplishments. Since there is no end to divine knowledge it is unwise to assume, as Moses did, that one may know it all. Such wisdom requires realization of the essence of things, whereby one is able to distinguish between actions that are wrong in substance from those that may be wrong in appearance only. However, in defense of Moses, ordinarily speaking the task of a lawgiver is to adjudicate on the basis of the law, therefore, he did what he was supposed to do. On the other hand, Moses is more than a lawgiver, he is one of the prophets of distinction in the Qur'ān, thus it would not be unreasonable to expect a more nuanced response from a person of his stature to the three quranic acts of Khiḍr. Perhaps the story is meant to show how a lawgiver such as Moses *strives* to acquire the skills needed to know the "essence" of things. Yūsuf Alī summarizes the takeaway of the story of Moses' meeting with Khiḍr in four points. First, wisdom is not all encompassing; even a wise prophet such as Moses does not know everything there is to know. Second, we must always strive to expand our knowledge, which is what Moses was trying to do in this story. Third, the knowledge that Khiḍr was given was informed by the lived experience while Moses was acting mostly within a theoretical framework. And finally, the fourth point is that we must remain open to see the paradoxes in life where apparent loss may in fact turn out to be a real gain and vice versa. In the final analysis, "God's wisdom transcends all human calculation."[88]

The Khiḍr-Moses episode in the Qur'ān is a reflection and representation of the paradoxes of life.[89] It symbolizes the delicate balance between patience and faith as they were enjoined on Moses after he understood the meaning of those paradoxes explained to him by Khiḍr himself. What is perhaps implied by the story is that such wisdom is only attainable by the will, mercy, and the grace of God, and that even Moses' prophetic status was not sufficient to make him attain that "most subtle knowledge" (*ma'rifah*) because it is only known to those who have become instruments of God's will on earth. Moses was shown these events only "to illustrate the manner in which God may provide contrivances or reconditionings for the benefit of [God's creation]." God uses a person of faith selected from among the most ordinary group of people and inspires agency to act and implement divine will.[90] In this story, Moses is being given a front row seat facing the paradoxical situations which cannot be dealt with using only one kind of knowledge. The story shows the coming together of the subtle but momentary knowledge belonging to Khiḍr and the universal knowledge (revelation) Moses had received. Moses' lens of seeing was the law which is derived from universal principles but the situations he faced when he was Khiḍr could not be solved with law alone. Because of the differences in their respective forms of knowledge or expertise, and in order to understand the subtleties of the situations in the quranic episode Moses needed to follow Khiḍr.[91]

In spite of the contextual and universal aspects of their knowledge respectively, Khiḍr and Moses combined did not possess even a fraction of divine knowledge. Al-Zamakhsharī reminds us by referring to the story where Khiḍr and Moses are riding in a boat (*safīnah*) and they saw a bird taking a drop of water from the sea. Khiḍr said to Moses, "your knowledge and my knowledge combined is like this drop of water if compared to the ocean of God's knowledge."[92] In one sense Khiḍr appears to be superior to Moses in this story. It may imply that Moses' encounter with Khiḍr is actually his encounter with the aspects of the divine in an attempt to remind Moses of the infiniteness of knowledge. In this, there are "glimmerings of a theophany" in the personage of Khiḍr who as God's servant is as human as Moses, and yet he seems to embody the divine attribute of mercy (eternal salvation) and divine knowledge (eternal prescience).[93] In short, it may be summed up as a divine test of Moses.[94] Most classical exegetes do not regard Khiḍr as superior to Moses. Zuhaylī in his *Tafsīr al-munīr* quoted the Sunni jurist, Abū 'Abdullah al-Qurṭubī, who stated that Moses' knowledge was based on *waḥy* (divine revelation) whereas that of Khiḍr's was based on *ilhām* (divine inspiration) therefore the former outranks the latter. Further, he notes that whatever Khiḍr's knowledge (and actions) may symbolize, in social context rulings of the law (*aḥkām al-sharī'ah*) cannot be established on the basis of exceptional situations like that experienced by Khiḍr.[95]

I have argued that Khiḍr is an embodiment of God's mercy *because of* the knowledge he has been given by God. This is how he is viewed in Muslim cultures as well as portrayed by the scholars and commentators of the Qur'ān. There is an intimate link between Khiḍr's knowledge and his charisma, i.e., between his divine mandate and his ability to perform "miraculous" and "magical" acts of healing for the sick and to offer guidance for those who seek him out. It is such acts or the believability of Khiḍr's ability to perform such acts which has transformed him into a figure of note among the ordinary believers and a venerable teacher for the mystically inclined. Khiḍr's role as a repository of divine knowledge makes him a person who reflects divine light (*al-nūr*) in the metaphoric sense of light as the source of spiritual countenance (*jalāl* or *tajallī*). Granted that interpreting Khiḍr's role in this fashion will mostly likely not be welcomed by everyone. However, among the Sufis as well as in popular Muslim piety Khiḍr is a familiar figure and, for many, an indispensable guide to spiritual excellence. In the next three chapters I will provide further arguments in support of the connections between textual and historical articulations regarding Khiḍr and the myriad of roles he plays in mystical as well as in the folk traditions prevalent in Islamicate/ Islamic cultures.

NOTES

1. The word "*fatah*" meaning "young man" here refers to Moses' servant. This companion/ attendant is said to be Yūsha' bin Nūn also known as Joshua. Al-Zamakhsharī, *Al-Kashshāf*, 395 and al-Baghdādī, *Tafsīr al-Khāzin*, 203.

2. Qur'ān 18:60.

3. "*ḥuqub*" generally means eighty years or simply a long time. Al-Zamakhsharī, *Al-Kashshāf*, 395; al-Baghdādī, *Tafsīr al-Khāzin*, 204.

4. Muḥammad Shafī', *Ma'ārif al-Qur'ān* (Karachi: Dār al-Ma'ārif, 1978), 5:591.

5. Shāh Walī Allāh, *A Mystical Interpretation of Prophetic Tales by an Indian Muslim: Shāh Walī Allāh's Ta'wīl al-Aḥādīth*, trans. J. M. S. Baljon (Leiden: E. J. Brill, 1973), 39–40.

6. Al-Baghdādī, *Tafsīr al-Khāzin*, 203.

7. Shafī', *Ma'ārif al-Qur'ān*, 591.

8. Ibid. See also al-Baghdādī, *Tafsīr al-Khāzin*, 209; he includes here what he considers to be Khiḍr's advice to Moses: "You do not seek knowledge so that you tell other people; you seek it so you may practice it."

9. Al-Zuhaylī, *Tafsīr al-munīr*, 294.

10. Exoteric and esoteric are complementary to each other; literally the "outward" and "inward" of all things. The Q. 57:3 states that God is "the First and the Last, The Evident (*al-ẓāhir*) and the Immanent (*al-bāṭin*); and [God] has the full knowledge of all things." Thus, the *ẓāhir* of Moses and the *bāṭin* of Khiḍr together represent the highest level of knowledge: the realization of the Real in its near Totality. Glasse, *The Concise Encyclopedia of Islam*, s. v. "Ẓāhir," 430.

11. Cf. Muḥammad ibn 'Alī al-Shawkānī, *Fath al-qadīr* (Riyādh: Dār 'Alam al-Kutub, 2003), 3:299.

12. Al-Zuhaylī, *Tafsīr al-munīr*, 298.

13. Tha'labī says in his *Tafsīr al-kabīr* that judging from most of the traditions attributed to Prophet Muḥammad, Khiḍr is one of the prophets; cited in Ibn Ḥajar al-'Asqalānī, *al-Zahr al-naḍir*, 26.

14. Sultān Ḥasan, *'Irfān al-Qur'ān*, 113. Māwardī also regards Khiḍr as an angel who appeared in human form. Ibn Ḥajar al-'Asqalānī, *al-Zahr al-naḍir*, 30.

15. Abū Ḥayyān believed that Khiḍr was a *walī* for a group of mystics but he contends that majority opinion is that he was also a prophet. Quoted in Ibn Hajar al-'Asqalānī, *al-Zahr al-naḍir*, 29–30; see also Abū Ḥayyān al-Ghirnāṭī, *al-Baḥr al-muḥīṭ fī al-tafsīr* (Cairo: Dār al-Kitāb al-Islāmī, 1992). Al-Baghdādī in his *Tafsīr al-Khāzin* does not regard Khiḍr as *nabī* (205–7). For him the reason Moses asked Khiḍr for "instruction" is because God asked him (Moses) to do so and not because Khiḍr is equal or superior to Moses.

16. Ḥifzur Raḥmān, *Qiṣaṣul Qur'ān* (Delhi: Nadwatul Musannifīn, 1975), pt. I, 545.

17. See Sayyid Quṭb, *In the Shade of the Qur'an, Fī Ẓilāl al-Qur'ān*, translated by Adil Salahi, vol. 11 (London: The Islamic Foundation, 2007), cited in Franke, *Begegnung mit Khidr*, 368–69. According to Franke, Quṭb goes against the exegetical tradition by rejecting the need to identify the "servant" by name in order to fully relate to the quranic passage in question. Those who follow this narrative would not see Khiḍr as a religious figure playing an important role in Muslim salvation history.

18. Ibrāhim ibn Fathī 'Abd al-Muqtadar, *Kashf al-ilbās: 'amma ṣaḥḥa wa-mā lam yaṣiḥḥu min qiṣṣat al-Khiḍr Abī al-'Abbās* (Jeddah: Dār al-Muḥammadī, 1997), 10–11; and Maḥmūd Marākibī, *Musā wa'l-Khiḍr*, 4.

19. Marākibī, *Musā wa'l-Khiḍr*, 107–8.

20. Reynold A. Nicholson, *Studies in Islamic Mysticism* (Cambridge: The University Press, 1921), 141.

21. Ḥasan, *'Irfān al-Qur'ān*, 113.

22. Cf. al-Shawkānī, *Fatḥ al-qadīr*, 3:299ff. A contemporary scholar Ṣalāḥ al-Khālidī also refers to it as a basis for Khiḍr's prophecy; see his major work on the tales of the prophets *Ma 'qiṣaṣ al-sābiqīn fī al-Qur'ān* (Damascus: Dār al-Qalam, 1989), 2:178; cf. al-Zuhaylī, however, contends that *raḥmah* refers to *wilāyah* (*Tafsīr al-munīr*, 288).

23. Cf. Ramaḍān Yūsuf, *al-Khiḍr baynā al-wāqi' wa'l-tahwīl*, 62–63.

24. Hashim Amir-Ali, *The Message of the Qur'ān: Presented in Perspective* (Rutland, VT: Charles E. Tuttle Company, 1974), K-30, Sec. 328–330.

25. Sale, *The Koran*, 244.

26. Hūd and Ṣāliḥ are two of the four Arab prophets mentioned in the Qur'ān.

27. May be compared to "gnosis" in English or *erfān* in Farsi which is regarded as the very summit of the spiritual path in Sufism. Consequently, an *'ārif* is the one who has attained *ma'rifah*—the one who possesses esoteric knowledge and exists in a state of absolute love of God.

28. See Ḥifzur Raḥmān, *Qiṣaṣ al-Qur'ān*, pt. I, 545; cf. Ian Richard Netton. "Theophany as Paradox: Ibn 'Arabī's Account of al-Khiḍr in his *Fuṣūṣ al-Ḥikam*," *Journal of the Muhiyiddīn Ibn 'Arabī Society* 11 (1992): 18.

29. Netton, "Theophany as Paradox," 18.

30. Cf. al-Zamakhsharī, *Al-Kashshāf*, 397; where he says, Moses could not seek knowledge from someone less in knowledge since he was indeed the most knowledgeable in his time, implying, as it were, that Khiḍr had a status comparable to Moses.

31. Ramaḍān Yūsuf, *Al-Khiḍr bayna al-wāqi' wa-al-tāhwīl*, 62–63. His argument rests on three points. The other two are, as mentioned above, that *raḥmah* refers to *nubūwwah*; and Moses could not seek discipleship of a non-prophet.

32. Muḥyiddīn Ibn 'Arabī, *La vie merveilleuse de Dhū-l-Nūn l'Égyptien*, trans. Roger Deladrière (Paris: Sindbad, 1988), 30.

33. Sands, *Ṣūfī Commentaries on the Qur'ān in Classical Islam*, 83. This is the view of Sahl al-Tustarī, an early classical Qur'ān scholar with a Sufi leaning. Many later orthodox scholars seemed to have followed him and agreed with his views. For more on this, see al-Zuhaylī, *Tafsīr al-munīr*, 16.

34. For instance, al-Baghdādī, *Tafsīr al-Khāzin*, 205–7.

35. Ḥifzur Raḥmān, *Qiṣaṣul Qur'ān*, 538; cf. Thackston, *The Tales of the Prophets*, 208. Also al-Baghdādī in his *Tafsīr al-Khāzin* refutes any such claims (that Khiḍr's meeting was with Mūsā bin Mīshā as said by Kā'b al-Ahbār instead of Mūsā bin 'Imrān) by some scholars contending that if Moses mentioned with Khidr was different than the one who received the Torah, the Qur'ān would have clarified it; see *Tafsīr al-Khāzin*, 203; cf. al-Zuhaylī, *Tafsīr al-munīr*, 287.

36. Newby, *The Making of the Last Prophet*, 114. The weak *ḥadīth* is used by some so as to avoid the conflict of rank between Prophet Khiḍr, the instructor of Prophet Moses who is also a messenger (*rasūl*) and therefore has a higher rank, so to speak. See Elboudrari, "Entre le symbolique et l'historique Khadir im-mémorial," 34.

37. Netton, "Theophany as Paradox," 18.

38. Paraphrasing Q. 18:65.

39. 'Abd al-Razzāq al-Qāshānī, *A Glossary of Sufi Technical Terms*, trans. Nabil Safwat (London: The Octagon Press, 1991), 84.

40. Translation by M.A.S. Abdel Haleem; slightly modified.

41. *The Bezels of Wisdom*, trans. R.W.J. Austin (New York: Paulist Press, 1980), 250.

42. For more on this see Ibn Ḥajar al-'Asqalānī, *al-Zahr al-naḍir*, 29–30.

43. John Renard, *Friends of God: Islamic Images of Piety, Commitment, and Servanthood* (Berkeley: University of California Press, 2008), 264–65.

44. For a Sufistic understanding of terms *nabī* and *walī* see Michel Chodkiewicz, *Seal of the Saints: Prophethood and Sainthood in the Doctrine of Ibn 'Arabī* (Cambridge: The Islamic Texts Society, 1993), chap. 3 "The Sphere of *Walāya*"; see also Claude Addas, *Ibn 'Arabī ou la quête du Soufre rouge* (Paris: Gallimard, 1989).

45. Chodkiewicz, *Seal of the Saints*, 92.

46. Edward W. Lane, *Manners and Customs of the Modern Egyptians* (London: J.M. Dent, 1914), 238.

47. See Schimmel, *Mystical Dimensions of Islam*, 7.

48. Moses received "guidance" (revelation) as well as "mercy" from God whereas Mary received only blessings and "mercy." Cf. Qur'ān 6:154, 7:52; 19:21.

49. Nicholson, *Studies in Islamic Mysticism*, 141.

50. 'Abdullah Yūsuf 'Alī, *The Meaning of the Holy Qur'ān* (Brentwood, MD: Amana Corporation, 1992), 727, note 2411.

51. Schwarzbaum, *Biblical and Extra-Biblical*, 18. It is also related that once Khiḍr sat on a pile of dry grass and leaves and out of his blessings they turned green; cf. al-Baghdādī, *Tafsīr al-Khāzin*, 205.

52. Jan Knappert, *Islamic Legends: Histories of the Heroes, Saints, and Prophets of Islam* (Leiden: E.J. Brill, 1985), 1:116.

53. Yūsuf ʻAlī, *The Meaning of the Holy Qur'ān*, 727, note 2411.

54. *Ṣaḥīḥ Bukhārī*, hadith #3400; al-Baghdādī, *Tafsīr al-Khāzin*, 205.

55. A. H. Johns, "Moses in the Qur'ān: Finite and Infinite Dimensions of Prophecy," in *The Charles Strong Lectures 1972–1984*, ed. Robert B. Crotty (Leiden: E.J. Brill, 1987), 135.

56. Ibn Kathīr al-Damishqī, *Qiṣaṣ al-ʻanbiyā*,' 535.

57. In many Muslim cultures wearing a green garment represents a higher spiritual status; green clothing is often associated with Prophet Muḥammad and many other Sufis and saints.

58. See Schimmel, *And Muhammad is His Messenger*, 39.

59. Nicholson, *Studies in Islamic Mysticism*, 13.

60. Ibn Ḥajar al-ʻAsqalānī, *al-Zahr al-naḍir*, 66.

61. Al-Qārī al-Harawī, *al-Ḥadhar fī ʻamr al-Khaḍir*, 106.

62. "Fish is the emblem of the fruit of secular knowledge." Yūsuf ʻAlī, *The Meaning of the Holy Qur'ān*, 747, note 2408.

63. John Renard, *Windows on the House of Islam: Muslims Sources on Spirituality and Religious Life* (Berkeley: University of California Press, 1998), 345.

64. Muḥammad Shafīʻ, *Maʻārif al-Qur'ān*, 592.

65. Yūsuf ʻAlī, *The Meaning of the Holy Qur'ān*, 726, note 2410.

66. Al-Shawkānī, *Fatḥ al-qadīr*, 3:299.

67. "The salt sea of this world represents, like Moses, exoteric knowledge, whereas the Waters of Life are personified by al-Khiḍr." See Martin Lings, *Symbol and Archetype: A Study of the Meaning of Existence* (Cambridge: Quinta Essentia, 1991), 75.

68. Najm al-dīn Abū Ḥafṣ al-Nasafī quoted in Sachiko Murata, *The Tao of Islam* (Albany: State University of New York Press, 1992), 160.

69. Yūsuf ʻAlī, *The Meaning of the Holy Qur'ān*, 901, note 3111. The "World of Light" and the "World of Darkness" are again allegorical references to the spiritual world and the corporeal world, respectively. For a fuller discussion see Murata, *The Tao of Islam*, 160.

70. The Abbasid Caliph Al-Muʻtasim (d. 842) was honored by a poet for his connection with Khiḍr or for being Khiḍr-like. In Yāqūt al-Ḥamawī's *Muʻjam al-buldān*, he is addressed as such: "You ranged with power through all the land, As though you sought al-Khiḍr's trail." Shihāb al-Dīn Abī ʻAbdullāh Yāqūt al-Ḥamawī, *Muʻjam al-buldān*, vol. 1 (Beirut: Dār al-Kutub al-ʻIlmīyah, 1990), translation from Wadie Jwaideh, *The Introductory Chapters of Yāqūt's Muʻjam al-Buldān* (Leiden: E.J. Brill 1959), 2.

71. Dale F. Eickelman and James Piscatori, eds., *Muslim Travellers: Pilgrimage, Migration, and the Religious Imagination* (Berkeley: University of California Press, 1990), xii.

72. Ibid.

73. Ibn Ḥajar al-ʻAsqalānī, *Al-Zahr al-naḍir*, 37.

74. Ibid., 36–37.

75. Qārī al-Harawī, *Al-Ḥadhar fī ʻamr al-Khaḍir*, 78.

76. Ibid., 86.

77. Bediuzzaman Said Nursi, *Letters* (Istanbul: Sözler Publications, 2001), First Letter, 21–23.

78. Attributed by Shaʻrawi, quoted in Louis Massignon, *The Passion of al-Hallaj: Mystic and Martyr of Islam*, trans., Herbert Mason (Princeton: Princeton University Press, 1982), 2:305, 330.

79. Al-Khālidī, *Maʻ qiṣaṣ al-sābiqīn fī al-Qur'ān*, 182.

80. Ibid.

81. Orthodox *'ulamā'* tend to be loyal to established norms and status quo. Thus, if Khiḍr is considered a prophet, Muḥammad is higher than him; if Khiḍr is deemed a *walī*, then Abū Bakr, the first of the four Sunni caliphs who succeeded Muḥammad, is to be regarded above him in rank because of the latter's proximity to the Prophet. Ibn Kathīr Damishqī, *Qiṣaṣ al-anbiya'*, 538. Similar arguments can be found in other conservative treatments of the issue. See for example, Haydar Nuʻaysah, *Al-Khiḍr* (Damascus: Dār al-Dhulfiqār, 2006); and ʻAbd al-Muqtadar, *Kashf al-ilbās*.

82. Qārī al-Harawī, *al-Ḥadhar fī ʻamr al-Khaḍir*, 88. *Qabd* and *basṭ* are two contrasting mystical states representing, as it were, the two states of utter despondency and utter happiness respectively.

83. For more on this see René Guénon, *Symbolism of the Cross* (London: Luzac, 1975), 12, also note 2.

84. Quoted in Ibn Ḥajar al-ʻAsqalānī, *Al-Zahr al-naḍir*, 113; and al-Zuhaylī, *Tafsīr al-munīr*, 16.

85. Ibn Ḥajar al-ʻAsqalānī, *Al-Zahr al-naḍir*, 113. This idea resembles the notion of a *mujaddid*, a reformer and a "renewer" of faith who is said to appear in every age.

86. A *dervīsh*—the one who has given everything for the sake of God—is naturally a "fool" by worldly standards or simply the one who aspires to become a Sufi (*mutasawwif*).

87. Farid ud-Din ʻAttar, *The Conference of the Birds. Mantiq ut-Tair*, trans. C. S. Nott (London: The Janus Press, 1954), 17.

88. Yūsuf ʻAlī, *The Meaning of the Holy Qur'ān*, 725, note 2404.

89. Sufis have extensively used the Khiḍr-Moses parable to show the value of paradoxes for life and particularly if one is trying to grasp mystical truths. Sufis are of course not the only ones who recognize the importance of paradoxes as a teaching tool. One of the most eminent psychologists of the twentieth century, Carl G. Jung, wrote about his "meetings" with Khiḍr through dreams. In an attempt to help his patients understand that paradoxes are a useful way to reconcile with reality, Jung utilized the episode of Khiḍr and Moses in his therapeutic counseling. Mohammed Shallan, "Some Parallels Between Sufi Practices and the Path of Individuation," in *Sufism, Islam and Jungian Psychology*, ed. J. Marvin Spiegelman et al. (Scottsdale: New Falcon Publications, 1991), 91.

90. Walī Allāh, *A Mystical Interpretation of Prophetic Tales,* 40–41.

91. Similarly, Vollers describes the issue in terms of theodicy; what may seem wrong to us (in Khiḍr's actions) may be right in God's judgment.

92. Al-Zamakhsharī, *Al-Kashshāf*, 395.

93. Netton, "Theophany as Paradox," 12.

94. It is about the symbolic knowledge which is here being represented through Khiḍr's actions and transferred through him to Moses. Symbolic knowledge, as Richard Martin has noted, is unlimited and "is not about the world as encyclopedic knowledge is." For more on symbolic knowledge and its relevance see his excellent article on "Structural Analysis and the Qur'an: Newer Approaches to the Study of Islamic Texts," *Journal of the American Academy of Religion Thematic Issue* 47 (December 1979): 670.

95. Al-Zuhaylī, *Tafsīr al-munīr*, 16.

Chapter 3

Khiḍr in Sufism

Bernard McGinn, who wrote extensively on aspects of Christian mysticism, acknowledged that to define mysticism is a problematic task. Mysticism is often regarded as a controversial dimension of religious practice and thus may be seen through the lens of a variety of categories or frameworks rather than any single master narrative. McGinn notes three general ways of viewing mysticism. Firstly, as part of religion; secondly, as a way of life; and, thirdly, as a process of communicating the inner experience of the presence of the divine.[1] The subject of this chapter may be located primarily in Islamic mystical thought, or more appropriately in Sufi writings. Inasmuch as Khiḍr lies within the realm of Sufism, it would be apt to say that he has been received in all the three different ways within the Islamicate tradition.

As already noted, the figure of Khiḍr is connected to the quranic text, the *tafsīr* literature, the *hadīth*, the *qiṣaṣ al-'anbiyā'*, a vast body of Sufi literature, as well as various folk traditions, many of which remain fluid and ever changing. The Khiḍr phenomenon and its associated traditions have taken up such a huge space within the Islamicate traditions and cultures that it is impossible to do justice to this topic in a single work. In this chapter, I will primarily focus on the religious and mystical understandings of Khiḍr's role and how they may be connected with the symbolism of "light" and spiritual or inward "illumination" which many Sufis claim to have received through him.[2] Nowhere is there more emphasis on seeking knowledge of and from God than in the mystical dimension of faith—the esoteric understanding of Islam. In Sufism, the seeker strives to be a *mu'min*; to not only seek knowledge but to implement it in one's life as part of one's spiritual practice. The secret of such knowledge, it is said, does not lie in isolation from or renunciation of the world. Rather it is found by being in the world and in seeking it from all available avenues. Al-Ṭabarī, citing an early Muslim scholar Ibn Abbās, states that after the Israelites were saved "from the people of Pharaoh" one of them asked Moses: "is there on earth anyone who knows more than you . . . ?" To which Moses said, "'No.' So God sent Gabriel . . . who said . . .

'Indeed, there is a man on the shore of the sea who knows more than you.'"[3] In effect, Moses is reminded here that "knowing" requires more than what we know and that we should never stop learning.

Sufis are among those who seek such wisdom and divine knowledge. The first "recorded appearance of the term *ṣūfī* dates from the middle of the second century" of Islam (8th century CE) when it was apparently "applied in Kūfa to the famous Jābir ibn Ḥayyān."[4] Sufis aspire to be "near" God; many were recognized in their own time as "friends of God" or saints. It is believed that the concept of *wilāyah* (sainthood) was first introduced into the technical vocabulary of Sufism by Hakīm al-Tirmidhī who lived in the 8th and 9th centuries. However, *taṣawwuf* (mystical practices and traditions of piety) existed prior to that time. The term *wilāyah* (or *walāyah*) would be familiar to the readers of the Qur'ān where it appears twice (8:72 and 18:44).[5] In early Islam mystics and pious individuals were not called Sufis; the term became known later. Referring to Muslim piety traditions, Chodkiewicz notes, "the thing existed before the word" *taṣawwuf* came along. Similarly, in later periods the word *taṣawwuf* did not always mean that the practice was authentic. Imām Hujwīrī, lamenting the decline of spiritual practice in his time (11th century), reportedly said, "*taṣawwuf* is today a name without reality, whereas it was once a reality without a name . . . the pretense is known and the practice unknown."[6] The Sufi path, according to Seyyed Hossein Nasr, is an "inward journey" where one's goal is to know the self and the source from where we came as well as our final destination, which does not sound as controversial a description as it has been made to be in some conservative Muslim circles. Nasr's statement is based on the quranic affirmation: "to God we belong, to God we shall return" (*innā lillāh-i-wa innā ilayhi rāji'ūn*). It is said that change is inevitable and everything around us is going through transformation which entails, at least for those who believe, that there is "life" after the physical earthly life. Sufi's want this belief to be the front and center of their journey here on earth as it offers a perspective and enables them to make choices based on that reality. This conscious way of living becomes the "path" for many. Nasr contends that the Sufi path, "leads from the desert of outwardness, forgetfulness, selfishness, and falsehood to the Garden of Truth, wherein alone we can realize our true identity and come to know who we are."[7] For Sufis, this self-knowledge is instrumental in moving from ordinary consciousness to higher states of consciousness where an individual can attain a deeper perspective on reality.

KHIḌR AS AN INITIATIC PRINCIPLE

As mentioned previously, Khiḍr is said to have drunk from the "water of life." For this reason, he is described as the one who has found the source of life, "the Eternal Youth."[8] He thus becomes the mysterious guide and an immortal saint in the popular religious piety. For the Sufis, Khiḍr is seen as one of the spiritual poles (*aqṭāb*, plural of *quṭb*) of the inhabited universe. In that, Khiḍr's status as a *quṭb* also corresponds to the notion of the "hidden Imām" in Shīʿī piety where the figure of the Imām functions as an invisible yet active guide to the living community of believers.[9] Annemarie Schimmel describes the role: "Sometimes the mystics would meet him on their journeys; he would inspire them, answer their questions, rescue them from danger, and, in special cases, invest them with the *khirqa[h]*, which was accepted as valid in the tradition of Sufi initiation."[10] Khiḍr is the initiator of those who seek the esoteric realities and those who strive on the path to someday becoming worthy of being a "Friend of God." The state of such a friendship (*wilāyah*) requires a long journey on an arduous path; arduous because of the struggle between ego on one side and the longing for the divine on the other. This initiatory function of Khiḍr is characteristic of his being a *quṭb* (or spiritual pole) and hence timeless. Moreover, Khiḍr's affiliation with his initiates is also timeless and "transhistorical" in the sense that it is part of the "tradition whose line is vertical . . . and whose moments are independent of the causality of continuous physical time" which Ibn ʿArabī has called the '*tajdīd al-khalq*' or the recurrence of the creative act.[11] Khiḍr is the hidden initiator of those who walk the mystical path like those from the Uwaysī *ṭarīqah*. Seekers in this particular Sufi order do not receive their initiation by a living master, instead they begin their mystical journey either by following the guiding light of the teachings from earlier masters or by being "initiated by the mysterious prophet-saint Khiḍr."[12] Here Khiḍr becomes an immortal personification of the 'initiatic principle' as he performs the role of a master/teacher in the invisible hierarchy of saints (*awliyā,*). He is indispensable to those who accept his discipleship, and he is always "present" for the disciple, without being physically there. The idea of one's teacher being present despite his/her physical absence is part of a wider spiritual matrix than just for the followers of Khiḍr. Sufis have long taught that for "the disciple the *shaykh* is always mysteriously present, especially during the rituals. The *shaykh* never dies . . . even if he has physically left this world. His spiritual guidance (*irshād*) and assistance continue even after death."[13] The figure of Khiḍr often invites the seeker to journey beyond the limitations of reason, into imaginal worlds. At times, the apparent contradictions symbolized by Khiḍr can be helpful just as paradoxes can make one see the range of possibilities instead of just the polar extremes.

Khiḍr represents mercy (*raḥmah*) a recognized attribute of prophecy, yet he is also known by his servitude (*'ubūdiyyah*) to the truth and to all the creatures of God.[14] In this, Khiḍr can be said to represent the servant-leader ideal so much emphasized in contemporary spiritual discourse.

The important role of a spiritual teacher becomes evident as one realizes the limitations involved in monitoring and guiding one's own journey toward God-realization. But not all Sufis have a physically present teacher. Khiḍr gained enormous reputation and popularity in the Sufi tradition due to his role as an initiator and a spiritual guide who is not physically there with the student. He nevertheless guides in his absence; this is what he is known for. Several Sufi orders began with claims (made by someone who would likely become known as the founder of the group) of being initiated by Khiḍr. It is yet another way of initiation through "a source other than a human master." A great many Sufis have said to have received *khirqah* from Khiḍr and that includes Ibn 'Arabī, one of the more well-known Muslim figures in the West.[15] By the early Middle Ages, Sufism had blossomed into a major force among the competing expressions of faith. In this milieu, Khiḍr had come to symbolize "the third path" to the knowledge of God, purely and constantly supernatural, giving access to the divine mystery (*ghayb*) itself.[16] He is invoked by almost every Sufi and mentioned by scholars of the Qur'ān and the *ḥadīth*. In the writings of "Abd al-Karīm al-Jīlī, Khiḍr rules over "men of the hidden world" (*rijāl al-ghayb*)—who are the exalted saints and angels.[17] Khiḍr is counted among those who, in the classical Sufism, are called the *abdāl*, ("those who take turns") a designation within the ranks of the *awliyā'* of Islam.[18] In a divinely instituted hierarchy of such saints, Khiḍr holds the rank of their "spiritual head." They are called *abdāl* because they apparently become a "substitute" for Khiḍr and take turns in "helping in his mission of assisting and saving good men in danger and distress."[19] The initiatory function of Khiḍr is characteristic of his being a *quṭb* in the hierarchy of saints. For Ibn 'Arabī, Khiḍr is one of the four *awtād* (pillars who hold the spiritual world in its place, as it were):[20] Idrīs (Enoch) is the *quṭb* in that hierarchy; then are the two imams, Jesus and Elijah and the fourth is Khiḍr—a pillar (*watad*) of knowledge and truth.[21] Through these four pillars God protects the "purity" of religion. Each of them has been assigned a distinct function: the first protects the faith (*īmān*), the second and the third protect sainthood (*wilāyah*) and prophethood (*nubūwwah*), and the fourth protects the mission (*risālah*). It is also held that of the four "living" prophets, "two of them, Idrīs and Jesus, dwell in the celestial spheres, and the other two, Elijah [Ilyās] and Khaḍir, dwell on this earth unseen by most mortals."[22] Thus the *awtād* hold the spiritual world just as, in the words of the Qur'ān, the mountains hold the earth like "pegs."[23]

Louis Massignon (d. 1962), the famous Catholic scholar of Islam, had much to say about Khiḍr. He understood Khiḍr as archetypal initiator of those who seek a spiritual path. Khiḍr initiated Moses by way of a series of tests (referring to the three episodes in the quranic narrative which were at first offensive to Moses), which were guided by the vision that "exceeds the literality of Good according to the Law."[24] Massignon saw himself as one of those whom Khiḍr had initiated to the path; he was said to be "in spiritual consonance with the *khadiriyyah* inspiration" having been visited upon by "the gentle breeze of the solitary initiator-al-Khiḍr."[25] This claim is not insignificant if it is indeed made to explain Massignon's quiet diplomacy during Vatican II on behalf of Islam and its recognition by the Council as part of the Abrahamic family of religions alongside Judaism and Christianity. For his efforts to be inclusive of Muslims as believers in God, Massignon was seen by some of his fellow Catholics to be dangerously stepping at the outer boundaries of his faith, even though he remained firmly established in his home tradition despite his love for Sufism. It is perhaps in this sense that Khiḍr provided Massignon the "vertical presence" allowing him to operate above the "law" as it were without violating any of it in essence.[26] For Massignon, Khiḍr may be hidden from most of us at present, but he will appear again to assist the Mahdi and Jesus at the end of times, so to speak.[27] In character with his mystical vision, Massignon suggests a role for Khiḍr in the eschaton. Indeed, Khiḍr is busy repairing the "cracks" in the "traditional edifice" in order to keep it intact and instrumental. Khiḍr's return at the end of times will serve as evidence of his freedom "from the limitations of time and space," and of his leadership as, in Laude's words, "the prophet of verticality."[28] Khiḍr will then guide the faithful to Jerusalem "to join Jesus son of Mary."[29]

In the Qur'ān, Khiḍr is called a "servant" of God. Such a designation implies a high status and at the same time a sense of loyalty to divine law. In Islam, the goal of existence is said to be to cultivate deep appreciation for and servanthood towards God. The Sufi path helps one do that firstly by breaking the ego which prevents individuals from reaching the state of humility necessary for servanthood (*'ubūdiyyah*). For Laude, in a mystical sense, besides servanthood, Khiḍr also represents the "freedom in God, which is . . . the other side of servanthood. Servitude towards God at each and every instant is actually the pathway to a spontaneous and potentially infinite freedom."[30] Laude explains this as Massignon's attempt to present Khiḍr (and Ilyās) as someone whose servitude (*'ubūdiyyah*) transcends law and who is thus transformed into a universal mystical trope. However, there is a slippery slope here due to the largely subjective nature of assessment involved which is used to determine a person having reached the status of a "true servant." Indeed, many have claimed to reach "true servanthood" by way of achieving the "freedom in God" which supposedly releases them for the obligations of the "law" or practices which are binding on Muslim believers. For traditionalists like Seyyed Hossein Nasr, *'ubūdiyyah* is related to the quranic term for worship (*'ibādah*) as in: "We [God] created human beings and jinn so they would worship [God]" (Q. 51:56). Thus, from an Islamic perspective the primary purpose of human existence is to "worship God" which can be interpreted to mean learning how to attain a "perfect state of servanthood."[31] A person's entire life is a journey of discovering one's true self and one's purpose by trying to cultivate humility through practicing the rituals of faith (*arkān*) such as daily prayers, and other actions like fasting, pilgrimage, and almsgiving at appropriate times during the year. For Sufis, there are additional spiritual practices that vary from school to school, and are aimed at striving (*jihād*, "to strive") for servanthood. This striving symbolizes a sacred journey, towards the realization of "what it means to be fully human." Once our ego realizes its full servanthood or *'ubūdiyyah*, it also becomes clear that "as servants we can never become the Lord."[32]

This prudent analysis of the path is crucial because some Sufi schools of thought and practice have focused intensely on the goal of "becoming one" with Reality, or al-Ḥaqq, the Truth, which is one of the quranic names for God. Muslim sages have left ample warnings for those who heed their message that it is important to distinguish between the path and the goal. The desire and striving for "union" with God may be a noble goal but its attainment is a different matter and much harder to quantify. Sincere practice is indeed fundamental to reaching the experience; however, excessive piety and obsessively pursuing one's "desire for union with God itself distances [the seeker] more than anything else from God."[33]

Historically as well as in contemporary times there have arisen numerous pseudo-mystical movements which claim to represent higher spiritual realities. Such movements, and those individuals who identify with them, have done great harm to the reputation of *taṣawwuf*, as they deviated from the *sharī'ah* claiming to be "one with God" having achieved mystical knowledge and experience. They see themselves as treading the mystical path at the expense of the observance of the *sharī'ah*. Many such individuals have laid claims regarding their encounter with Khiḍr who supposedly gave them such knowledge and the authority to what amounts to innovation in matters of faith (*bid'a*). Theologically speaking, it is not sustainable to reconcile Sufism with a practice that intentionally excludes *sharī'ah*. Sages from earlier periods when Sufi thought and practice was still nascent warned of these dangers and sought to distinguish between the *mutaṣawwif* (true seeker) and the *muṣtawif* (pretender to mystical knowledge); between a "true Muhammadan" and the "shopkeeper sheikh."[34] Similarly, the famous Sufi and scholar, Abū Ḥāmid Muḥammad al-Ghazālī (d. 1111), in his *Kīmiyā-e sa'ādat*, defends the Sufi way from allegations by Orthodox Muslims and argues that Prophet Muḥammad's piety and Sufi disciplines have much in common. At the same time, he insists that for the Sufi path to be authentic it cannot claim to be above the necessity of observing the ritual requirements outlined in the *sharī'ah* including the *arkān* (the Five Pillars).[35] Most practitioners of Sufism who contemplate the prophecy of Khiḍr and consider him their "hidden" *shaykh*, as it were, do not disregard the *sharī'ah*; instead they begin their journey within it.[36] For those who seek an encounter with Khiḍr, it is said there are certain conditions that need to be met. Firstly, the person should be a follower of the *sunnah* (prophetic example); secondly, the person should have no greed left for this world; thirdly, the seeker should be kind and gentle towards everyone.[37] Therefore, the *sharī'ah* is a pre-requisite and essential for one to be initiated in the *ṭarīqah* or the "path" because the path emanates from and exists within the *sharī'ah*.

If the esoteric reality of Islam (*ḥaqīqah*) is likened to the center of a circle, the exoteric form of it (*sharī'ah*) is the circumference of that circle. And the radius proceeding from the circumference to the center is the mystical path (*ṭarīqah*) leading a pilgrim, as it were, from *sharī'ah* to the *ḥaqīqah*; "from outward observance to inner conviction, from belief to vision, from potency to act,"[38] and most of all from the human realm to the divine realm. If the circumference represents the wholeness of reality, the center symbolizes its uniqueness and oneness (*tawḥīd*). This description is also helpful in demonstrating the relationship between esoteric and exoteric aspects of faith; each is differently constructed and yet both are centered on Reality. It may also be used to frame the Khiḍr-Moses relationship as mutually dependent. Each is given only part of the domain where they may exercise their authority; each of them needs the other to see the wholeness of truth. Sufis in general regard the *sharī'ah* as integral to the path, however, there are also groups and individuals who consider the spiritual path to be "above" the law, even if they continue to observe/practice the pillars of faith enshrined in the *sharī'ah* for other reasons. Similarly, piety is integral to the practice of Islam, yet many puritanical and orthodox-leaning Muslims frown upon practices that they consider "extra-Islamic." The Khiḍr-Moses story may indeed be instructive for both kinds of practitioners. Khiḍr does not operate independent of divine will and law, as he noted in his explanations for the three acts. Similarly, *sharī'ah*-centric, law-abiding Moses is amenable to be guided by a spiritual figure who appears to be "amoral" in the story.[39] The gap between the two positions seems wide and may only be bridged by taking a position of humility.

THE MASTER-DISCIPLE RELATIONSHIP

The "vertical dimension" of the spiritual relationship (between God and the seeker) depends entirely upon divine initiative even when human effort appears to be instrumental. As already discussed, Khiḍr's actions in the quranic story were in their entirety directed by divine will, as part of the verse Q. 18:82 clarified towards the end of the encounter between Khiḍr and Moses (. . . I did not do [these things] of my own accord . . .). The role Khiḍr played was that of an agent. Spiritual knowledge is "illuminative and unitive, a knowledge whose highest object is the Truth." This knowledge comes in three stages: *'ilm al-yaqīn* (knowledge of certainty) *'ayn al-yaqīn* (the eye of certainty), and *ḥaqq al-yaqīn* (the truth of certainty).[40] The Sufi knows by God or through God because, in the final analysis, human beings can hardly lay claim to acquiring knowledge through independent means. Just as we are spiritually dependent for our existence on the Source of all beings, similarly we are utterly reliant for our knowledge and actions. Nothing is originally from us, strictly speaking. A Sufi saying explains this dependence on God: "we exist in this world, but we subsist in another." In other words, we may be physically "here" but our subsistence, our ability to breathe and be alive through that act of breathing, is determined elsewhere. Our food may be of this earth, but *why* (not just how) that food sustains us, that is determined on a different plane.

Sufism is a path that begins with repentance (*tawbah*) and leads one to a higher state of awareness. Through a series of steps and stages (*maqāmāt*, pl. of *maqām*) one may achieve such higher virtues that open oneself to the mysteries of the divine presence. This process is generally seen as unfolding in the "passing away" (*fanā'*) in God and in "surviving" *(baqā')* as a transformed person. It is believed in mystical circles that to attain such a state of being one needs a trained instructor, someone who has already walked that path. Often the instructor is both physically and spiritually present and is in communication with the seeker even though only the spiritual dimension of such a relationship is essential. The Khiḍrian trope offers a variant to this traditional master-disciple relationship. Khiḍr as the Sufi master and instructor is absent as a physical being and yet fully present in the lives of innumerable seekers of the divine light who find themselves dependent upon his guidance for their spiritual journey. How is it that Khiḍr, an otherworldly spiritual guide, can relate to a disciple who materially and organically exists in the time-space continuum? Henry Corbin suggests reimagining the disciple's relationship with Khiḍr to be dissimilar to what someone would have with an earthly teacher. The thought that it is dissimilar opens the mind to seeing other possible modalities at work including dreams. Questioning the nature of such a relationship is to question the historical existence of Khiḍr whereas Khiḍr, as many insist, is "transhistorical" and, by virtue of being "immortal," also transcendent.[41] Attempts to explain how Khiḍr can be in many places at once and be always present for his disciples is problematic to say the least.

> If, taking the standpoint of analytical psychology, we speak of Khidr as an archetype, he will seem to lose his reality and become a figment of the imagination, if not of the intellect. And if we speak of him as a real person, we shall no longer be able to characterize the difference in structure between Khidr's relationship with his disciple and the relationship that any other *shaikh* on this earth can have with his.[42]

Hence the experience of being a disciple of Khiḍr "invests the disciple, as an individual, with a transcendent, 'transhistorical' dimension."[43] It is an experience which cannot be explained using the space-time matrix of our existence and sense perception.[44]

There are countless stories in mystical literature about experiences of meetings and forming relationship with Khiḍr. Often narrators acknowledge their dependency upon Khiḍr's instruction and guidance. These stories have been passed down for generations as oral wisdom and are part of the ethos. The Central Asian religious group, the Uwaysī order, considers these stories as fundamental to the practice of the mystical path. This Sufi order is named after Uways al-Qaranī (d. 657) of Yemen, a contemporary of Prophet Muḥammad. Uways became a Muslim without ever meeting the Prophet in person.[45] However, he regarded Muḥammad as his physically absent but spiritually present teacher and shaykh. There emerged a model named after Uways for people with no visible human guide. It became acceptable to follow a teacher who may be geographically separated (or is invisible for some other reason) and yet may be "present" and "available" to the disciples. Uwaysis are known to regard Khiḍr as their guide and a hidden master. Indeed, some Sufis would argue that anyone who commits to the mystical path may receive instructions from Khiḍr from the world of the unseen (*'ālam al-ghayb*). Like the Uwaysis, many individuals and groups rely on Khiḍr's guidance or other "physically absent instructor[s]."[46] They believe it is possible to connect directly not just with Khiḍr, but also with other prophets and saints, thus the Khiḍrian model becomes a paradigm for the master-disciple relationships more generally. Accounts of Sufis' communication and their spiritual relationship with hidden saints are recorded in the *History of the Uwaysīs* written in the early seventeenth century.[47] Besides that of the Uwaysīs, there are in the literary tradition numerous instances where Khiḍr is said to have played an important role as a guide and a helper. One prominent example within the literary *genre* in medieval times is the *Dāstān* or romance story of Amīr Ḥamzah, which originated in the eleventh century.[48] Khiḍr appears in the *Dāstān* as a rescuer of the hero (Amīr) and his companion ('Amar). He instantly saves the distressed from hunger and thirst, ferries people across bodies of water safely onto dry land, and counsels those struggling with making a righteous decision. In the *dāstān* all sorts of characters familiar to a Muslim reader (religious, historical, as well as fictional) are woven into the narrative of the stories. These no doubt add an element of believability to works of fiction. Like in other genres, Khiḍr always plays the familiar role of being a "savior" and does miraculous things, always by the leave of God, reciting the "Great Name" before performing extraordinary things. Here he is seen to empower those who are on the side of the good (like the hero, Amīr Ḥamzah) and helps destroys the ones (a villain of the story, Malunah Jadu) who seek to harm others.[49]

The story of Khiḍr reminds us of the importance of the notion of discipleship even for those who may have already assumed the role of a teacher. It illustrates the need for knowledge at a time when it seems there is nothing more to be learned. The ethics or propriety (*adab*) that informs the master-disciple relationship is evident in an episode in the life of Ibn 'Arabī. It is between him and his spiritual teacher Shaykh 'Urayb, which also involves Ibn 'Arabī's first encounter with Khiḍr. Ibn 'Arabī reports that once he disagreed with the Shaykh on a matter of secondary importance. Later when he left the Shaykh, Khiḍr appeared to him and told him, "Accept what the Shaykh says!" So Ibn 'Arabī repented. But as the story goes Ibn 'Arabī was right in the matter of disagreement, nevertheless, *adab* required him to be submissive to one who was superior in rank. This was the reason why Khiḍr "did not tell him he was mistaken but simply [that] he should submit to his master." Addas continues: "although [Ibn 'Arabī] repented of his attitude he would not budge from his position. As a disciple, *murīd*, Ibn 'Arabi was hierarchically inferior to 'Urayb and owed him his obedience; as a gnostic (*'ārif*) endowed with an inner certainty (*basīrah*), he spoke the truth and in this particular instance surpassed his master."[50]

The role of being a Sufi teacher demands rigor, openness to the divine, and the experience of a lifetime. Moses' encounter with Khiḍr is an example of such rigor where strong faith is called upon to direct one's actions that are seemingly illegal, abhorrent even. Servitude to God alone enables the person to earn the heart of being a master-teacher. It is through servitude alone that one may hope to attain that most subtle knowledge, *ma'rifah*, which is sought by many but is given to a select few. When God destines one to attain such knowledge, God institutes a divine experience in favor of such a person and an encounter with Khiḍr is one such experience. The 14th-century Indian Sufi master, Sharafuddin Maneri (d. 1381), interpreted the Khiḍr-Moses encounter as a means for Moses to learn how to be like a Sufi master. In one of his famous letters to a fellow Sufi companion Maneri describes the "qualifications" of a shaykh:

> Khiḍr taught Moses the five stages of becoming a Sh[ay]kh. . . . The first is the submission of servanthood. . . . Second is an aptitude to receive truth directly from God without any intermediary; the third is a submission distinguishable from the first submission by a very special grace; the fourth is the honor of receiving divine knowledge of God without any intermediary; and the fifth is the riches of receiving infused knowledge.[51]

Sufis use language that is sometimes objectionable to the legal minded. For the orthodox scholars too, the spiritual claims or aspirations can appear grandiose and, for some of them, border on heresy. Maneri's words echo the teachings of the mainstream Sufi schools in the Muslim world, but they become suspect because of the apparent attempt to bypass the channels of scholarly authority of traditional religious teachers (*'ulamā'*). Maneri was hardly the first to speak in this fashion. Scores of others, including the 8th-century Sufi teacher Rābi'a of Basra, attempted to deconstruct the dichotomy that exists between hell and paradise, self and Self, male and female (and the separate rules that govern their affairs). In her masterful attempt to portray the grandeur of the eternal dwelling place of souls, beyond the world of petty legal disputes, for example, over how to correctly stand in prayer, Rābi'a lays out the essence of what it means to love God.

> In love, nothing exists between breast and Breast.
> Speech is born out of longing, true description from the real taste.
> The one who tastes, knows; the one explains, lies.[52]

Rūmī too says something similar when he speaks of the futility of legal wranglings between the *'ulamā'* and between them and others, especially as it relates to the language of love vis-a-vis legalism.

> Out beyond ideas of wrongdoing and rightdoing, there is a field. I'll meet you here.
> When the soul lies down in that grass, the world is too full to talk about.
> Ideas, language, even the phrase *each other* doesn't make any sense.[53]

Both Rābi'a and Rūmī started out as disciples and in the course of their own spiritual journeys acquired (received, granted, learned) the skills and rigor necessary for the role of becoming teachers in their own right. They belonged to different epochs and places, schools of thought and each received knowledge differently. Together they represent the highest and the exemplary among Sufi masters. Each left a legacy that inspired countless others. Each modeled the practice of spirituality differently which speaks to the diversity of forms and schools. Rābi'a and Rūmī are but only two among the numerous Sufi masters that have enriched the mystical traditions in Islam. Some of them we know well and others not so much and yet the master-disciple tradition continues and with them the renewal of spiritual life. It has been argued that the Khiḍr-Moses story may be seen to inform the "practice of discipleship with a living master."[54] As already seen in the previous chapter, this is problematic due to the widely accepted hierarchy of prophets where Moses is placed among the top five while Khiḍr's status as a prophet is not even universally recognized. Thus, clearly, the Moses-Khiḍr story is not as straightforward as it may appear. What is clear from the story is the importance for any seeker to remain open to learning, even from Khiḍr and even when one is as highly stationed as Moses. Rūmī explains it as follows: "If so exalted a figure as Moses sought [Khiḍr], how much more should a lesser person submit to his tutelage."[55]

KHIḌR AND LIGHT

Khiḍr is said to possess gnosis (*ma'rifah*), a kind of divine insight. Khiḍr is the one on whom God had bestowed mercy and given knowledge from God (Q. 18:65). Khiḍr's knowledge may also be seen as a conduit for receiving divine light (*al-Nūr*) which can be compared with gnosis. An unnamed mystic described it in the following words. "If gnosis were to take visible shape, all who looked thereon would die at the sight of its beauty and loveliness and goodness and grace, and every brightness would become dark beside the splendour thereof."[56] This idea of distinguishing between worldly brightness and divine splendor makes it plain that there is a kind of illumination (*kashf* or unveiling) of the soul which happens as a result of divine knowledge. This notion of "inward illumination" is found in many religious traditions and Sufism is no exception.

Illumination of the mysteries of *'ālam al-ghayb* has been sought by mystics from all walks of life and was promoted by individual Sufis as well as some schools of Sufi practice since the 9th century. One of the schools which deals with the theme of "light" and illumination, having to do with *ma'rifah* or spiritual knowledge, is known as al-Ishrāqiyyah, the philosophy of illumination, which was founded by Shihābuddīn Suhrawardī (d. 1191).[57] According to Henry Corbin, Suhrawardī was seminal in bringing out the "oriental" dimension of Islamic wisdom—a dimension without which, by implication, the Western or Semitic aspects of Islam would remain incomplete. Suhrawardī, among others, sought to maintain the unity of philosophy and mystical experience.[58] At the same time, according to Corbin, the extra-Islamic elements within the "theosophy of Light" (*ḥikmat al-Ishrāq*) are related to ancient Persian ideas that were prevalent prior to Islam. The "light-infused ontology"[59] of Suhrawardī seems to have influenced a number of major Muslim thinkers who in turn opened new frontiers for perceiving the notion of light in Islamic mystical discourse. The notion of divine knowledge as "light" and its symbolic meanings arose as a result of trying to interpret the so-called "Light verse" -Q. 24:35

(Sūrat al-Nūr)- that refers to a "lamp" which reflects divine light:

> God is the Light of the heavens and earth. His Light is like this: there is a niche, and in it a lamp, the lamp inside a glass, a glass like a glittering star, fueled from a blessed olive tree from neither east nor west, whose oil almost gives light even when no fire touches it—light upon light. God guides whoever He will to his Light; God draws such comparisons for people; God has full knowledge of everything.[60]

Taking their cue from this allegorical narrative many Sufistic interpreters of the Qur'ān theorized about the symbolism of the lamp and its light. The expression "mystical lamp" became popular in Sufism and was understood as an "illuminating device" that gives the Sufi an enigmatic and extraordinary status compared with other human beings. The idea of a lamp lit with the "blazing fire" of divine love symbolizes higher station (*maqām*) held by individuals as a result of their knowledge and wisdom. The "lamp" is said to reside in the *qalb* (spiritual heart or intellect which the Sufis identify as the organ that lies at the core of one's being) of a person, through which one connects with God. Al-Ghazālī's famous treatise (*Mishkāt al-anwār*) speaks of the mystical lamp that "burns" in the heart and warms the soul of the seeker.[61] The lamp here signifies the archetypes or most beautiful names of God (Q. 7:180).[62] Numerous other references to the lamp can be found in the writings of Muslim mystics.[63] In his commentary on Sūrat al-Nūr, 24:35, Ibn 'Arabī considers "niche" (*mishkāt*) as an outer cloak of the heart to protect from passions (*ahwā*"). The glass within the niche represents the heart even as it is transparent allowing the light to shine through because it (the heart) has attained the level of purity and has been enabled to reflect divine radiance.[64] Ibn 'Arabī regards the "lights" (*anwār*, pl. of *nūr*) as the "Divine Sayings which appear in the 'niche' of the Prophet [Muḥammad], who manifests the glory and beauty of these lights exactly as they are in reality."[65]

The light motif is used in a variety of ways in the Islamic tradition. Many scholars and mystics have alluded to the notion of light as an allegory for mystical insight and as a precursor to religious experience. In addition to the metaphor about the niche, Ibn 'Arabī wrote of spiritual light as something which he personally experienced. He reported that in 1198 as he prayed in Azhar mosque, located in the city of Fez, he witnessed something quite extraordinary: "I saw a light that seemed to illuminate what was before me, despite the fact that I had lost all sense of front and back, it being as if I had no back at all. Indeed during this vision I had no sense of direction whatever, my sense of vision being, so to speak, spherical in its scope, I recognized my spatial position only as hypothesis, not as reality."[66] By relating this experience Ibn 'Arabī claimed to have reached what he calls "the Station of Light."[67] In this vision of reality, the "normal coordinates of space and time are suspended and become mere hypothetical."[68] What is at stake in experiences like these is the very idea of how we understand reality. Ibn 'Arabī asserts that human beings exist at the crossroads of two kinds of reality: one that is not really a reality as such—this worldly reality; and the other, a reality that connects human beings, and them alone, to God. This dimension is part of the spiritual "inheritance" from God given to human beings who are God's vicegerents (Q. 2:30). Whether human beings are able to visualize, actualize, and realize this inheritance within their lifetime or not is another matter; some clearly do as Sufis through the ages have claimed. Spiritual light is one of the keys to the realization of this inheritance. For Ibn 'Arabī light is "synonymous with knowledge of God and knowledge of the Unity of Being."[69] He often mentioned "those illuminated ones" referring to other Sufi masters and *awliyā'*. He believed that the *qalb* is the place where God dwells, and the seeker should "illumine it with the lamps of the celestial and divine virtues. "[70]

Similarly, al-Ghazālī in his *Iḥyā' 'ulūm al-dīn* (*Revival of the religious sciences*) speaks of those whom the uncreated light illumines with its brilliance.[71] He also has his own "highly developed light metaphysics" where he identifies illumination as the third degree of *tawhīd*.[72] This light motif is often expressed in terms of "veils" and the separation through them between divine reality and the world of matter. Thus, we find a description within Sufi thought of the path from darkness to light which involves "seventy-thousand veils" and at least half of these are said to be the "veils of light."[73] The goal of the seeker is to become "refined" by going through each of these veils until the seeker (*sālik*) has attained the freedom from the "taint of darkness." The symbolism of light and freedom from darkness are synonymous and they imply a high degree of self-consciousness as in knowing "light as light" and freedom as the state of being free.[74] The unveiling of each of these invisible barriers is equivalent to illuminating the spiritual self to a degree which otherwise experienced darkness, where darkness equals ignorance. The connection between light (*nūr*) and gnosis (*ma'rifah*) has many other connotations, articulated by numerous Muslim thinkers and mystics. The light is also seen as the light of certainty (*al-yaqīn*). Without this light one remains in the state of ambiguity insofar as one's faith is concerned. Thus, *nūr* within a believer's heart (*al-qalb*) allows him/her to "see" what is not visible to the naked eye. Hence a believer who is endowed with the "light" of certainty is said to have attained the *r'uyāt al-qalb* (visitation of the heart) and through which the believer is endowed with extraordinary powers of discernment (*firāsah*). Thus, notions such as inward illumination and spiritual light (*al-nūr*) can be said to represent divine knowledge and the wisdom that accompanies such knowledge.[75] Sufi accounts above point to the importance of the symbolism of light in mystical experience. Based on the foregoing, I propose that Khiḍr's knowledge may also be seen as a conduit for receiving divine light.

In his work on the symbolism of the role played by Khiḍr, Patrick Franke speaks of the idea of "sacralization of spaces in the traditional world of Islam"[76] as well as the notion of "encountering Khiḍr."[77] Franke's work deals with accounts of Khiḍr's appearances in specific places that allowed the stakeholders to declare those places as sacred. This sacralization of space coincides with accounts of seeing or even meeting with Khiḍr. This allowed the person to claim special spiritual status and a confirmation of and blessing on their mystical quest. If appearance of Khiḍr in a particular place is "sacralization of space" it may be argued that encountering Khiḍr is the "sacralization of being" or of experience. It is through an encounter with Khiḍr that many have come to be regarded as Sufis or aspiring to be one. Meeting with Khiḍr somehow became the norm in the Sufi experience.[78] There are countless reports by Sufis and scholars throughout Muslim history who thought Khiḍr to be "alive" and active; and stories of him appearing to people are given as evidence of such claims. Among the many personal accounts of meetings with Khiḍr, Ibn 'Arabī may have left one of the most intricate reports concerning his meeting the mysterious saint. Ibn 'Arabī writes that while he was on the port of Tunis, Khiḍr appeared to him as if coming from over the water but he was not wet, and then he proceeded towards a distant light house reaching it while taking only a few steps.[79] Franke's work showcases a collection of accounts by Sufis who claim to have met Khiḍr and have thus gained what are variously called mystical insights, secret knowledge, divine mysteries, and so on.[80] The knowledge and other gifts claimed by Sufis who have encountered Khiḍr shows two things simultaneously. First, it shows that Khiḍr's high spiritual status allowed the mystically inclined to gain a spiritual status for their own purposes, be they interested in pursuit of divine proximity or in asserting their right as inheritors of spiritual authority and attaining the role of a Sufi master. The first pursuit denotes a purely spiritual quest, and the second perhaps a more politically tainted quest for power and control of an institution or group. As Franke notes, Khiḍr was almost always "instrumentalized as a symbol of religious authorization."[81] Second, by the very nature of such accounts and their proliferation, Khiḍr gains universal appeal, and his veneration grows steadily. This explains the wide dissemination of the Khiḍr legend in predominantly Muslim societies. Franke attests to the fact that his collection of Sufi accounts of meeting with Khiḍr allowed him to map out the "general historical phenomenology of the veneration of this figure within the Islamic world."[82] Information about and claims regarding an encounter with Khiḍr did not always come through the Sufis themselves; many times, they are made on behalf of a Sufi teacher by their disciples and/or the masses who wish to believe in such stories of hope and renewal. Sometimes, the veneration of Khiḍr blends in with reverence for the Sufi master where the followers begin to identify their teacher as Khiḍr. Said Nursi cautions regarding this point in his *Mektubat*:

> Saints who attain to direct vision and knowledge of reality have reported virtually unanimously their adventures with Khidr and these elucidate and provide this level of life. One of the degrees of sainthood . . . is even called the degree of Khidr. A saint who reaches it receives instruction from Khidr and meets with him. But it sometimes happens that such a person is mistakenly thought to be Khidr himself.[83]

In Sufi poetry, Khiḍr sometimes takes on the role of the cup-bearer (*sāqi*) offering the possibility of an encounter with the divine.[84] Here cup is the symbol of mediation or guidance and, simultaneously, a reference to initiation to be on the path (*ṭarīqah*) that eventually leads to "immortality" and "friendship" with God. Here are a few examples of those who reported to have seen or have met Khiḍr. 'Imad al-dīn 'Alī Kirmānī (d. 1371) was a jurist, Sufi, and a poet known to have written in in the genre of *ghazal* and the *mathnawī*; the latter being "a poem based on independent internally rhyming lines."[85] In one of his later works of poetry written in 1364 called the *Ṣafā-nāma* ('The Book of Purity') also known as *Mu'nis al-abrār* (The Companion of the Pious), Kirmānī speaks of an encounter with Khiḍr that appears almost as a qualification announcement or a declaration of credentials of being a mystic.[86] Sharafuddīn Manerī, the noted Sufi who lived in India is said to have been visited by Khiḍr. The legend has it that he was recognized as having saintly qualities at birth and while still an infant, Khiḍr came to him and "rocked his cradle" as an indicator of Maneri's (to be realized) spiritual achievements.[87] Sufi Hasan Khwājā' (d. 1725) also reported a qualifying event where Khiḍr appears to have pointed to him as someone who has reached a high spiritual status.[88]

Just as Khiḍr has been used to transform profane space into a sacred one (this is what Franke's work tries to show) I argue that the Khiḍr symbol has also been used to transform individuals—according to Sufis, their souls—journeying from the inner darkness of ignorance to attaining knowledge of and proximity with God and thus achieving the station of light. If we apply this analysis to the story of Khiḍr, two aspects of Khiḍr's presence seem to converge: a manifestation of God's mercy (*raḥmah*) and a reflection of divine light (*al-nūr*). Khiḍr's knowledge is primarily esoteric (*'ilm al-bāṭin*) and thus his being a conduit to divine knowledge can be viewed as his being a dispenser of divine light simultaneously, since God in Islam is both the "source of all knowledge" (*Al-'Alīm; Al-Khabīr*) as well as "source of esoteric light" (*Al-Nūr*). Khiḍr makes divine knowledge manifest for Moses in the quranic episode and thus he brings him to "light," as it were, from being in the "dark" about the true nature of things.[89] It may be noted that Khiḍr's role as a prophet can be maintained within the classical understanding of quranic interpretation and other religious literature, while his role as a revealer of "divine light" is mainly developed and sustained within Sufism. Inasmuch as Khiḍr is seen as a repository of divine knowledge and the initiator of those who seek divine proximity, i.e., those who are on the path, Khiḍr functions as an "illuminator" of souls. For knowledge and light are allegories that may be considered two sides of the same coin. As guardian of the symbolic lamps that illuminate every corner of the *qalb* (heart) of the seeker, Khiḍr remains a servant of God like other human beings. He performs spiritual service for seekers on behalf of God and by the leave of God, as noted by Sufis of all ranks. Khiḍr's "miraculous" actions do not make him divine or semi-divine. His continued presence as reported by many may be a mystery, but he remains a mortal. No credible *ṭarīqah* or Sufi order will entertain the idea of collapsing the divine-human boundary whereby divinity may be attributed to a mortal. However, stories of boundaries being crossed do exist. In the next chapter I will focus on folkloristic aspects of the Khiḍr story where the boundaries between orthodox renderings of the divine command and its popular manifestations and associated practices are not as clearly defined and maintained as in some of the Sufi-leaning traditions.

NOTES

1. Bernard McGinn, *The Presence of God: A History of Western Christian Mysticism*, vol. 1, *The Foundations of Mysticism* (New York: Crossroad, 1991), xv.

2. This is not to be equated with illumination of the mind alone but rather with a kind of spiritual realization that is more inclusive of one's totality of being. In religious discourse this occurs as a result of disciplined piety on the part of the seeker and a compassionate gaze (which a Christian mystic may recognize as dispensation of grace) on the part of God.

3. Abū Ja'far Muḥammad ibn Jarīr al-Ṭabarī, *The History of al-Ṭabarī (Ta'rīkh al-rusul wa'l mulūk)* vol. 3 *The Children of Israel*, trans. & annotated by William M. Brinner (Albany: State University of New York Press, 1991), 10.

4. Chodkiewicz, *Seal of the Saints*, 27.

5. For *wilāyah* see Chodkiewicz, *Seal of the Saints*, 47, and Renard, *Friends of God*, 260 and 264.

6. Schimmel, *Mystical Dimensions of Islam,* 20. See also, 'Alī ibn Uthmān al-Hujwirī. *The Kashf al-mahjūb: The Oldest Persian Treatise on Sufism by al-Hujwiri*, trans. Reynold A. Nicholson, Gibb Memorial Series, no. 17 (London: Luzac, 1959).

7. Seyyed Hossein Nasr, *The Garden of Truth: The Vision and Promise of Sufism, Islam's Mystical Tradition* (New York: HarperOne, 2007), 6–7.

8. Corbin, *Creative Imagination in the Sufism of Ibn 'Arabi*, 56.

9. Seyyed Hossein Nasr, *Sufi Essays* (Albany: State University of New York Press, 1991), 58.

10. Schimmel, *Mystical Dimensions of Islam*, 106. For *khirqah*, see Cyril Glasse, *The Concise Encylopedia of Islam*, s. v. "Khirqah," 225. It is described as "a rag"—a sign of worldly poverty. It is placed during an act of initiation of a disciple into the order by a Sufi master as cloak (also called "*muraqqa'ah*") over the disciple or if not done physically using actual cloth, *khirqah* can be placed by communicating it through other means (such as a dream or a vision as in the case of Ibn 'Arabī who is said to have received it from Khiḍr).

11. Corbin, *Creative Imagination in the Sufism of Ibn 'Arabi*, 90ff.

12. They are called Uwaysīs after the name of Uways al-Qaranī, a contemporary of the Prophet who lived in Southern Arabia. See Schimmel, *And Muhammad is His Messenger*, 22; Corbin, *Creative Imagination in the Sufism of Ibn 'Arabi*, 32, 53–54.

13. Nasr, *Sufi Essays*, 59.

14. Patrick Laude, *Massignon intérieur* (Lausanne, Suisse: Editions L'Age d'Homme, 2001), 34.

15. Claude Addas, *Quest for the Red Sulphur: The Life of Ibn 'Arabī* (Cambridge: Islamic Texts Society, 1993), 62. Addas reports that Ibn 'Arabī was invested with the "*khirqa Khaḍiriyya*, the 'initiatic mantle' transmitting the *baraka* of Khaḍir firstly at Seville in 592 [A.H.] and then at Mosul in 601 [A.H.]." See also Schimmel, *Mystical Dimensions of Islam*, 105–6; and Corbin, *Creative Imagination in the Sufism of Ibn 'Arabi*, 63–67.

16. Louis Massignon, *La Passion de Husayn Ibn Mansūr Hallāj* (Paris: Gallimard, 2010), 2:54.

17. Nicholson, *Studies in Islamic Mysticism*, 82.

18. Not a quranic doctrine but found in the *ḥadīth*; the *abdāl* are first mentioned in Imam Ibn Ḥanbal's *Musnad*; See Virginia Vacca, "Social and Political Aspects of Egyptian and Yamani Sufism," *Journal of the Pakistan Historical Society* 8, no. 4 (October 1960): 233–34.

19. Massignon quoted in Vacca, "Social and Political Aspects of Egyptian and Yamani Sufism," note 1.

20. Although it is said above that Khiḍr is a *quṭb*, that role differs from *watad* only in function; in rank they are equal to one other.

21. Ibn 'Arabī, *Al-Futūḥāt al-makkīyah*, 2:3, cited in Ḥusaynī, *Ḥayāt al-Khiḍr*, 119.

22. Chodkiewicz, *Seal of the Saints*, 93.

23. "Have We not made the earth as a wide expanse, and the mountains as pegs?" ("*awtādan*" = pillars), Qur'ān 78:6–7 as translated by Yūsuf 'Alī, *The Meaning of the Holy Qur'ān*.

24. Louis Massignon, "Elie et son rôle transhistorique, *Khadiriya*, en Islam," in *Élie le prophète*, ed. Gustave Bardy, vol. 2, *Au Carmel dans le Judaïsme et l'Islam* (Bruges: Desclée de Brouwer, 1956), 269–90, cited in Patrick Laude, *Louis Massignon: The Vow and the Oath* (London: Matheson Trust, 2011), 30.

25. Laude, *Louis Massignon: The Vow and the Oath*, xii.

26. Ibid., 30.

27. Massignon, "Elie et son rôle transhistorique, *Khadiriya*, en Islam," 161, cited in Laude, *Louis Massignon: The Vow and the Oath*, 35.

28. Laude, *Louis Massignon: The Vow and the Oath*, 35.

29. Massignon, "Elie et son rôle transhistorique, *Khadiriya*, en Islam," 152.

30. Laude, *Louis Massignon: The Vow and the Oath*, 30.

31. Nasr, *The Garden of Truth*, 12.

32. Ibid.

33. A caution attributed to Sufi Abu'l Ḥasan al Shādhilī, cited in Nasr, *The Garden of Truth*, 12.

34. This categorization is from the famous Indian Urdu poet Khwāja Mīr Dard, quoted in Schimmel, *Mystical Dimensions of Islam*, 20–21.

35. Abū Ḥāmid al-Ghazālī, *Kīmiyā-e sa'ādat* (Tehran: Markazi Publications, 1954).

36. Sufi accounts of struggle regarding faith often reflect their desire to seek Khiḍr's help. One such account is attributed to 'Abd al-Wahhāb bin Aḥmad al-Sha'ranī who invoked Khiḍr seeking help in how to maintain balance (*mīzān*) between esoteric practices and his fidelity to acts of faith which are part of *sharī'ah*. See al-Sha'ranī as cited in Elboudrari, "Entre le symbolique et l'historique Khadir immémorial," 25–26.

37. Ramaḍān Yūsuf, *Al-Khiḍr baynā al-wāqi'*, 344.

38. See William Stoddart, *Sufism: The Mystical Doctrines and Methods of Islam* (New York: Paragon House, 1985), 20.

39. Laude, *Massignon intérieur*, 34.

40. Nasr, *The Garden of Truth*, 30–31.

41. Corbin, *Creative Imagination in the Sufism of Ibn 'Arabi*, 54–55.

42. Ibid.

43. Ibid.

44. It is said that the saints of God are accustomed to receiving wisdom and guidance in nonconventional ways; one of these is Khiḍr's frequent visitation "with . . . [them] by translevitation." Elmer H. Douglas, *The Mystical Teachings of al-Shādhilī*, ed. Ibrahim M. Abu-Rabi' (Albany: State University of New York Press, 1993), 17 and note 9 on 248.

45. Vollers, "Chidher," 252–53.

46. Julian Baldick, *Imaginary Muslims: The Uwaysi Sufis of Central Asia* (London: I.B. Tauris, 1993), 3.

47. See Julian Baldick's translation and commentary on the *History of the Uwaisis* in his book *Imaginary Muslims*.

48. Annemarie Schimmel, *Classical Urdu Literature from the Beginning to Iqbāl* (Wiesbaden: Harrassowitz, 1975), 204. For the *Dāstān*'s origins in mediaeval Persia and later development in India, see Frances W. Pritchett, trans. and ed., *The Romance Tradition in Urdu: Adventures from the Dāstān of Amīr Ḥamzah* (New York: Columbia University Press, 1991).

49. Pritchett, *The Romance Tradition in Urdu*, 168–69.

50. Addas, *Quest for the Red Sulphur*, 64.

51. Sharafuddīn Manerī, *The Hundred Letters*, trans. and ed. Paul Jackson (New York: Paulist Press, 1980), 30.

52. Charles Upton, *Doorkeeper of the Heart: Versions of Rabi'a* (Putney, VT: Threshold Books, 1988), 36.

53. A passage from a poem by Jalāl al-Dīn Rūmī, "A Great Wagon," in *Essential Rumi*, trans. Coleman Barks (New York: HarperOne, 2004), 36.

54. Halman, *Where the Two Seas Meet*, 21.

55. Jalāl al-Dīn Rūmī cited in John Renard, *All the King's Falcons: Rumi on Prophets and Revelation* (Albany: State University of New York Press, 1994), 85.

56. An unnamed mystic quoted in Reynold A. Nicholson, *The Mystics of Islam* (London: Arkana-Penguin Books, 1989), 7.

57. J. Spencer Trimingham, *The Sufi Orders in Islam,* with a new foreward by John Voll (New York: Oxford University Press, 1998), 140–41.

58. Corbin, *Creative Imagination in the Sufism of Ibn 'Arabi*, 20–21.

59. Ian Richard Netton, *Allāh Transcendant: Studies in the Structure and Semiotics of Islamic Philosophy, Theology, and Cosmology* (London: Routledge, 1989), 157.

60. Translation by Abdel Haleem, *The Qur'an*, 223.

61. Miguel Asín Palacios, *La espiritualidad de Algazel y su sentido christiano* (Madrid & Granada: Imprenta de Estanislao Maestre, 1934–41), 371.

62. Abū Ḥāmid al-Ghazālī, *Mishkāt al-anwār: The Niche for Lights*, trans. W.H.T. Gairdner (London: Royal Asiatic Society, 1924).

63. For example: "When God kindles that lamp in the heart of His servant, it burns fiercely in the crevices of his heart [and] he is lighted by it," in A. J. Arberry, *Sufism: An Account of the Mystics of Islam* (Mineola, NY: Dover Publications, 2002), 50; and " while the inner lamp of jewels is still alight, hasten to trim its wick and provide it with oil," in Idries Shah, *The Sufis* (New York: Anchor Books, 1990), 146.

64. Ibn 'Arabī, *Al-Futūḥāt al-makkīyah*, 1:434.

65. Muḥyīddīn Ibn 'Arabī, *Divine Sayings: 101 Ḥadīth Qudsī. The Mishkāt al-Anwār of Ibn 'Arabī*, trans. Stephen Hirtenstein and Martin Notcutt (Oxford: Anqa, 2004), 12.

66. Muhyiddin Ibn 'Arabi, *Sufis of Andalusia: 'Rūḥ al-quds' and 'al-durrah al-fākhirah' of Ibn 'Arabī*, trans. R. W. J. Austin (London: Allen & Unwin, 1971), 30.

67. Stephen Hirtenstein and Michael Tiernan, eds., *Muhyiddin Ibn 'Arabī: A Commemorative Volume* (Element, 1993), 55. Cf. Adam Dupre & Peter Young, "The Life

and Influence of Muhyiddin Ibn 'Arabi" in *Union and Ibn 'Arabi: Proceedings of the First Annual Symposium of the Muhyiddin Ibn 'Arabi Society* (Durham: Durham University, April 1984), 1–10.

68. Peter Coates, *Ibn 'Arabi and Modern Thought: The History of Taking Metaphysics Seriously* (Oxford: Anqa, 2002), 164.

69. Ibid., 133.

70. Miguel Asín Palacios, *El-Islam cristianizado,* 2nd ed. (Madrid: Plutarco, 1931), 423.

71. Abū Ḥāmid al-Ghazālī, *Iḥyā' 'ulūm al-dīn* (Delhi: Kitāb Bhawan, 1933).

72. Schimmel, *Mystical Dimensions of Islam*, 96.

73. Attributed to W.H.T. Gairdner in Nicholson, *The Mystics of Islam*, 15–16.

74. Muhammad Iqbal, *The Development of Metaphysics in Persia: A Contribution to the History of Muslim Philosophy* (Whitefish, MT: Kessinger Publishing, 2005), 116.

75. Nicholson, *The Mystics of Islam*, 51.

76. Patrick Franke, "Khidr in Istanbul: Observations on the Symbolic Construction of Sacred Spaces in Traditional Islam," in *On Archeology of Sainthood and Local Spirituality in Islam: Past and Present Crossroads of Events and Ideas,* ed. Georg Stauth, Yearbook of the Sociology of Islam 5 (Bielefeld: Transcript Verlag, 2004), 45.

77. The title of the book by Patrick Franke, *Begegnung mit Khidr*.

78. The notion of meeting with Khiḍr is found even in non-Muslim westerners who came in contact with the Islamicate cultures. As already mentioned, Carl G. Jung, the well-known psychiatrist and author, wrote in his autobiography that he dreamt of Khiḍr several times and then goes on to elaborate on the symbolism of these dream images connecting them to other events in his life. Jung in fact made significant use of the figure of Khiḍr in his writings and identified him as one of the archetypes. See Carl Gustav Jung, *Four Archetypes: Mother, Rebirth, Spirit, Trickster*, trans. R.F.F. Hull (London: Routledge, 2003). Jung also used the Khiḍr-Moses parable to teach his patients the need of learning through paradoxes. For Jung, the parable of Khiḍr-Moses opens with Moses' desire to follow Khiḍr on his journey to seek wisdom from the latter. However, Moses is soon shocked to witness three acts by Khiḍr which apparently (exoterically speaking) contradict divine law and each time he questions Khiḍr about these. At the end, Khiḍr unveils the reasoning behind his acts and it becomes clear to Moses that there is more than what meets the (exoteric) eye, hence the paradox.

79. Ibn 'Arabī, *Al-Futūḥāt al-makkīyah*, 1:86.

80. Franke notes that as part of his doctoral dissertation, which was on the subject of Khiḍr, he collected one hundred and fifty texts from various times and regions. Franke, "Khidr in Istanbul," 45; Cf. *Begegnung mit Khidr*.

81. Franke, "Khidr in Istanbul," 48.

82. Ibid., 45.

83. Bediuzzaman Said Nursi, "First Letter," *Letters* (Istanbul: Sözler Publications, 2001), 23.

84. Franke, *Begegnung mit Khidr*, 287.

85. J. T. P. de Bruijn, et al., "Mat̲h̲nawī," in *Encyclopaedia of Islam,* ed. P. Bearman, et al., 2nd ed., http://dx.doi.org/10.1163/1573-3912_islam_COM_0709.

86. J. T. P. de Bruijn, *Persian Sufi Poetry: An Introduction to the Mystical Use of Classical Persian Poems* (Surrey UK: Curzon Press, 1997), 120.

87. Paul Jackson, S.J., *A Jesuit Among Sufis* (Gujarat: Sahitya Prakash, 2017), 117.

88. Alexandre Papas, "Soufisme, pouvoir et saintete en Asie Central: Le cas des Khwajas de Kashgarie (XVIe-XVIIIe siecles)," *Studia Islamica* 100/101 (2005): 178.

89. Moses' objections to Khiḍr's actions were precisely because he (Moses) was in the "dark" and did not have the knowledge of those things that lay behind each of Khiḍr's actions. Thus, Khiḍr had to explain the hidden meanings behind each act so Moses could understand. Both had knowledge; Moses was given the *sharī'ah* or the law (exoteric knowledge), while Khiḍr was endowed with *'ilm ladunnī* or the knowledge of the unseen world (esoteric knowledge). For a Sufi view of the categories of knowledge and prophetic mission, see Corbin, *Histoire de la philosophie islamique*, 68, 80–81.

Chapter 4

Khiḍr in Folklore

Islam like other Middle Eastern religions is an "emissary" religion in the sense that prophets are said to give directions for moral action. The "prophet is not God's vessel," but an instrument for God, a messenger. "For prophets God is omnipotent, transcendent and personal, far beyond human ken, but nonetheless active and moral, ordering humanity onto the right path."[1] Seen from the textual perspective, the role of prophets is straightforward; they provide the rules of the road for individuals to follow. Historically speaking, the interpretational matrix of the time would determine how the rules are implemented socially, culturally, and legally. The goal from an orthodox Muslim perspective is not to become "one with God" (achieve mystical union) but rather to faithfully live the "will of God" (*sharī'ah*). On the other hand, in mystical understanding, the prophet is also a saint which implies that such a person operates on multiple levels, including what we may refer to as legal and spiritual. Sometimes the prophet can be seen to be commanding the law and at other times reflecting divine compassion. And in the small hours of the night the same prophet would be beseeching God for forgiveness, something Muḥammad was known for and what many Sufis and spiritually inclined Muslims tend to do. In this chapter I look at how these understandings impact our view of a prophet like Khiḍr since he is uniquely situated between the textual and the mystical realms of belief and practice. A further complication regarding Khiḍr is that his relevance and functions are also acknowledged and recognized in the sphere of popular religion. In a sense Khiḍr is an indispensable figure with whom everyone needs to contend, regardless of the perspective/s they hold (textual, literal, mystical, historical, literary, aesthetic, folkloristic or any number of combinations of these).

Khiḍr is a prophet, no doubt; and yet, he is also a saint. One might argue that he became a saint over time because of what may be called his "extra-legal" approach to matters at hand. Khiḍr is believed by many to be what Lindholm calls an "exemplary saint [and] a magical being . . . [who is] granted special powers as a result of a spiritual identification with the supernatural."[2] It appears that through the figure of Khiḍr the Qur'ān and the Islamic tradition add a new dimension to the emissary aspect of prophets, i.e., that which pertains to sainthood. If the "emissary" prophet leads the believer to what Lindholm calls the "arduous ethical path of piety,"[3] the saintly prophet's job is to fulfill that need which speaks to the "magical" and the "imaginal" dimensions of the path. As symbolic as the person of Khiḍr is, his symbolism has been expressed most effectively in literature and is enacted in practices that are part of the subcultures of Islam. Some may argue that this is indeed due to the providential role folklore plays in disseminating symbolic doctrines.[4] It is in the nature of popular piety to take upon or to draw from folk tales and legends which apparently fulfill "spiritual" or devotional needs of many seekers. The legends do not remain the same when they travel from one culture to another. This is precisely the case with legends that sustain the Khiḍr narrative as well as those inspired by the Khiḍr-Moses encounter.[5]

In his recent study, Jibril Latif rightly notes that "the Khiḍr of folklore has a wide range, from helper of the wayfarer, to sometimes agent of subversion in moral systems. The expressions of al-Khiḍr made in folkloric contexts are not representatives of Islamic practice per se."[6] However, as noted earlier, who is to say what is Islamic? To qualify as "Islamic" one must consider the canonical and the textual, but these alone are not sufficient. To make meaning from the text requires context and the "context is boundless."[7] Such is the case with Khiḍr; the context for studying Khiḍr is indeed boundless and so are the meanings assigned to all the various aspects inspired by the Khiḍr narrative. Marshall Hodgson opined that this boundless context is best labeled "Islamicate," by which he meant anything which was not "devotional" or "confessional" in the strict sense. But that will not do, as we have seen that among Sufi groups Khiḍr is often situated in the center of both the devotional and the confessional. The lines are often blurry on what is confessional depending on which Islam we are considering. In Shi'ism, the belief in the hidden Imam whose guidance is continuously received by select individuals is part of the "confessional" while Sunnis may find that problematic. Similarly, the lines are blurry when it comes to the appropriation of Khiḍr whether it is the religious, social, literary, cultural or any combination of these various settings. Shahab Ahmed argues that "*islām* is . . . in the first semantic instance, *action and activity* by the individual human being . . . it is something a person *does*, and it is by doing *islām* that a person makes himself or herself . . . a Muslim."[8] Insofar as a non-Muslim is concerned, a wide range of activities may still fall under "Islamic" even when these are not considered confessional or even devotional for some Muslims. For example, countless non-Muslim who visit the shrines of Muslim saints in many countries around the world—from Shahab Ahmed's measure at least—could be seen to engage in an Islamic activity without their being Muslim. Whether they are dubbed

Islamic or Islamicate, for the purposes of this inquiry it is sufficient to note that the expressions of Khiḍr made in folkloric contexts are rooted in the Islamic texts and traditions that constitute the streams of theology and culture.

Khiḍr is known in a variety of ways engaging in acts that fulfill different needs of ordinary believers. As noted earlier, in hagiography Khiḍr is viewed as one of the four prophetic figures recognized as being "alive" or what one might call "near-immortal."[9] Khiḍr is so regarded because he apparently drank from the "Water of Life."[10] Traditions like this often thrive on folklore as well as literary texts which express such ideas in ambiguous and/or in poetic forms. Poetry gives rise to folklore and folklore in turn preserves some aspects of the tradition and reshapes others. In Muslim cultures, the heritage of Khiḍr has been transmitted mainly in two directions: in mystical and literary genre on the one hand and in popular cultural beliefs and practices on the other. In both areas the multivalent person of Khiḍr has inspired numerous ideas concerning his role and mission.[11] This articulation not only reflects the wide reach of the Khiḍr legend with many of its specific nuances, but also highlights how the notion of immortality lends itself to being a tool for explaining Khiḍr within the Muslim tradition. In popular sub-cultures in the Muslim world, Khiḍr's voice continues to echo in the hearts of many. It can be heard far and near as Mounir Hafez assures us announcing his (Khiḍr's) credentials of being an initiator and a guide, who is appropriately stationed at the meeting point of where different forms of knowledge converge.

> I am the one stationed at the Confluence of the Two Seas;
> I am the one who drinks from the source of the Source.
> I am the guide of the fish in the sea of divinity;
> I am the initiator of Moses.[12]

This chapter considers select examples of the cultural and folkloric manifestations of the Khiḍr story found in West Asian (Middle Eastern) and South and Southeast Asian cultures and traditions. These examples, rooted as they are in religious and hagiographical discourse, will help us see the process of cultural appropriation of the Khiḍr-Moses episode. In order to grasp the full import of what Khiḍr story has to offer we must look at all that he has inspired. We must consider the symbolic representations anchored in Khiḍr's story and the various viewpoints emanating therein so as to understand his significance and meaning for the present.

KHIḌR AS A SYMBOL OF IMMORTALITY

The concept of the immortality of the soul can be found in many ancient civilizations. Archeologists' findings speak to the beliefs held by the earliest known human ancestors which included continuing on after death. Their evidence lies in the artifacts found at ancient burial sites such as walking sticks, utensils, and in some cases, companion animals to help the traveler in the next world. These simple beliefs and burial practices were not limited to prehistory; they were later found in emerging civilizations as sophisticated articulations of the concept of immortality. Pythagoras believed that the human soul was immortal and was capable of independent existence and that its imprisonment in the body was only temporary. Plato also distinguished between matter and the immaterial and, therefore, affirmed the existence of a "rational soul" which was indestructible.[13] The philosophers' understanding of the abiding soul did not necessarily imply personal immortality as later emphasized by Christian thinkers who referred to it as resurrection of the body and the soul. Earlier Zoroastrian and Jewish worldviews also maintained such a view of an ongoing journey beyond earthly existence. In Islamic thought immortality (*khulūd*) is acknowledged as part of one's primary belief structure. Believing in God, the unseen (*al-ghayb*), and the afterlife (*al-ākhirah*) are required articles of faith and they infer immortality of some kind. Legal and theological schools within Sunni and Shi'a traditions share this belief even if they differ in their understandings of how this immortality will be experienced by an individual. Apart from the beliefs in the afterlife and resurrection of the body and immortality of the soul, which are accepted without rational explanation, the idea that any human being can live on this earth indefinitely as Khiḍr is said to be doing is not feasible.[14] Thus, we find a rupture in the Khiḍr's meta narrative; specifically, between the textual foundations (the Qur'ān and the *ḥadīth*) and its mythic receptions as found in folklore and some forms of Sufi practice.

Khiḍr and the concept of immortality are often linked because, as noted earlier, Khiḍr stands for the things that require a lasting presence; people need saving and that does not change from one era to the next. When we consider that the concept of Khiḍr is firmly grounded in the textual tradition and that he provides a bridge, however narrow, between popular and orthodox beliefs, it is no surprise that his legend has reached far and wide. Khiḍr, "the Green One" ("Khiḍr-le-vert"), has been associated with aspects of regeneration and "greening" and he is believed to wander in the wilderness helping those in distress. The notion of Khiḍr being an "eternal wanderer"[15] and his notoriety as "evergreen" originated in connection with the idea that Khiḍr drank from the "water of life" which is also the reason for his supposed immortality.

Khiḍr's quranic story suggests that he played a crucial role of initiating Moses in the knowledge he (Moses) apparently did not have. The story has inspired many interpretations centered on the idea of searching for a teacher who would provide a perspective on reality that is otherwise not available. In Sufism, where necessity of a spiritual teacher is emphasized, the Khiḍr-Moses episode became the prototype for all those later mystic voyages in search of a spiritual guide—both seen and unseen.[16] The story may also be viewed as an attempt to provide a perspective on knowledge and its two primary domains—the exoteric and the esoteric—the two "seas" of knowledge that complement one another. Apparently, Moses lacked this "knowledge of the two seas" hence the importance assigned to his encounter with Khiḍr. However there are other explanations for what the Qur'ān meant by the meeting of the two seas (*majma' al-baḥrayn*); for example, in popular pre-Islamic myths the meeting place of the two seas was also believed to be the "dam of Alexander" where, according to later tradition Khiḍr and Ilyās meet each year. Yet another perspective on the "two seas" analogy is offered in terms of the very two persons who are said to be meeting, namely Moses and Khiḍr, since they are, symbolically speaking, repositories (or oceans) of divine knowledge.[17]

Legends and myths need some grounding in order to take hold and to maintain these for any sustained period. Even non-Islamic ideas can be entertained and recited in support of the myth, especially if these can help keep the power of the myth somewhat intact. Khiḍr being immortal is an intriguing notion and one way to process that idea is through the analogy of re-birth or being re-born. If Khiḍr was reported to have been "alive" at various times by different people who lived—in some cases—centuries apart, it might make sense to someone who believes in myths, that it can happen not because a mortal like Khiḍr can ceaselessly live like a human, but because, like Hermes, he is re-born in every age.[18] Even as Khiḍr is considered a much sought-out figure whose spiritual attainments remain earthbound, he is also seen as someone who has transcended the material world while still being able to interface with the living. It is by virtue of this "transcendence" that he is able to maintain his immortal status. Khiḍr symbolizes an approach to immortality by way of spiritual ascent, but he also epitomizes the perfectibility of the human soul by virtue of being a ruler of the "world of the suprasensory" (*'ālam al-ghayb*), the world inhabited by the "invisible ones" (*rijāl al-ghayb*). The mysterious / mythic country referred to by 'Abd al-Karīm al-Jīlī in his *al-Insān al-Kāmil* called "Yūh" is precisely the place which is said to be governed by Khiḍr. He is the charismatic overlord of the people of Yūh, initiator of prophets (he initiated Moses in the quranic episode), and master of *'ālam al-barzakh* (the realm of the intermediate state or the inter-world). Spiritual pilgrims enter this "northern most region" of the earth with his permission into a timeless state of being.[19]

Khiḍr became a repository of things that were previously not nameable. Among the personas he assumed, Khiḍr is known as the venerated *shaykh* and a "vigilant guardian" consoling those who seek his help. He is the incessant traveler, helper, and teacher of those who do not possess a physical master, and Khiḍr's greenness is believed to symbolize intense spiritual activity. The color association is sometimes used to distinguish Khiḍr from Moses and Jesus as they are associated with white and black respectively. Moses with white because it is the "color of law" and Jesus with numinous black, the "color of sacrifice." The color symbolizes the specialization for each of these figures, but also their major preoccupation, which in the case of Khiḍr is being a wanderer and helper of travelers on the path. That path may be taken to mean a literal journey from one physical place to another or it may be understood as an inner spiritual journey. Wherever Khiḍr's feet touch the place turns green; whomever Khiḍr blesses, that person is restored to wholeness, intellectually, physically, and spiritually. It is said that Khiḍr is from Mount Qāf, a place between paradise and the material world; a place which marks the boundary between the visible and invisible worlds.[20] It is in the so-called "high north" where physical reality of the world ceases to make any sense; where a ship may sink but water or drowning does not kill the person, where light is capable of illuminating the intellectual and spiritual self. It is a place where no evil can survive.[21] Khiḍr speaks all languages and is a *khalīf* (caliph, vicegerent) of God on earth. He appears unexpectedly to protect people from danger, even without their knowing. Khiḍr and Ilyās (Elijah) are not always recognized unless the people they visit are given the privilege. Every year Khiḍr and Ilyās spend Ramaḍān in Jerusalem, perform pilgrimage together and then go their separate ways to help people.

Khiḍr is a guide and so is his colleague Ilyās but in a different way; both share some common traits. Apart from the ones noted earlier, there is the notion that just as Ilyās justified the killing of the prophets of Baal (1 Kings 18:20–40), a justification exists for Khiḍr's killing of the youth in the quranic story. Both acts were a kind of "necessary suffering" in order to benefit those who are affected.[22] In popular stories it is not just Khiḍr and Ilyās who play the rescuer roles; in the *Dāstān of Amīr Ḥamza*, even the patron of Khiḍr and Ilyās, Āsifa Basafā ("pure woman") helps to rescue the hero of the story from his evil captors.[23] In the *Dāstān*, Khiḍr is referred as "Hazrat," a title of respect, or as "Khwājā" a title reserved for persons of high rank. In line with his reputation as a savior and a miracle-worker, Khiḍr's water-flask appears to be always full no matter how many people have taken a drink from it.[24] According to al-Ghazālī, Khiḍr and Ilyās are known to appear together and carry out their tasks in coordination, especially during the *hajj* (pilgrimage) when travelers most need help.[25] In his "Kitāb dhikr al-mawt wa mā ba'duhu," which is part of his larger work *Ihyā' 'ulūm al-dīn*, al-Ghazālī mentions the appearance of Khiḍr and Ilyās at the time of the death of the Prophet Muḥammad, which in a way symbolizes the "immortality" of the Prophet's message and the continuation of his legacy till "the end of times." Their appearance to Muḥammad on his deathbed is particularly interesting in that both Khiḍr and Ilyās can be regarded as immortal as a means to an end rather than for an end in itself. They are agents to the continuing mission—the coming of the message of God on earth—which began with Adam and Eve and which will be renewed through various channels till the day of resurrection (*yawm al-qiyāmah*).[26] The appearance of Khiḍr and Ilyās together is also recorded by Rūmī[27] who saw them as two different and yet inseparable beings, both of whom are tasked with transforming the earth into a "heavenly" state. Sometimes the two figures are conflated because of their common characteristics.[28] In other places they are substituted for each other, attributing similar characteristics to both interchangeably.[29]

KHIḌR IN POPULAR LEGENDS

There are various facets of the person of Khiḍr both in folk literature and popular piety. These aspects have in turn generated numerous spinoff stories and legends. Much of this literature is in the domain of folk traditions as well as in some forms of Sufism. Although the epithet "al-Khaḍir" first surfaced within the Islamic, more specifically in the *tafsīr* literature in the first century of Islam, other conceptual elements associated with Khiḍr such as "immortality," "water of life," and "regeneration" are pre-Islamic themes that have existed in connection with myths and legends across space and time. In fact, these themes (and many more) converge into an archetypal figure known in the European tradition as the "Green Man." The Green Man archetype and associated legends manifest themselves throughout the Western world spanning many centuries.[30] Below is a brief accounting of some of the various ways in which Khiḍr has continued to live in people's hearts and though traditions, practices, and memorials; in sacred spaces, and in writings of Sufis and saints. The selection here is limited to West Asia (Middle East) and South and Southeast Asia.

Khiḍr in West Asia

There are numerous symbolic representations of Khiḍr and they can be found in nearly every corner of the earth, wherever Muslims reside. The legend has truly lived up to its universal quality as it has spread far beyond the confines of its place of origin in West Asia. Today Khiḍr enjoys global fame and is venerated in many cultures around the world. In Palestine and the surrounding regions, there are reportedly hundreds of sites where the "cult of El-Khadr" thrives in ancient shrines dedicated to Khiḍr and at times simultaneously to other spiritual figures.[31] The parallel "cult of Elijah" also exists in the same region and Elijah (Ilyās) shares many of those shrines with Khiḍr. As a result, Khiḍr has been called the "Muslim version of Elijah" based on their similar characteristics.[32] The resemblance between Khiḍr and Elijah (Ilyās) is so close that in many regions where the former is venerated, the latter also came to be known as "the Green One."[33] Many such shrines which are visited by Muslims in remembrance of Khiḍr are also visited by Christians in memory of "Mar Elias" (Ilyās / Elijah) and/or "Mar Giries" (Saint George). Khiḍr has been equated with Saint George because they both appear (Khiḍr only in some versions of the story) as horsemen. The universality of Khiḍr legend has been acknowledged to the extent that "in the cult of the Christians, [Khiḍr] is in practice almost always S[aint] George."[34] Thus Khiḍr is honored by all creeds in Palestine.[35] Mahmoud Ayoub, in his essay on cultural parity and shared Muslim and Christian saints, states that in historic Palestine and in regions to the north, saints and shrines have always enjoyed a wider popularity and were never limited to a single group or community. Different religious communities have been known to acknowledge shared cultural heritage and practices centered around religious figures and buildings but also around other cultural markers such as food, clothing, and literature. Khiḍr is one of these shared figures[36] who continues to be revered, most often in association with Elijah (Ilyās) and Saint George.[37] Christians and Muslims still visit sites and shrines where these figures share the space as well as practices emanating from ancient customs and traditions of piety. Shrines are spread across the region, but they appear to be concentrated in the following places: Mount Carmel, Mount Hermon, Western Galilee, Lod, and Taybeh.[38]

In a recent study Robert D. Miller II suggests a connection that goes further in the past arguing that many of the shrines in the Middle East attributed to Saint George were built on ancient sites associated with the "Canaanite storm god Baal." Miller notes that based on his archeological and geographical research, he believes that there is a "cultic continuity from Baal [of antiquity c. 1300 BCE to Saint] George," which now extends to Khiḍr since the early Middle Ages. Expanding on the idea first suggested by Hassan Haddad in his 1969 study on "'Georgic' Cults and Saints of the Levant" Miller argues that the myth of Baal continues in the name of Saint George and the key connection seems to be the "slaying of the dragon."[39] For him, Khiḍr becomes yet another link in the mythic chain thus connecting the ancient figure of Baal with the Middle Eastern Christian and Muslim veneration of Saint George and Khiḍr. But Miller's thesis does little to clarify the lack of images associating Khiḍr with dragon slaying.

Khiḍr is considered immortal and alive but at the same time he has hundreds of shrines and memorial tombs in many parts of the world. In most cases such places are considered simply as memorials where Khiḍr is reported to have appeared, even though the place may happen to be someone's tomb. Often such places are subsequently identified with Khiḍr more than the person reportedly buried there. There is also an interesting example of a place where a shrine structure is dedicated to Khiḍr ("El-Khuḍr") but there is no tomb inside since Khiḍr is believed to be still alive.[40] Another way in which Khiḍr's tombs are explained is by arguing that Khiḍr's soul has passed through those who are buried in such shrines by way of metempsychosis[41] or that these shrines may be seen as hierophanies[42] or a manifestation of divine knowledge that Khiḍr possessed. For Khiḍr to have so many places identified with him is further proof that "he has in fact no fixed abode [and] is always on the move."[43] In many parts of Turkey there are "memorials" and "stations" (*maqāmāt*) to commemorate the appearances of Khiḍr, Elijah or both.[44] Khiḍr is said to have appeared in Sophia Mosque, and there is a station (*maqām*) of Khiḍr at the Ali Pasha Mosque in Istanbul. In fact, the term *Khidrlik* in many towns of modern Turkey became a generic name for a holy place.[45] Arguably, it can be confusing for some as these saintly figures and personalities in these "cults" appear to inhabit shared spaces with interchangeable names. In the popular traditions of Turkey, Khiḍr and Ilyās have gained much fame and functionality. In the spring of each year a festival is celebrated in parts of the country called "Khiḍr-Ilyās" (*Hidrellez* in Turkish). It is believed that on the 5th of May, where Khiḍr and Ilyās "both of them immortal after having drunk from the 'Water of Life,' come to meet and their meeting place is often pictured as a spot by the seashore."[46] This day is also regarded by "seamen as the opening of their season."[47] In some regions of Turkey the festival is known as "Khiḍr day" which is observed at the beginning of the spring sometimes celebrated as the "feast of Lydda" (*'Īd Lydd*)[48] The place Lydda or Lod in Israel is the original site of the festival, where Khiḍr shares the shrine with Saint George which is believed to be the latter's native city. The festival takes place in the vicinity of the fourth-century church called Saint George's Church in Lod[49] which is adjacent to the mosque of "El-Khiḍr." According to Ethel Sara Wolper, festivals and traditions associated with Lydda became well-known in central Turkey as many older sites from pre-Muslim conquest, which were known after Saint George were gradually renamed after Khiḍr.[50] The fact that historically speaking a Christian festival has been celebrated for centuries by both Muslims and Christians is a testament to the fluid spiritual and devotional borders that mark popular religion despite the deeply entrenched and established orthodoxies of these two religions.

Besides being the object of veneration and a cause for festivity, in Israel/Palestine Khiḍr also functions as a "renowned saint-physician for nervous and mental troubles." His numerous shrines are visited simply to seek cures for mental disorders.[51] It is also customary to make vows—"the practice of incurring voluntary obligations"—at these shrines. Through such vows deliverance is sought from "disease, death, or danger, [and] success in enterprises, bestowal of an heir, and the like."[52] Vows differ from one saint to another but such vows which incur voluntary obligations and are bound by conditions are known as *nudhūr muqayyadah* ("bound vows") as they are separated from those of another class called *nudhūr muṭlaqah* ("free vows"), which have no conditions attached to them.[53] A typical formula of a vow made out to a saint may resemble this verse recited at the shrine of "Khiḍr-Saint George": "O [Khiḍr] Ever Green, two birds come to you; The one with feathers (i.e., well-grown), the other with darkened eyes (i.e., still very young). I take as a vow upon myself, if these two remain alive, I shall offer sacrifices and pay my dues to [Khiḍr]."[54]

Jerusalem plays an important role in early Muslim writings on eschatology. Incidentally, there are also a number of places associated with Khiḍr there, including in the *haram* itself. The most notable of these are the "Bāb al-Khiḍr" (the gate), "Maskan al-Khiḍr" where Khiḍr supposedly resides, and the "Miḥrāb al-Khiḍr."[55] According to the 11th century scholar Ibn al-Murajjā there is also the sacred *maqām* (place, or station) of al-Khiḍr near the "Dome of the Prophet [Muḥammad]."[56]

As noted by Miller, the Georgic cults of the Levant associate Saint George with the myth of the slaying of the dragon. In Beirut, Lebanon, the place where the dragon supposedly lived and where it was killed by Saint George, we again see Christians and Muslims coming together; Christians visiting Saint George and Muslims celebrating Khiḍr.[57] The similarity between Khiḍr, Saint George and other figures was not limited to the roles and perceptions of these saints. It extended to the architecture of Christian places associated with figures that were claimed by both Christians and Muslims. This apparently prompted the statement concerning the Syrian Orthodox Monastery of Mar Behnam in Mosul that if we "remove all Christian symbols, especially the cross . . . the decoration of Mar Behnam could be moved bodily without profanity to any mosque."[58]

In Syria, Khiḍr's is said to have appeared in the Great Mosque of Damascus. To many, he represents an agency of God's wisdom who transcends time and hence provides a bridge between the past and the present through his appearances. A few famous people have reportedly met Khiḍr in that mosque. Khiḍr supposedly prays each night near the tomb of John the Baptist inside the Great Mosque of Damascus, which is where Khiḍr's *maqām* is also located.[59] If one needs more evidence beyond the numerous references of Khiḍr's presence in the Mosque, there is also an engraving referring to this, although it is quite small and easily missed by most visitors.[60] The proximity of the tomb of John the Baptist and Khiḍr sites in the Great Mosque accentuates the "link between Damascus and the saintly figures whose presence in Damascus predated the Muslim conquest."[61] This connection at once sanctifies the place beyond its connection with Muslim history and situates it in the larger Islamicate tradition. These links also speak to the inter-relationality of these religious traditions as well as to the commonality of their cultural heritage.[62]

Like in Lebanon (Beirut), where the connections between Khiḍr and Saint George can be gleaned through the inscriptions at the old Saint George Cathedral,[63] in Iraq, Khiḍr is often linked with both Saint George and Saint Behnam. The two saints are sculpted above the gate of a building near Mosul, known on the map as "monastery of al-Khiḍr."[64] Muslims in Mosul have for centuries venerated Khiḍr in Al-Aḥmar (red) mosque located on the banks of the Tigris, which is also known as *maqām* al-Khiḍr.[65] Khiḍr's connection with Saint George also links him with Saint Sergius who like Saint George and Khiḍr is viewed as a powerful protector and miracle worker. In Rusafa, Syria the shrine dedicated to Saint Sergius and where his cult has thrived for centuries is frequented by Christians and Muslims.[66] He has often been seen together with Saint George as the protector "soldier-martyr" saint. Saint George and Saint Sergius continue to be among the most revered saints in the Middle East.[67] In Mosul, like several other places in the Middle East where Khiḍr is revered along with Saint George, shrines are frequented by women who would come to pray for healing and for other needs. There were rituals associated with their visits such as the practice, not unlike divination, where while seeking favors from the saint, the visitor would throw a handkerchief or some other light object towards the sculpture. If the object landed on the sculpture, it would be interpreted as a sign of their prayers being heard.[68] These and numerous other ways of perceiving Khiḍr's role, and of giving him a function that transcends time and place, are symbolic of his immortal personality, both in a legendary sense and also and eventually—as it gradually becomes part of a continuing tradition—in a spiritual sense. In one of her recent essays on Khiḍr's connection with places and buildings, Wolper states:

> The act of associating these cities with prophets and saints became a way to assure their holy status. Because of Khiḍr's immortality, adding a Khiḍr *maqām* to a sacred area with multiple religious associations emphasized God's

> authority . . . [and] also further legitimized the long-standing nature of Muslim claims to these sites. At the same time, the presence of Khiḍr sites in areas with multiple religious associations brought attention to some of the shared themes in many of the religious and cultural traditions of the Near East. As one of God's servants who had tried to help Moses and others in their search for immortality, Khiḍr, in his ability to transcend the boundaries of time and space, embodied the differences between human and divine knowledge.[69]

Wolper writes about the "new type" of Khiḍr appearing in the post crusades period. With dynastic changes in the Near East as well as "changing frontiers" in the 12th century and later, the image of Khiḍr changed and he took on new personas inspired by new realities on the ground. Besides immortality and multiple cultural belonging, the hero now needed "strength and bravery . . . [and] military prowess."[70] Like other Christian saints who were seen as "mounted horseman" slaying some fearsome creature, Khiḍr, the humble saint, now began to appear on horseback. Khiḍr was not alone in being on the receiving end of an image change, taking on characteristics originally associated with Saint George; there were also Saint Theodore, Saint Sergius and Mar Benham who were sometimes described in macho-like terms.[71] Khiḍr, fashioned as a horseman and potentially armed, must have looked nothing like that the one Sufis sought out and wrote about since the eight century in their pursuit of divine knowledge. Instead, the Khiḍr of the medieval period having a variety of sites including those found inside mosques, monasteries, and churches appeared more like a military savior. This new type of Khiḍr (according to Wolper) became a favorite of the rulers in the region who needed a legitimizing force that combines the spiritual and the military aspects to provide a stronger grip on power. For Wolper, Khiḍr can be seen as one of the "composite figures" who provided a bridge for cultural, social, and even religious interactions between communities separated by orthodox constructions of their respective religious belief systems. The monastery in Mosul (Iraq) dedicated to Mar Behnam contains two images believed to be those of Saint George and Saint Behnam. Later an additional structure was built near the site with included a *maqām* of Khiḍr.[72]

Another example of Khiḍr as a "composite figure" is found in the buildings associated with the *tekke* (Sufi center) of Elwan Çelebi located in north-central Turkey. Having its origins in the 14th century, the building complex has attracted visitors seeking the blessings of saints including Khiḍr-Ilyās. However Christian elements of the cult and the site were also part of the narrative despite its "cultural transference" of the place transforming it into a Muslim space.[73] In most of these instances where places and buildings are known to belong to multiple communities and traditions, several reasons can be deduced to be at work. They include theological and spiritual reasons for sure, but also others that may be rooted in the social and political forces of the time. According to Wolper, one of the main reasons for "cultural transference" was to "mark the continuity and significance of these figures within a newly formed sacred landscape."[74]

The figure of Khiḍr is full of paradoxes from the very start of the narrative. He is said to have instructed Moses (a sign of higher status), although they are equals of sorts; he is immortal, subservient to divine law and yet he does things that seemingly defy law. Khiḍr is a spiritual guide to countless people, without having met (many of) them. In his role as a resident of—and visitor to—numerous sacred sites, many of them not originally Muslim, Khiḍr is an expression of "the paradoxical idea of how Muslim and Christian beliefs and heroes [can] mix in local landscapes"[75] and yet have global implications.

Khiḍr in South and Southeast Asia

In the folklore of the Indian subcontinent, Khiḍr has emerged as a "substitute for the Hindu gods of the water" and is well-known among and revered by sailors and fishermen.[76] Khiḍr is often represented as an "aged man," a mendicant (*faqīr*), often wearing green and moving with ease through the waters with a fish as his vehicle.[77] As Islam spread through the subcontinent it brought with it not only new political and theological ideas, but also literary and mystical traditions and practices. In popular culture many such doctrines and literary stories intermingled with the local myths and rituals resulting in new and composite stories, symbols, and traditions. In the popular folklore of north India, Khiḍr is known in a variety of ways: "Khwājā Khizr," "Pīr Badar," "Rājā Kidar," and so on.[78] "Khwājā Khizr" still appears in many Indian folk tales including some that preceded the advent of Islam. He is at the center of many fertility and agricultural cultic rites.[79] It is safe to say that the figure of Khiḍr played a significant role in the reformulation of the popular religion of the subcontinent because it gave new directions to the imagination of those who believed in his supposed magical powers. Khiḍr in other words became "the depository of all kinds of ancient myths and popular rites" which were prevalent in the region, especially in northern India.[80] If in Palestine/Israel Khiḍr is identified with Elijah (Ilyās) and Saint George, in India he is reminiscent of Somā and Gandhārvā, two figures from Vedic mythology who correspond to the two prominent functions of Khiḍr as "guardian and genius of vegetation and of the Water of Life."[81] At times he is also depicted as the patron of learning.[82] But it is mainly Khiḍr's association with the color "green" (and hence with vegetation) that his connection to a north Indian "festival of vegetation" known as "Khaddī" could be explained.[83] "Khaddī," named after Khiḍr, is an occasion to invoke the spirits of regeneration as it marks the growth of vegetation in spring, parallel perhaps, to "Hidrellez" in parts of Turkey.

According to some legends, Khiḍr is connected with sea-travel and is regarded as a patron of travelers and protectors of those in distress. Sailors in particular, if they are believers in the "cult" of Khiḍr, expect his help and protection from hazards of being at sea. The expressions of their devotion to Khiḍr differ in each of the many different cultures where these beliefs are prevalent. The fishermen of the Punjab "worship" Khiḍr instead of the river Indus; and among some groups he is also known as "the Muslim substitute for Ganga, the mother."[84] It is in connection with Khiḍr being their patron-saint that fishermen and sailors invoke his name every time a boat is launched into the sea.[85] Besides sailors, pilgrims to the sacred rivers also launch small boats with "black sails" (which supposedly turn white if accepted by the Khwājā) and other offerings in the hope that their sins will be made to pass.[86] In Punjab there is also an elaborate ceremony surrounding the digging of wells which involves numerous rituals including the placing of little bowls of water around the proposed digging site as a "magical means of measuring the water supply."[87]

Khiḍr maintains a foothold in many Southeast Asian cultural and folk traditions as well. Some of these stories arrived with the Sufis but the deeper cultural resonances between the Javanese and South Indian ethos may also explain his presence in many parts of Java. Su Fang Ng in her recent study on "Alexander the Great" spoke about the "globalist" nature of legends such as that of Alexander in part because of their suitability as "transcultural vehicle[s] for ideas of empire."[88] One could argue that Khiḍr story spread in Muslim lands for similar reasons except the empire in this case would be the transnational Islamic empire of faith. The power of legends connected to larger faith traditions do evoke a sense of global connection and offer meanings for local contexts, including for those in power. In the Malay world, stories of Alexander, Islamicized as *Hikayat Iskandar Zulkarnain*, take the form of a "conversion narrative." The hero is transformed through his supposed conversion to Islam which is followed by his commitment to "convert the world."[89] Khiḍr plays a significant role in elevating Alexander to a position of eminence as he (Khiḍr) is the agent of Alexander's conversion thus helping to connect peoples of the world, east and west. From here Khiḍr emerges as a teacher and initiator of new converts. He is at once global (like Alexander) and local (also like Alexander turned Iskandar).[90] Here is an excerpt that captures the significance of Khiḍr imprinted in Malay history through the narratives attributed to Alexander, the ruler of the world.

> Iskandar establishes sovereignty largely not by military means but through the spiritual persuasion of the prophet Khidir. This conversion integrates the world's

> peoples into a pan-Islamic kinship. So capacious and universal is this community of Islam that it can include the most apparently outré of beings, including even non-human *jinns*.[91]

The Malay text *Hikayat Iskandar* ends with a lesson on morality elevating "universalism" over conquest and expansion of the empire. Similar narratives are found in other parts of Southeast Asia which produced their own versions of the Alexander stories and further popularized not only Iskandar and his moral vision but also the role Khiḍr plays in anchoring Iskandar in these narratives.

In Java, in line with Islamic cultural notions, Khiḍr came to be regarded as a prophet because of his status as a spiritual teacher and because the Qur'ān speaks of him as a recipient of esoteric knowledge. Stories about Khiḍr appear in many Javanese literary texts from the modern period where he is sometimes referred to as "Hilir" or "Kilir."[92] Albertus Laksana in his illuminating study on Javanese pilgrimage practices has reported on many appearances of Khiḍr. Sunan Kalijaga, one of the prominent saints in Java is said to have been initiated by Khiḍr, which is quite significant for the role he plays in Muslim Java. Despite Kalijaga's Hindu past and the composite "Javano-Islamic" identity his association with Khiḍr (regarded in Javanese culture as a teacher of "the highest level of Islamic mystical knowledge") is seen as a strength and one of the reasons for Kalijaga's "elevated status among other [saints] in Java."[93] Khiḍr is also known through literary texts such as the Romance of "*Wandering santri Asmarasupi*," a poem which includes passages on Islamic theology and mysticism.[94]

Khiḍr, the Metatron, and Enoch

It is not uncommon for people to add new characteristics upon the heroic figures they come to identify with their cause. It is natural therefore that diverse ancient concepts and roles came to be intertwined with one another in almost indistinguishable ways. Some have even ventured to compare Khiḍr with the Metatron, the Jewish mystical angelic figure. Patrick Laude notes that the Khiḍr character, like that of the Metatron, is a useful illustration "of the monotheistic way of integrating the demiurgic principle" with the idea of the one God.[95] He argues that the "ambivalent status" of these two figures in the Bible and the Qur'ān, suggests a unique way to maintain the monotheistic foundation of the two religions while at the same time keeping the door open to the idea that created beings can be brought near the majesty and the mystery of divine presence. Indeed, there are some similarities between the Metatron and Khiḍr; for example, they are both identified with Enoch (Idris in the Islamic tradition). Metatron's "prophetic and salvific" aspects are connected with Enoch while Khiḍr's prophetic and salvific qualities are compared with Idris's whom the Qur'ān identifies as a "man of truth . . . a prophet" who was "raised . . . to a high station" (Q. 19:56–57).[96] Additionally, in Judaism the Metatron is seen as an angel, even a "supreme angel." For Muslims, Khiḍr is a prophet and a saint, while some regard his saintly status as more important than his prophetic qualifications (that of prophesying based on his knowledge from God). In the same vein, both the Metatron and Khiḍr have been conceived as "intermediaries" in their respective traditions, which brings us back to the question of the need for a demiurgic principle in the first place. According to Laude, the "intermediary status is typical of demiurgic characters as it refers to the ambiguities of the dimension of divine immanence."[97]

In Rabbinic literature, Enoch is considered an angel, a "prince of the Face." In Kabbalist thought he is identified as metatron and represents the supreme emanation of the Shekinah.[98] The Qur'ān also speaks of *as-sakīna* (tranquility) which God sends into the hearts of true believers (*mu'minīn*) and into the world in general.[99] Prophets, saints, and pious individuals are often regarded as having received *sakīna* which grants them inner peace and charism as they radiate God's "presence"[100] in the world. Khiḍr is known to have been endowed with (by way of quranic attribution) God's "own" knowledge; consequently, it is not surprising that he became entwined with the figure of Enoch (Idrīs) who has possessed some of the same qualities as Khiḍr. Thus, the mystery of the *Shekina/al-sakīna* appears to be shared by all three Abrahamic faiths.[101]

The stories of divine presence and illumination are widespread, and some are reminiscent of the Khiḍrian way of doing things. In the Iberian Peninsula, a legend identifies a 16th century figure, David Reubeni, nicknamed the "Jew with a shoe," as the Wandering Jew.[102] When a stranger, almost beggar-like person comes in the shop to buy a shoe, he is turned away by the proprietor, but the latter immediately realizes his mistake and runs after the beggar to apologize. Apparently, this beggar is a prophetic figure, a "Wandering Jew," not unlike (and often conflated with) an Elijah-like (or Khiḍr-like) figure. The stranger is symbolic of the traveler Khiḍr-Ilyās.[103] The moral of the story is that one should be hospitable even to a stranger as he/she may turn out to be the very savior whom one seeks in times of need. Associating the craft of shoemaking with prophecy, the story also suggests that the path to illumination necessitates humble beginnings as the work in a shoe shop is perceived to be a lowly occupation.[104]

While the theological debate goes on as to whether Khiḍr is alive, and if so, how, seekers around the world continue to report on their encounter with the ever-present guide and see him as helping them towards the straight path (*ṣirāt al-mustaqīm*). As explored above, it is precisely for this aspect of

Khiḍr's life that the understanding of his role as a guide and symbolism as a hero become important in the development of Muslim popular traditions. Even as Khiḍr is seen as an elusive and invisible figure, his functionality plays a major role in the Muslim tradition. To many he is an embodiment of divine wisdom (*ḥikma*). Khiḍr is a model for humankind because of the way he is remembered as a prophet and a guide, and for his saintly charism described in the religio-cultural narratives. Khiḍr is alive not only through those thousands of individuals who have reportedly personally "encountered" him, he is also present and may be found in the verses of many poets such as Jalāl al-Dīn Rūmī, Farīd al-Dīn 'Attār, Shams al-Dīn Ḥāfiẓ, Asadullah Khān Ghālib, and Muḥammad Iqbāl. These mystics and/or poets have also "immortalized" him in their own way; through verses that invoke immortal subjects such as the search for love, truth, and divine knowledge. Khiḍr has influenced the lives of many literary persons and mystics, ascetics and people of piety. Since becoming part of the Islamicate tradition, the Khiḍr legend has manifested in various forms and in myriad places and it continues to thrive. The story of Khiḍr has played a particularly important role in folklore and popular mysticism in many Muslim societies. To his followers and devotees, Khiḍr, even in his absence, physically speaking, offers an intriguing opportunity for self-discovery and self-empowerment. He makes people realize the sense of their agency, allowing them to comprehend the notions of immortality and universal power as co-existing; not as opposites but rather as complementary.[105]

Irfan Ahmad in his recent work argued that religion exists at the intersection of what are often dubbed as "folk" and "scriptural" traditions.[106] From the foregoing it is clear that there is truth in that claim and that Khiḍr story intersects all aspects of life and faith, culture and history, text and context. It is not possible to do justice to a figure like Khiḍr if we tried to delineate his personhood, role, and legacy within either the folk or the scriptural domains. In fact, to get a fuller picture, it is necessary to look at each of the ways he is understood and described, appropriated and reconstructed. The chapters above have tried to show the sectional views of Khiḍr, in the Qur'ān and *tafsīr* literature, among Sufis and in folk traditions and legends. In the next chapter, I will explore how Khiḍr symbolism has been used in poetry, focusing on one of the most well-known poet-philosophers of South Asia, Muḥammad Iqbāl. In his poetry, Iqbāl invokes the figure of Khiḍr in ways that stretches the metaphor of Khiḍr's role and value quite differently than found in the thought of many of the Persian Sufi poets such as Hāfiz and Rūmī. Analyzing Khiḍr in Iqbal's thought suggests that there is a paradigm shift—from seeing a Khiḍr-like person to be a necessity for the seeker to seeing him as a luxury and even a distraction. For Iqbal, as we shall see, it is better to *be* like Khiḍr, than to spend life searching for him.

NOTES

1. Charles Lindholm, *The Islamic Middle East: An Historical Anthropology* (Oxford: Blackwell Publishers, 1996), 37.
2. Ibid.
3. Ibid.
4. Cf. Lings, *Symbol and Archetype*, 83–84.
5. In South and Southeast Asia, the Khiḍr legend "became entwined with those of other mythical or semi-mythical figures of the local religions." Giorgio Levi della Vida, "al-Khaḍir," *Enciclopedia Italiana* (Roma: Instituto della Enciclopedia Italiana, 1950), 20:177; Cf. A. Augustinovic, *"El-Khadr" and the Prophet Elijah*, 10.
6. Latif, "The Green Man," 30.
7. Culler, *Literary Theory*, 68.
8. Ahmed, *What is Islam?*, 101.
9. The other three being Idrīs (Enoch), Ilyās (Elijah), and 'Īsā (Jesus). Schimmel, *Mystical Dimensions of Islam*, 202. These prophets are believed not to have tasted earthly death yet. This is entirely due to divine will and intervention, which, however, does not imply attribution of divinity or any magical powers to these prophets. From the Islamic perspective they are only human even if their experience of death is delayed.
10. In essence Elixir (*al-Iksīr*), which originally was the term for "externally applied dry-powder used in medicine," which would transform base metal into gold. In its Greek sense it is also believed that elixir purifies the soul and prolongs life. M. Ullmann, "al-Iksīr," *The Encyclopaedia of Islam* (Leiden: E.J. Brill, 1971), 3:1087.
11. For connections between myth, narrative and history and how they inspire and enrich religious traditions, see the excellent work by Claude Gillot, "Mythe, récit, histoire du salut dans le Commentaire coranique de Tabari," *Journal Asiatique* 282 (1994): 237–70.
12. "Je suis celui qui stationne au Confluent des Deux Mers, / Je suis celui qui s'abreuve à la source de la Source; / Je suis le guide du poisson dans la mer de la divinité, / Je suis l'initiateur de Moïse." Mounir Hafez, *Khidr: Le Bon Génie* (N.p.: Bibliothèque d'Orient et d'Occident, 2008), 7–8. Available online at: http://www.moncelon.fr/mounirhafez.htm. English translation by Jean-Pierre Lafouge.
13. Julien Ries, "Immortality," trans. David M. Weeks, in *The Encyclopedia of Religion,* ed. Mircea Eliade (New York: McMillan, 1987), 7:140.
14. The notion of immortality as a whole is a difficult one to grasp in the historical-material sense. In hagiography, it lends itself to all manner of myth that sometimes leads to flights of fancy. Perhaps the advice of René Guénon may help digest this concept better. He suggests that we consider it as "effective immortality" as opposed to "virtual immortality," where Khiḍr is spiritually present, regardless of whether he is actually alive. Guénon, *Symbolism of the Cross*, 12, also note 2.
15. Schwarzbaum, *Biblical and Extra-Biblical Legends*, 17.
16. Nancy N. Roberts, "A Parable of Blessing: The Significance and Message of the Quranic Account of 'The Companion of the Cave,'" *The Muslim World* 83, nos. 3–4 (July-October 1993), 297. See also Augustinovic, *"El-Khadr" and the Prophet Elijah.*

17. Hafez, *Khidr: Le Bon Génie*, 9.

18. Garth Fowden speaks of the "notion of immortalization" and the idea of finding oneself "on the edge of bodily extinction" as equivalent to the "rituals of death and rebirth" (*The Egyptian Hermes: A Historical Approach to the Late Pagan Mind* [Princeton: Princeton University Press, 1986], 84). Hermes Trismegistus, the legendary son of Zeus and Pleiad Maia in Greek mythology, is said to have been immortal. Hermes was made famous by his appearance in Homer's *Iliad* and *Odyssey* where he is depicted as a "friendly" person, which qualifies him as a protector of cattle and sheep as well as of travelers. He is said to be "closely connected with deities of vegetation" and also appears as the "messenger of the gods." See William Smith, *A New Classical Dictionary of Greek and Roman Biography, Mythology and Geography* (New York: Harper & Brothers, 1878), 400; and *Encyclopedia Britannica*, s.v. "Hermes," access February 9, 2022, https://www.britannica.com/topic/Hermes-Greek-mythology.

19. See Jīlī's *Kitāb al-Insān al-Kāmil,* cited in Henry Corbin, *Spiritual Body and Celestial Earth: From Mazdean Iran to Shi'ite Iran*, trans. Nancy Pearson (Princeton: Princeton University Press, 1977), 148–49; Nicholson, *Studies in Islamic Mysticism*, 82.

20. Chapter 50 of the Qur'an is called "Qāf" partly because it begins with the Arabic letter qāf. Interpreters have often sought to explain the mystery behind these opening letters in various ways (there are other chapters in the Qur'ān that begin with letters of the alphabet). The Qāf here is often explained as the name of a mountain. See Wheeler, *Moses in the Quran and Islamic Exegesis*, 99.

21. Hafez, *Khidr: Le Bon Génie*, 6.

22. Arnaboldi, "Élie Le Verdoyant," 3.

23. Pritchett, *The Romance Tradition in Urdu*, 214–15.

24. Ibid., 112–13.

25. Abū Ḥāmid al-Ghazālī, *Iḥyā' 'ulūm al-dīn*, 1:285, cited in Al-Ghazālī, *The Remembrance of Death and the Afterlife*, trans. T. J. Winter (Cambridge: Islamic Texts Society, 1989), 71.

26. There are evidently other versions of this story mentioned in Ibn Kathīr's *Bidāyah,* which do not take this appearance to be historical. Al-Ghazālī, *The Remembrance of Death and the Afterlife*, 71.

27. Renard, *All the King's Falcons,* 86.

28. Alessandro Grossato, *Elia e al Khidr: L'archetipo del maestro invisibile* (Venise: Fondazione Giorgio Cini; Milan: Edizioni Medusa, 2004), 155ff.

29. Arnaboldi, "Élie Le Verdoyant," 2.

30. William Anderson's work is a testimony to the popularity of this truly universal figure. See his *Green Man: The Archetype of Our Oneness with the Earth* (London & San Francisco: HarperCollins, 1990). Another example of Khiḍr's possible influence is found in the 14th century English folk story of *Sir Gawain and the Green Knight* where the latter may be a representation of Khiḍr. In that story, the Green Knight tempts the faith of the title character, Sir Gawain three times. Some parallel tropes between the two stories include 1) chivalry and the test of one's heroic abilities and/or patience as in Moses being tested by Khiḍr's three seemingly bizarre actions 2)

immortality—the Knight is beheaded but did not die; similar to Khiḍr's longevity and continued "presence" and 3) mystery surrounding the Knight who dons different appearances keeping Sir Gawain on his toes; again similar to Khiḍr whose appearances vary depending on the genre. Other connections have been suggested by Su Fang Ng and Kenneth Hodges in their insightful essay, "Saint George, Islam, and Regional Audiences in *Sir Gawain and the Green Knight*," *Studies in the Age of Chaucer* 32 (2010): 257–294.

31. Augustinovic, *"El-Khadr" and the Prophet Elijah.*

32. George K. Anderson, *The Legend of the Wandering Jew*, 409.

33. Augustinovic, *"El-Khadr" and the Prophet Elijah,* 52. See also Meri, "Re-Appropriating Sacred Space," 237–64.

34. For instance, in Tayibeh there is a shared shrine known as "El Khadr [but] the saint today venerated is in fact St. George under the name of El Khadr." Augustinovic, *"El-Khadr" and the Prophet Elijah*, 25–28 & 64.

35. Taufik Canaan, *Mohammadan Saints and Sanctuaries in Palestine* (London: Luzac, 1927), 120.

36. Mahmoud Ayoub, "Cult and Culture: Common Saints and Shrines in Middle Eastern Popular Piety," in *Religion and Culture in Medieval Islam,* ed. Richard G. Hovannisian and Georges Sabbagh (Cambridge: Cambridge University Press, 1999), 103-15.

37. Augustinovic, *"El-Khadr" and the Prophet Elijah,* 12.

38. Robert D. Miller, II, *Baal, St. George, and Khidr: A Study of the Historical Geography of the Levant* (University Park: The Pennsylvania State University Press, 2019), 9.

39. Ibid., 1.

40. Hasluck, *Christianity and Islam Under the Sultans,* 327.

41. A clearly non-Islamic idea, however, adopted as a reasonable explanation for Khiḍr's continuous "existence," by some. Sale, *The Koran*, 244. Metempsychosis (*taqammus*) is transmigration of the soul from one body to another. There are supposedly four kinds of metempsychosis: First is *naskh*, where the soul takes a body of the same species as it inhabited previously. Modern day Druze believe that human soul is a *naskh*. Second is *maskh* where a human soul enters the body of an animal or another inferior being. Third is *faskh,* which is a state where the human soul becomes completely separated from the body and goes to lower living being such as a plant. And finally, *raskh* is taken to mean inert, firmly rooted and immovable; it implies that the human soul goes into something inanimate like a stone or a rock. Information kindly supplied by Mahmoud Ayoub.

42. A hierophany is a manifestation of the sacred in material objects and phenomena in a way that they, the objects, assume the reality as such. For more on this, see Eliade, *The Sacred and the Profane,* 20–22.

43. Augustinovic, *"El-Khadr" and the Prophet Elijah,* 52.

44. Hasluck, *Christianity and Islam Under the Sultans*, 327–29.

45. Ibid., 329.

46. P. N. Boratav, "Khiḍr-Ilyās," in *The Encyclopaedia of Islam*, new ed. (Leiden: E. J. Brill, 1979), 5:5.

47. Hasluck, *Christianity and Islam Under the Sultans,* 324.

48. Ibid., 320. See also Canaan, *Mohammadan Saints and Sanctuaries in Palestine,* 215; and Ayoub, "Cult and Culture," 109. It is also mentioned that this "Khiḍr day" is the same as Saint George's day which is 23rd of April. William Anderson, *Green Man,* 29.

49. One of the earliest descriptions of this joint Christian-Muslim festival is found in Shams al-Dīn al-Muqaddasī's *Aḥsān al-taqāsīm fī ma'rifat al-aqālīm* (Leiden: E. J. Brill, 1877), cited in Amikam Elad, *Medieval Jerusalem and Islamic Worship: Holy Places, Ceremonies, Pilgrimage* (Leiden: E. J. Brill, 1995), 135.

50. Ethel Sara Wolper, *Cities and Saints: Sufism and the Transformation of Urban Space in Medieval Anatolia* (University Park: The Pennsylvania State University Press, 2003), 97.

51. Canaan, *Mohammadan Saints and Sanctuaries,* 120.

52. Ibid., 130.

53. Ibid., 137.

54. Ibid., 137–38. For different vows at such shrines, see also Augustinovic, "*El-Khadr" and the Prophet Elijah*, 58.

55. Elad, *Medieval Jerusalem and Islamic Worship*, 117.

56. Ibid., 75. Elad also notes that there is a house of Khiḍr and Ilyās near the Temple Mount.

57. Helen Gibson, "St. George the Ubiquitous," *Saudi Aramco World* 22, no. 6 (November–December 1971): 4–5.

58. Jules Leroy, *Monks and Monasteries of the Near East*, trans. Peter Collin (Piscataway, NJ: Gorgias Press, 2004), 182.

59. Wolper, "Khiḍr and the Politics of Place," 153–54. Wolper rightly notes that having Khiḍr and John the Baptist in proximity not only allowed them "to be worshiped within one sanctuary, but in so doing emphasized a discourse of conversion and continuity" which helps maintain the dialogue of traditions.

60. Rudolf Kriss & Hubert Kriss-Heinrich, *Volksglaube im Bereich des Islam* (Wiesbaden: Otto Harrassowitz, 1960), 1:213.

61. Wolper, "Khidr and the Changing Frontiers," 133.

62. As noted above, apart from Jerusalem and Damascus, numerous Khiḍr sites are found in Turkey where Christians and Muslims have coexisted and have been interacting for many centuries.

63. R. Du Mesnil du Buisson, "Le lieu du combat de Saint Georges à Beyrouth," *Mélanges de l'Université Saint-Joseph*, 12 (1927): 250–65.

64. J. M. Fiey, OP, *Assyrie chrétienne. Contribution à l'étude de l'histoire et de la géographie ecclésiastiques et monastiques du Nord de l'Iraq* (Beirut: Librairie Orientale, 1965), 2:575–76.

65. For more on this, see *Etudes Carmélitaines: Elie le Prophète*, vol. 2, *Au Carmel, dans le Judaïsme et l'Islam* (Paris: Desclée, 1956), 256–90.

66. Elizabeth Key Fowden, "Saint Serge chez les Arabes." *Les Dossiers d'archéologie* 309 (2005–2006): 55–56.

67. Elizabeth Key Fowden, *The Barbarian Plain: Saint Sergius between Rome and Iran* (Berkeley: University of California Press, 1999), 4. For many other Khiḍr sites

in the Middle East, see also Denys Pringle, *The Churches of the Crusader Kingdom of Jerusalem: A Corpus*, vol. 2 (Cambridge: Cambridge University Press, 1998).

68. Fiey, *Assyrie chrétienne*, 577.

69. Wolper, "Khiḍr and the Changing Frontiers," 134.

70. Ibid., 136.

71. Ibid.

72. Ibid., 139, 142.

73. Ibid., 144.

74. Ethel Sara Wolper, "Khiḍr, Elwan Çelebi and the Conversion of the Sacred Sanctuaries in Anatolia," *The Muslim World* 90 (Fall 2000): 316.

75. Wolper, "Khiḍr and the Changing Frontiers," 146.

76. Currie, *The Shrine and Cult of Mu'īn al-dīn Chishtī*, 10; See also Friedlaender, "Khiḍr," 695.

77. Coomaraswamy, "Khwājā Khadir and the Fountain of Life," 173.

78. "Khwājā," "Pīr," and "Rājā" are the honorifc titles that show an elevated status of Khiḍr, both spiritual as well as mythical. The source of the first two is the Islamic understanding of the spiritual master; the third, however, seems to have been given to Khiḍr for his identification with water and rainfall. "Rājā" or king in pre-modern Indian folklore is often depicted as "half-priest, half-king" and is often held responsible for controlling the weather and hence the harvest. See William Crooke, *Religion and Folklore of Northern India* (London: Oxford University Press, 1926), 29, 72.

79. For an account of some of these cults, see Crooke, *Religion and Folklore*, 62–63, 247.

80. Friedlaender, "Khiḍr," 695.

81. Coomaraswamy, "Khwājā Khadir and the Fountain of Life," 176.

82. John A. Subhan, *Sufism, Its Saints and Shrines. An Introduction to the Study of Sufism with Special Reference to India and Pakistan* (Lucknow: Lucknow Publishing House, 1960), 118.

83. For more on "Khaddī" see Crooke, *Religion and Folklore*, 32.

84. Curry, *The Shrine and Cult of Mu'īn al-dīn Chishtī*, 10. For connections between Khiḍr and other Indian myths and fables, see Coomaraswamy, "Khwājā Khadir and the Fountain of Life."

85. Friedlaender, "Khiḍr," 695.

86. Crooke, *Religion and Folklore*, 62.

87. Ibid.

88. Ng, *Alexander the Great from Britain to Southeast Asia*, 76–77.

89. Ibid., 81.

90. Ibid., 84–85.

91. Ibid., 111.

92. Theodore G. Th. Pigeaud, *Literature of Java* (Dordrecht, Netherlands: Springer, 1970), 3:122, 248.

93. Laksana, *Muslim and Catholic Pilgrimage Practices*, 32–33.

94. Nancy K. Florida, *Javanese Literature in Surakarta Manuscripts*, Vol. 1: *Introduction and Manuscripts of the Karaton Surakarta* (Ithaca: Cornell Southeast Asia Program Publications, 1993).

95. Patrick Laude, *Divine Play, Sacred Laughter* (New York: Palgrave Macmillan, 2005), 30.

96. Ibid., 32.

97. Ibid., 31.

98.Arnaboldi, "Élie Le Verdoyant," 8.

99. The Qur'an 48:4—"It is He who sent down tranquility into the hearts of the believers, to add faith to their faith. To God belong the forces of the heavens and the earth. God is Knowing and Wise."

100. Karen Armstrong, *Muhammad: A Biography of the Prophet* (San Francisco: Harper Collins, 1993), 224.

101. Arnaboldi, "Élie Le Verdoyant," 5.

102. François Delpech, "De David Reubeni au Juif Errant: dans les pas du 'Juif au soulier.'" *Revue de l'histoire des religions* 229 (2012): 56.

103. Ibid., 58–59.

104. Ibid., 60.

105. François de Polignac, "Une 'dualité' du pouvoir? Empire terrestre et inspiration divine dans la légende arabe d'Alexandre et de Khidr," in *Representing Power in Ancient Inner Asia: Legitimacy, Transmission, and the Sacred*, ed. Isabelle Charleux, et al. (Bellingham: Western Washington University, 2010), 347.

106. Irfan Ahmad, *Religion as Critique: Islamic Critical Thinking from Mecca to the Marketplace* (Chapel Hill: The University of North Carolina Press, 2017), 53.

Chapter 5

Khiḍr in Muḥammad Iqbāl's Poetry

Khiḍr is known as the immortal guide in the Islamicate tradition; he is the Muslim equivalent of Elijah, a prophet by some accounts and a mysterious "servant of God" and a saint in others. In popular piety, Khiḍr is venerated at numerous sites and sacred spaces that often belong to multiple communities. In Sufism, Khiḍr remains an indispensable master-teacher figure for millions who follow the mystical path. Many have made use of the symbolism that Khiḍr carries—in Sufi writings as well as in folk literature. Khiḍr's name is also invoked in classical forms of poetry in various Islamic languages including Arabic, Farsi, and Urdu, and his archetypal roles have captured the imagination of writers and thinkers across the religious and cultural boundaries.[1] Among the Western poets the figure of Khiḍr appeared in Goethe (d. 1832) who had a deep interest in the *dīwān* of Ḥāfiẓ which is where he most likely encountered Khiḍr. While responding to the beauty and tranquility of "the East" Goethe found in Ḥāfiẓ, he expressed his appreciation in the following words:

> North and South and West are crumbling,
> Thrones are falling, kingdoms trembling:
> Come, flee away to purer East,
> There on patriarch's air to feast,
> There with love and drink and song,
> Khiser's spring shall make thee young.[2]

Poets in the Muslim world, and many others, have invoked Khiḍr for the purpose of highlighting their respective visions of mystery and divine workings in the world. There are literally hundreds of references and allusions to Khiḍr in the writings belonging to different genres and cultures. These writers and poets have immortalized Khiḍr by treating him as a significant link in the mystical chain of divine emissaries and saintly figures. To Rūmī, Khiḍr epitomizes the role of spiritual leadership as he, unlike many other prophets, was always wholly occupied with God in the sense that he was not concerned about the "law" or the *sharī'ah* which prophets like Moses and Muḥammad were tasked to teach.[3] Khiḍr embodied actions that were apparently against the law and yet they were in accord with the will of God. Khiḍr's actions were symbolic of the truths that were hidden from the uninitiated. Rūmī expresses this notion in his Mathnavī:

gar Khizar dar baḥr-e kashtī rā shikast
ṣad durustī dar shikast-e Khizr hast[4]

If Khiḍr were to break the ship in the sea
A hundred good reasons lie in Khiḍr's deed

Khiḍr was content with being a mysterious helper behind the scenes. He was blessed with the "water of life" and the knowledge he was given from God. Thus, Khiḍr was beyond both the fear of death and worries of exoteric applications of the law. He had "drunk" from the "well spring of spirit, whose water not only reflects real things, but contains the real. Flowing through all of creation as the evolutionary sap that robes the world in green, the water elevates all beings to a new stratum of existence."[5] Here lies what some regard as the "immortal" aspect of Khiḍr, integrating various symbols in his person: water, vegetation, and the color green, and the very idea of renewal.

A GUIDE FOR THE SEEKERS OF IMMORTALITY

Following in the footsteps of Rūmī, Iqbāl also uses the image of Khiḍr to bring out the unlimited potential of human beings (towards the goal of attaining immortality), to fulfill the responsibility entrusted (*amānah*) by God through various prophets (*raḥmah*) as well as through revelation (knowledge; '*ilm ladunnī* in the case of Khiḍr). To Iqbāl, the person of Khiḍr represents more than just a guide on the way or Khizr-i rāh as he calls him; rather, he sees Khiḍr as an embodiment of the secret of immortality.[6] He is, in other words, both an "immortal guide" as well as a "guide to immortality." In the former sense Khiḍr exists as part of a long tradition in Islam where believers, especially those who are spiritually inclined, draw upon him for guidance. Here Khiḍr's continued guidance is contingent upon his immortal existence and is also its proof.[7] In the latter sense, what guides the seeker to immortality is the state of being where Khiḍr is considered the epitome of such a state known as *maqām al-Khiḍr.* This state of being is the state of positive action. For in Iqbāl as in the ancient epic of Gilgamesh, the virtue of "action" is life itself, and so long as there is action, there is life.[8] Gilgamesh, the Sumerian hero who in many ways is parallel to Khiḍr in his role as an immortal guide, is a good example of demonstrating the virtue of action.[9] In Iqbāl, however, Khiḍr occupies a rather nuanced role; a role that both corresponds to and yet distinguished from that given by many earlier mystically- inclined poets. In this chapter I will explore the role of Khiḍr in Muḥammad Iqbāl's thought, highlighting passages in Iqbāl's Urdu and Farsi collections where he makes use of the Khiḍr motif to convey his message of activism and self-reform.

Muḥammad Iqbāl (d. 1938), the poet-philosopher of the Indian subcontinent, is famous for his bold, uplifting, and inspiring poetry. Iqbāl was a poet first, and remained that throughout his life, but he was also a philosopher by training. The combination of the two gave him a somewhat dynamic and a captivating style of writing which greatly appealed to Muslim readers and audiences. Iqbāl was one of the most sought out Muslim intellectuals of the twentieth century; both the religiously inclined as well as the literary minded drew inspiration from him.[10] He left several collections of poetry, and yet his tone, like his main message, was prophetic. In his verses, he utilized serious tropes to make his arguments instead of what we might see in a typical poet whose message, even when prophetic, often draws on symbols of love and passion.[11] Through his poetry, which deeply reflected his philosophical thinking, Iqbāl sought to "awaken" the Muslim mind and to caution the masses to the growing indifference towards values in the name of rational thought and material progress. He had a deep reverence for spiritual traditions, in particular for Sufism, but the form of spirituality he advocated required "activism" rather than resignation from the world as such. Iqbāl was opposed to what he saw as "decadent" forms of spirituality masquerading in the name of authentic Islam.[12]

Iqbāl's philosophy of "action" is visualized and rendered mostly in verse where he has effectively used the symbolism of Khiḍr to convey his message against stagnation and *taqlīd* (unquestioned following of traditions) and in support of a regenerative, life-giving action. The preeminence of Khiḍr in Iqbāl's thought is nowhere more obvious than in his poem titled "Khizr-i rāh" (The Guide), which is one of the last poems in the collection called *Bāng-i darā* (The Call of the Way) Iqbāl's first published collection of Urdu poems.[13] Here Iqbāl describes Khiḍr as an unseen but pre-eminent guide to a searching believer. In "Khizr-i rāh" Iqbāl explores a vision of life, which, although seemingly ravaged by the passing of time, in truth represents a dynamic nature of reality. Out of the ordinary movement of life evolves a "rhythm"—reflective in the story of Khiḍr—unceasing and unhindered, where death is viewed as but a small way station in a long journey. It is in the context of Khiḍr, then, that for Iqbāl in the midst of "the devastating aspect of time" emerges another concept of time which can be described as a "ceaseless duration." From this perspective life is not measurable in serial time; it is rather seen as "overflowing, eternal and evergreen."[14]

The theme of eternity despite our bondage in this serial time permeates Iqbāl's other poems as well. In *Asrār-i khudī* (The Secret of the Self), *Payām-i mashriq* (Message from the East) and also in *Nawā-i waqt* (The Melody of Time), Iqbāl often speaks about such notions as the problem of time, human destiny, and the human-divine relationship, each of which can be found to have relevance in the story of Khiḍr who appears frequently in Iqbāl's poems. At times, Khiḍr is mentioned in relation to the "greening of the mountain tops" or as part of a narrative describing the foiled attempt of Alexander who is searching for the "Fountain of Life." In each instance, there is a sense of an indefatigable wanderer searching for life. Like many other poets in history Iqbāl used the imagery of Khiḍr to enhance his message of optimism by using the metaphor of immortality.

jafā kashī kā Khizr kahīye un kisānoṅ kō
yē sabẓ kartē haiṅ kōhsār kī chatānoṅ kō

Call these farmers the embodiment of Khiḍr;
As they turn the mountain rocks into green

and,

hāth dhō bayth āb-i-ḥaywāṅ se Khudā jāney kahāṅ
Khizr ne uskō chupā kar aye Sikandar rakh diyā[15]

Give up searching for the living water as God knows whither;
O Alexander, Khiḍr has hidden it.

Iqbāl depicts the figure of Khiḍr as a spiritual guide par excellence.[16] He himself drew spiritual guidance from Khiḍr. In the following verses from "Khizr-i rāh," Khiḍr responds to some of Iqbāl's questions concerning the condition of the Muslim world:

kiyā sunātā hai mujhey turk-o 'arab kī dāstāṅ
mujh se kuch pinhāṅ nahīṅ Islāmiyoṅ kā sōz-o sāz[17]

Why tell me the story of the Turk and the Arab?
The tragedy of the people of Islam is nothing of a secret to me.

For Iqbāl Khiḍr represents more than just a guide (Khizr-i rāh), he sees Khiḍr as an embodiment of the secret of immortality. He revises the logic of viewing Khiḍr's role by proclaiming him both an "immortal guide" and a "guide to immortality." In the former sense, Khiḍr exists as part of a long tradition of attracting seekers to spiritual discipline. In the latter sense, the immortal status of this guide presupposes a state of immortality, which is the goal of all seekers. Thus, while Khiḍr's immortality ensures his continued guidance forever, what draws one to immortality is the state of being called *maqām al-Khiḍr*, where the personification with essential Khiḍrian traits become a reality. This state of being is the state of "positive action" because the virtue of "action" is life itself and so long as there is action and movement, there is life. Again, Iqbāl, putting the words in the mouth of Prophet Khiḍr, says:

> *pukhta tar hai gardish-i payham se jām-i zindagī*
> *hai yahī aye bekhabar rāz-i dawām-i zindagī* [18]
>
> Constant circulation makes the cup of life more durable,
> O ignorant one! this is the very secret of immortality.

This philosophy of action expressed in Khiḍrian terms is quite similar to the story of Gilgamesh. In the Epic of Gilgamesh, the Sumerian hero poses the perennial question of immortality, and by doing so it very much seeks to highlight Gilgamesh's attempt to achieve "eternal youth, [and] lasting fame." Gilgamesh, the king of Uruk, had seen people die despite their heroism and achievements; he wanted to defeat death and sought immortality. However, as the story reveals, all his attempts resulted in failure.[19] In the end, Gilgamesh finds the answer to the question of immortality in death itself, where death is seen as an utterly impersonal act—the "ultimate act, the act which comes when the gods command it."[20] It seemed to Gilgamesh that death is impossible to overcome, and immortality is nothing but an illusion of the mind. And yet when his "illusions of personal immortality are stripped away, there is only the act to maintain the freedom to act."[21] The immortality of the human soul is viewed not in the simplistic, dualistic opposition of the soul to the body, but rather in soul's interplay with the ego, which Iqbāl called *khudī*. Iqbāl says, "the life of the ego is a kind of tension caused by the ego invading the environment and environment invading the ego."[22] Thus, immortality is not simply being human and possessing a soul, rather it lies in the dialectic between the ego and one's surrounding/social conditions/environment which creates and maintains a tension between the two, contributing to the ever-enhancement and perfection of the ego drawing oneself away from the clutches of fatalism (*qismat*).[23] Ego in Iqbāl is seen as a "unity of mental states" and is "absolutely unique."[24] Selfhood or self-affirmation is this ego's worldly manifestation. Achieving this unity will allow the divine will to "flow through the human soul, filling and transforming it, until one reaches conformity with one's destined fate."[25] The development of the ego is the most important task that ultimately leads to the highest form of self-affirmation, that of being an "individual" who is self-contained, unique and centered. Thus, Iqbāl remembers McTaggart by saying the "universe is an association of individuals" and God himself is an individual although God represents the "Perfect Individual, the Absolute Ego, the Center of all centers."[26]

Iqbāl, like Rūmī, believed in personal immortality of the soul and that achieving this immortality required a strong determination on the part of each individual. In other words, it is by self-effort and strong will that one may attain it, just as we have seen in the example of Gilgamesh. Thus, the imagery and symbolism of Khiḍr in Iqbāl's thought highlights the need for serious and sincere effort (action) on the part of human beings. Iqbāl says, "personal immortality . . . is not ours as of right; it is to be achieved by personal effort."[27] This personal effort translates as "action" where an individual attains immortality by virtue of his/her will and an acquired power to act rather than by virtue of just being. Immortality is not a given, it is an "earned immortality."[28] Goethe, who was one of Iqbāl's Western mentors and whom he read and admired, echoes a similar philosophy of action; it includes "striving and willing" as keys to accomplishing: "He who toils forever striving, Him can we redeem."[29] This is similar to how Iqbāl's notion of *khudī* is conceptualized and it is also how he perceives Khiḍr—i.e., as someone who epitomizes striving and action. It is not surprising that Iqbāl is said to have had a meaningful engagement with Goethe despite their differences concerning the poetic style of Ḥāfiẓ of which Iqbāl was not a fan.

Immortality implies some sense of continuity beyond earthly life. In Iqbāl, this continuity is spelled out in terms of an ongoing development of the ego. As the ego in this earthly life seeks perfection by use of the physical structure—that is the body—it actually aims to survive this structure itself at death. Beyond death the ego survives, if it does, in a different state of consciousness which in the Islamic tradition is known as *'ālam al-barzakh*—a state between death and resurrection.[30] But the ultimate stage for the integration of the immortal ego is its attainment of eternity which, religiously speaking, is the same as paradise—the culmination of both life and love. Iqbāl writes:

jauhar-i zindagī hai 'ishq;
jauhar-i 'ishq hai khudī [31]

[If] the essence of life is love,
The essence of love is ego.

Even as the ego (*khudī*) contains the potential of perfection of the soul it seeks the guidance of those perfected egos that have, by their own striving as well as God's intervention, already had a glimpse of that elevated state of consciousness. Khiḍr, in Iqbāl's view, symbolizes one such guiding ego. As someone whom God calls "one of Our servants," Khiḍr typifies the act-bound ego, who is busy helping human beings realize the essence of divine will. Therefore, it is by virtue of his power to act that Khiḍr is immortal. For Iqbāl it is by nurturing the self (*khudī*) that we shall find the secret of Godhead (*ta'mīr-i khudī meṅ hai khudā'ī*).[32]

The concept of *khudī* (self or ego) may be said to be the central feature of Iqbāl's thought. He admonishes those who make no effort on their part and simply wait for a savior to appear, whether it is Khiḍr, Mahdi or Jesus. For Iqbāl, the ego is both "single and manifold . . . hidden and open,"[33] it is preserved as a separate entity, separate from the divine and yet completely dependent. Iqbāl's philosophy is opposed to the monistic view of reality held by some Muslim mystics, such as those of the school of Ibn 'Arabī, who argued in favor of the idea of *waḥdat al-wujūd* or the "unity of Being."[34] As mentioned earlier, Iqbāl conceives the idea of unity in terms of "will" rather than "being," arguing that there is no "universal life" from which we all emanated and hence we long for a reunification which will constitute the great oneness of all. Instead, he argues, God and human beings are distinct and there is hardly room for self-annihilation. Rather, we should aim for self-affirmation—which allows the full realization of the self. Unlike in pantheistic Sufism where the human soul supposedly "dissolves" or annihilates (*fanā'*) itself into the divine, in Iqbāl, the human determination (willpower) seeks to "unite" with the divine will (God's plan for humanity) which infuses and strengthens human effort while preserving its individuality and thus fulfilling the human goal of the "realization" of the self. To Iqbāl, the ego never merges itself into the "ocean" of the divine Godhead to the extent where it (like a drop of water meeting the ocean) completely loses its identity. But there hangs always this paradox of union in separation and separation in union:

khudī roshan zenūr-e kibriyāyī ast,
rasā'ī hāi aw az nā rasā'ī ast;
judā'ī az muqāmāt waṣālish,
waṣālish az muqāmāt-e judā'ī ast[35]

The Self is brilliant by the light of Divine grandeur,
its reachings are from its not-reaching;
Its separation is a station of the stations of union,
its union is one of the stations of separation[36]

THE PHILOSOPHY OF ACTION AS A PATH OF SPIRITUAL REALIZATION

Iqbāl wanted Muslims to believe in the philosophy of action and carve out their own path than to simply adopt the path chosen for them by others. He saw the struggle as between "us" vs "them"; between Arab-based early Islam vs Greco-Persian-based, Avicenna-induced medieval Islam; between Islam-inspired modernity vs West-inspired modernity and so on. For Iqbāl, intuition and spiritual experience cannot be subordinated to reason because the latter has its limits as for him Kant aptly demonstrated, although, ironically, using reason to do so.[37] Iqbāl spoke about *'ishq* (love) as the vital force that is sustained by the "dynamic, creative motion" necessary for the realization of the self-hood (*khudī*). He places *'ishq* above *'aql* (intellectual constructs),[38] because the latter cannot deliver humanity without the former.

Iqbāl was immensely influential in his time partly because there were not many intellectuals who were as vocal about both continuity and change. Iqbāl spoke about the rich heritage of Islam and the need to preserve it in a time of great change and in the midst of challenges that surrounded Muslims in the early part of the 20th century. His understanding of tradition was that it must be dynamic to remain viable and life-giving.[39] At the same time, he was loud enough to demand that Muslims direct the change on their own terms and pace. Iqbāl was well-liked by Muslims but for different reasons. To the traditionalists he appeared as a guardian of the rich Muslim heritage for which they felt safe and were comforted that Iqbāl was not a radical reformist like Mustafa Kemal Atatürk.[40] The progressives saw in Iqbāl someone who could articulate and lead the "movement of change" urgently needed to stop the marginalization and alienation of religion and to fight against the fast approaching, European-inspired materialism. David Kerr explains this movement as a "constant process of inner growth or evolution, in which universal principles and ethical norms find new and varied [manifestations] in different times and places." Such a process of change would work only if it preserved the principles and norms and at the same time inspired authentic reform.[41]

Iqbāl stood against the resigning spiritualism of his day, whose origin he attributed to the development of Persian Neoplatonism within the intellectual history of Islam.[42] Thus we can see that despite his love for Rūmī, Iqbāl rejected the pantheistic elements in Mawlana's thought. However, in Rūmī he saw more than pantheism; he saw an "advocate of spiritual development . . . [and] the infinite quest for God."[43] Through his poetry of "action" Iqbāl drove out all three: *the poet* from the tavern; *the Sufi* from his *khānqāh* (monastery) and *the preacher* from his mosque. His poetry is essentially a critique upon the perpetual inaction associated with these three roles, traditionally manifested by a self-centered poet, a resigned mystic, and a literal-minded cleric. Iqbāl indirectly addresses individuals who profess these roles by way of a dialogue with Khiḍr who as a symbol of life appealed to Iqbāl in almost every aspect of his philosophical worldview. Iqbāl was certainly not against these vocations, rather, he sought to drive out the stigma of spiritual and social stagnation which these roles and professions seemed to symbolize. One day, Khiḍr appeared to Iqbāl and said, "If the eye of the heart be open, the destiny of the world is unveiled." Iqbāl, therefore, questioned Khiḍr:

choṛ kar ābādiyaṅ rehtā hai tū ṣehrā naward,
zindagī terī hai be rôz-ô shab-o farda-ô dôsh;
zindagī kā rāz kiyā hai salṯanat kiyā chīz hai?
awr ye sarmāya-ô meḥnat meṅ hai kaisā kharôsh?[44]

Away from inhabitation you roam the desert;
your life is devoid of day and night; today and tomorrow;
What is the secret of life; what is kingship?
and what is this conflict between capital and labor?

To this Khiḍr replied:

kyūṅ ta'ajjub hai merī ṣeḥrā nawardī par tujhey?
ye tagā pūay damādam zindagī kī hai dalīl[45]

Why do you wonder over my rambles in the desert?
This constant motion is the potent sign of life.

and,

apnī dunyā āp peydā kar agar zindoṅ meṅ hai
sarr-i Ādam hai ẕamīr-i kun fakāṅ hai zindagī![46]

Create your own world if you are among the living,
Life is the secret of Adam, the conscience of life itself!

Iqbāl believed that "the world is not something to be merely seen or known through concepts, but something to be made and remade by continuous action."[47] Iqbāl's message is filled with optimism; he constantly reminds us to not lose hope. It is hope that motivates one to action that eventually leads one to self-determination and self-affirmation[48] as opposed to self-annihilation a la monistic Sufism. In this, he invites every individual to become, as it were, a substitute for Khiḍr just as the latter is seen to substitute for Moses' "perceptivity"[49] in the quranic episode narrating their encounter (Q. 18:60–82).[50]

But his optimism utilizes the figure of Khiḍr in an antinomian way as well. Reminding us of the "fool of God," who, unlike others, resists the temptation to seek help from Khiḍr, Iqbāl says:

aye khunak āṅ tashna kāṅdar āftāb
mī na-khwāhid az Khizar yak jām āb[51]

Happy is the man who, though thirsty in the sun,
Does not beg of Khizr a cup of water in such need

Iqbāl's reference here is to the notion of trust in God (*tawakkul*) serving as the anchor for one's faith. It seems that he wants us to look up to Khiḍr as a guide but not to become completely dependent on him. Instead, each seeker should strive to be Khiḍr-like. Hujwīrī in his *Kashf al-maḥjūb* mentions one of the "servants" of God named Ibrāhīm ibn Aḥmad al-Khawwās who was asked by Khiḍr for his company. Al-Khawwās refused, fearing that he "might put confidence in him [Khiḍr] instead of in God."[52] Similarly while protesting against *taqlīd*, Iqbāl says:

taqlīd kī ravish sey to behtar hai khudkushī,
rasta bhī ḍhūnḍ Khizr kā sawdā bhi choṛ de;
mīnār-i dil par apney Khudā kā nuzūl dekh,
awr intezār-i Mahdī wo 'Īsā bhī choṛ de[53]

Better annihilate yourself than to follow blindly;
forget the dealings with Khizr rather search on your own;
See the descent of divine in the sanctuary of your heart;
and quit waiting for Mahdi or Jesus.

Although Iqbāl's philosophy—not unlike some other schools of Sufism—validates Khiḍr's high function as a guide, it cautions against spiritual dependence on others (saviors included) for one's salvation. He regards *taqlīd* as synonymous with death, while creativity and self-motivated action for him represent life. Though Khiḍr is indeed a guide, sought out by many, he should be a *guide to action* rather than to a sort of spiritual resignation found among many mystics who invest great hopes in the supposed mediatory powers of their spiritual teacher (*shaykh*). Iqbāl appeals primarily to the heart rather than to the mind; his poems passionately call for action and seek to inspire enthusiasm.[54] His deep understanding of esoteric Islam furnishes him with a perspective that often lies dormant in secular poets and intellectuals. At the same time, Iqbāl's use of Khiḍr's symbolism is somewhat contrary to how Sufis and hagiographers envisioned Khiḍr's role in aiding the divine plan for salvation. He believes self-effort is key to achieving Khiḍr's help but too much reliance on Khiḍr's help defeats the purpose of seeking assistance in the first place, which is to ultimately become Khiḍr-like for others. A true poet is analogous to Khiḍr in that they both seek to guide others to the "Fountain of Life" (which, for Iqbāl, springs from self-determination and action) and hence the poet is likened to Khizr-i Rāh.[55]

fikr-ô bā māh-o anjum ham-nashīṅ,
zīsht rā nā āshnā khūb āfrīṅ;
Khizr-ô dar ẓulmāt-e aw āb-e hayāt,
zinda-tarāz āb-e chishmish kā'ināt[56]

His thoughts dwell with the moon and the stars,
he creates beauty in that which is ugly and strange;
He is a Khizr, amidst his darkness is the Fountain of Life,
All things that exist are made more living by his tears.

Such a person as described in these verses is not just a poet who calls people to action for just any reason but rather who calls people to "act" in the path of God, striving to achieve unity with the divine. Here Iqbāl combines the roles of a mystic and a poet into one, similar to Khiḍr who is at once a "knower" (a quality sought by mystics) as well as a proactive "guide" (a quality a true poet should possess). Such a person is called to be prophetic and to undertake action that may be seemingly defiant of God's law (as Khiḍr appeared to Moses in the story related in Sūrat al-Kahf, 18: 60–82) but in fact are divinely ordained and ultimately salvific. It is hardly surprising that such an ideal poet in Iqbāl's mind was none other the great teacher Rūmī, who is both a mystic—having attained the knowledge of God—and a poet, who communicates and transmits this knowledge to others in the most sublime manner. In one of his poems in *Bāng-i darā* Iqbāl says:

kām dunyā meṅ rahbarī hai merā
mithl-i Khizr-i khujasta pā hūṅ meṅ[57]

My task is to be a guide in this world,
Like Khizr I am always on the go.

Iqbāl saw himself as embodying the role of Khiḍr for his readers and followers. At the same time, he considered Rūmī to be his "Khizr"—as someone who had a tremendous influence on his (Iqbāl's) thinking and also on the style of his poetry.[58] Indeed his famous poem, "Khiẓr-i rāh" acknowledges this debt by noting that the spiritual guide in that poem is a representation of Rūmī.[59]

NOTES

1. Poetry is said to facilitate articulation of ideas considered inexplicable. Traditionally speaking poets and literary persons are said to have inherited metaphysical truths and reframed them in their own idiom for the benefit of those with little access to and/or interest in formalistic philosophical and theological traditions.

2. Johann Wolfgang Goethe, *Goethe's Reinke Fox, West-Eastern Divan, and Achilleid,* trans. A. Rogers (London: G. Bell & Sons, 1890), 199–200, cited in Seyyed H. Nasr, *Knowledge and the Sacred* (New York: Crossroad, 1991), 96.

3. Jalāl al-Dīn Rūmī, *Discourses of Rūmī [Fīhi mā fīhi],* trans. A. J. Arberry (New York: Samuel Weiser, 1972), 78, cited in Renard, *All the King's Falcons*, 85.

4. Jalāl al-Dīn Rūmī, *Mathnavī-e ma'navī* (Tehran: Rozaneh Publishing, 1999), 1:237.

5. Renard, *All the King's Falcons,* 86.

6. Muḥammad Iqbāl, *Bāng-i darā* (Lahore: Shaikh Muḥammad Ashraf, 1924).

7. A. Anwar Beg, *The Poet of the East* (Lahore: Khawar Publishing Cooperative Society, 1961), 115.

8. Iqbāl's philosophy is fused with a deep sense of aesthetic vitalism. He is critical of contemplation for its own sake and favors action and self-reliance. M. M. Sharif, *About Iqbal and His thought* (Lahore: Institute of Islamic Culture, 1964), 72.

9. For more on Gilgamesh's attempt as well as "realization" of immortality, see John Gardener and John Maier, *Gilgamesh: Translated from the Sin-Legi-Unnini Version* (New York: Alfred A Knopf, 1984).

10. See Abu'l Ḥasan 'Alī Nadwī, *Nuqūsh-i Iqbāl* (Lucknow: Majlis Taḥqīqāt wa Nashrīyāt-i Islām, 1994).

11. Asghar Ali Engineer, "Iqbal's 'Reconstruction of Religious Thought in Islam': A Critical Appraisal," *Social Scientist* 8, no. 8 (1980): 52.

12. Ibid., 53.

13. Muḥammad Iqbāl, "Khizr-i rāh," in *Kulliyāt-i Iqbāl: Urdu* (Lahore: Shaikh Ghulām Alī & Sons, 1984), 255–76.

14. S. Alam Khundmiri, "Conception of Time," in *Iqbal: Poet-Philosopher of Pakistan,* ed. Hafeez Malik (New York: Columbia University Press, 1971), 250.

15. Muḥammad Iqbāl, *Sarôd-i raftā*, ed. Ghulām Rasool Mehr & Sādiq Alī Dilāwarī (Lahore: Shaikh Ghulām Alī & Sons, 1959), 244–45.

16. Beg, *The Poet of the East*, 115–16.

17. Iqbāl, "Khizr-i rāh," in *Kulliyāt-i Iqbāl: Urdu*, 264.

18. Ibid., 258.

19. Gardner and Maier, *Gilgamesh*, 6.

20. John Gardner, *The Sunlight Dialogues* (New York: Alfred A. Knopf, 1973), 533.

21. Gardner and Maier, *Gilgamesh*, 6. The Epic of Gilgamesh is a story of despair but also hope; it is about struggle for immortality. It seeks to convey a message about life using the language of death expressed in verse.

22. Muhammad Iqbal, *The Reconstruction of Religious Thought in Islam* (Delhi: Kitāb Bhavan, 1998), 102.

23. Ibid.

24. Muhammad Maruf, "Allama Iqbal on Immortality," *Religious Studies* 18 (Summer 1982): 376.
25. Annemarie Schimmel, *Deciphering the Signs of God: A Phenomenological Approach to Islam* (Albany: State University of New York Press, 1994), 147.
26. Beg, *The Poet of the East*, 189.
27. Iqbal, *Reconstruction of Religious Thought*, 119.
28. Maruf, "Allama Iqbal on Immortality," 377.
29. Cited in Thomas Carlyle, *On Heroes, Hero-Worship and the Heroic in History* (Lincoln: University of Nebraska Press, 1966), xi.
30. Iqbal, *Reconstruction of Religious Thought*, 120.
31. Fayyaz Mahmood, "Iqbal's Attitude Towards God," in *Iqbal as a Thinker*, ed. Raziuddin, et al. (Lahore: Shaikh Muḥammad Ashraf, 1973), 277.
32. Ibid., 282.
33. Annemarie Schimmel, *Gabriel's Wing: A Study into the Religious Ideas of Sir Muhammad Iqbal* (Leiden: Brill, 1963), 103.
34. The notion of *waḥdat al-wujūd* as enunciated by Ibn 'Arabī is believed to be the idea that ultimate unity between the human soul and divine being is the culmination of one's spiritual journey. William C. Chittick, *The Sufi Path of Love* (Albany: State University of New York Press, 1985).
35. Muḥammad Iqbāl, "Khudī," in *Armughān-i hijāz*, in *Kulliyāt-i Iqbāl: Fārsī* (Lahore: Shaikh Ghulām Alī & Sons, 1973), 1003.
36. Schimmel, *Gabriel's Wing*, 139.
37. Iqbāl referring to Kant's *Critique of Pure Reason*; see Iqbal, *Reconstruction,* 5.
38. Fazlur Rahman, "Muhammad Iqbāl and Atatürk's Reforms," *Journal of Near Eastern Studies* 43, no. 2 (1984): 158.
39. David A. Kerr, "Muhammad Iqbal's Thoughts on Religion: Reflections in the Spirit of Christian—Muslim Dialogue," *Islamochristiana* 15 (1989): 28–29.
40. Iqbāl denounced Atatürk in *Jāvīd nāma* for "his Westernization policy" and for abolishing the Caliphate. Fazlur Rahman, "Muhammad Iqbāl and Atatürk's Reforms,"159.
41. Kerr, "Muhammad Iqbal's Thoughts on Religion," 31.
42. A. H. Kamali, "The Heritage of Islamic Thought," in *Iqbal: Poet-Philosopher of Pakistan,* ed. Hafeez Malik (New York: Columbia University Press, 1971), 211.
43. Annemarie Schimmel, *The Triumphal Sun: A Study of the Works of Jalāloddin Rumi* (Albany: State University of New York Press, 1993), 384.
44. Iqbal, "Khizr-i rāh," in *Kulliyāt-i Iqbāl: Urdu*, 256.
45. Ibid., 257.
46. Ibid., 259.
47. Iqbal, *Reconstruction of Religious Thought,* 198; cited in Fazlur Rahman, "Muhammad Iqbāl and Atatürk's Reforms," 158.
48. Reynold A. Nicholson, introduction to *Asrār-i Khudī*, *The Secrets of the Self,* by Muhammad Iqbal, trans. Reynold A. Nicholson (Lahore: Farhan Publishers, 1977), xiii.
49. Yusuf S. Chishti, *Sharh-i Asrār-i khudī* (Lahore: Ishrat Publishing House, n.d.), 276.

50. In his poem, "Asrār-i khudī," Iqbāl writes: "*Khizr bā shud Mūsa-i idrāk rā*" (Being a Khizr to the Moses of perception). Muḥammad Iqbāl, *Asrār-i Khudī, The Secrets of the Self*, trans. Reynold A. Nicholson (Lahore: Farhan Publishers, 1977), 24. Iqbāl often portrays various prophetic figures such as Adam, Abraham, Moses, and Khiḍr with having various strengths. At times Moses is seen as superior to Khiḍr and at other occasions, as in the case above, Khiḍr seems to be substituting Moses' superior perception (*idrāk*). Cf. Schimmel, *Gabriel's Wing*, 264.

51. Iqbāl, "Asrār-i khudī," in *Kulliyāt-i Iqbāl: Fārsī*, 24.

52. al-Hujwīrī, *The Kashf al-mahjūb*, 153, 290.

53. Muḥammad Iqbāl, "Ghazliyāt," in *Bāng-i darā,* in *Kulliyāt-i Iqbāl: Urdu*, 107, cited in Khalifa A. Hakim, *Fikr-i Iqbāl* (Lahore: Bazm-i Iqbāl, 1957), 20.

54. Cf. Beg, *Poet of the East*, 211. See also Nicholson, introduction to *Asrār-i Khudī*, viii.

55. Schimmel, *Gabriel's Wing*, 61.

56. Muaḥmmad Iqbāl, "Dar Ḥaqīqat-i shī'r wa iṣlāḥ-i adbiyāt Islāmiyah," in *Asrār-i khudī,* in *Kulliyāt-i Iqbāl: Fārsī*, 35.

57. Muḥammad Iqbāl, "'Aql-o dil," in *Kulliyāt-i Iqbāl: Urdu*, 41.

58. Sharif, *About Iqbal and His Thought*.

59. Schimmel, *Gabriel's Wing*, 264, 357. Schimmel also notes that in recognition of the spiritual connection Iqbal had to Rumi, the Turks have carved out a "*maqām*" for Iqbal in the garden adjacent to the mausoleum of Mawlana Rūmī in Konya. See her *Deciphering the Signs of God*, 55.

Conclusion

In the Introduction I mentioned Marshall Hodgson's preference for the term "Islamicate" to refer to aspects related to Islam and Muslims which were produced by non-Muslims and/or produced in non-Islamic contexts. For Shahab Ahmed that rationale does not hold up. He, therefore, seeks to release Hodgson from being bound by the notion that anything Islamic can only come from Muslims and therefore "ideas and behaviours that are evidently related to Islam, but which are thought and performed by people who are not themselves Muslims"[1] need to be filed under Islamicate. Ahmed sees "*islām* . . . [as an] *action and activity* by the individual human being . . . it is something a person *does*, and it is by doing *islām* that a person makes himself or herself . . . a Muslim"[2] or in the case of non-Muslims, makes something *Islamic*. There is a distinction between the actor, his/her context and the produced effect. Ahmed offers the example of a Sikh wrestler who, prior to entering the competition, invokes the name of 'Alī ibn Abī Ṭālib, the cousin and son-in-law of Prophet Muḥammad, who is known for his chivalry and "warrior-courage." The Sikh wrestler is not a Muslim and yet he finds it meaningful to imagine being like 'Alī. In this, Ahmed argues that:

> The Sikh wrestler *gives meaning to his Self by this engagement with the Con-Text of the Revelation of Islam* . . . [and even though he] is not Muslim . . . he has *committed himself to meaning-making in terms of Islam*. His act is *precisely* an Islamic act—it is meaningful in terms of Islam. Just as a Muslim makes meaning for him*self* in terms of Islam by engagement with the Con-Text of Revelation . . . so does a non-Muslim. It is the *commitment of the self to the making of meaning in terms of the hermeneutical engagement with the Revelation of Islam* that makes the action of the non-Muslim actor *Islamic*.[3]

Given what Ahmed suggests, one can argue that all the narratives about Khiḍr which were woven into the fabric of Muslim practice using stories and ideas from pre-Islamic era as well as their post-7th century connections with cultures around the world, are Islamic. Even though these narratives relied on the contributions by many non-Muslim actors and drew from sources that were not Islamic, by virtue of the fact that *what* these actors produced was "meaningful in terms of Islam" qualifies them as "Islamic."[4] Khiḍr can thus be viewed as a Muslim bridge between ideas and stories spread across time and space. He becomes a symbol of the collaborative transnational, transcultural, and interreligious legacy spanning centuries. Everyone with whom Khiḍr is connected and everyone he represents, works with, and appears besides, become part of the Islamic ethos because of the "meaning-making" process that these connections engender.

An interesting dimension of Khiḍr that emerges from the foregoing is that he appears to be a leveler of rank, a remover of distinctions based on worldly privileges of class and place. While he bestows spiritual status or rank, he does so indiscriminately; thus, he appears and helps any person regardless of class or caste, and not just *al-khāṣṣa* (the spiritual elite or the accomplished Sufis). The wide range of spaces inhabited by Khiḍr discussed here clearly indicates that Khiḍr is reachable regardless of who the seeker is and where she/he may be located. Among the Uwaysīs of Central Asia Khiḍr is the physically absent teacher of those who put their trust in him and are willing to toil on the path. For the Sufis or those aspiring to be one, an encounter with Khiḍr is a way to elevate one's spiritual status. The elitist idea that gnosis can be achieved only by the elect is contrary to how Sufism is blended in Muslim life and religion in cultures around the world. The story of Khiḍr appears to validate the foundational precepts of Sufism. Khiḍr as a popular figure can be said to be the most "accessible saint" in universal Islam. His availability to one and all counters the claim that only the elect may know the divine or have the ability and the means to seek *ma'rifah*. Inasmuch as Khiḍr touches the lives of human beings, even if he is imaginary to the rationalist, he allows the common person to feel this direct relationship with the transcendent and compassionate God, making God immanent and manifest in their lives. This hope-filled message may help strengthen the faith of those on the margins.

Finally, miracles or *mu'jizāt* which come as a result of the knowledge of the unseen (*'ilm al-ghayb*) are not due to personal abilities but are granted by God; this is true as much of Moses and other prophets as it is of Khiḍr. Even though in popular piety much good is often credited to his own doing, Khiḍr of the Qur'ān operates like the Jesus of the Qur'ān—the special acts they were able to perform were realized only by leave of God. It is God's doing, channeled through these human beings who acted as vessels, especially in those particular moments where the miraculous occurs. The powers are granted to Khiḍr and other prophetic figures by the grace of God and in the actual moment of the performance of those extraordinary deeds. This is to allow the dispensation of divine mercy through a medium which does not transgress the boundaries of theological principles. Prophet Muḥammad is said to have the power to intercede on behalf of his followers on the day of resurrection when the time to act will be no more. Similarly, the Khiḍr narrative allows for mediation through Khiḍr but with one key difference—in the case of Khiḍr, it is instantaneously available to a sincere seeker, although the purpose and nature of mediation in this case is quite different as it is temporal and procedural. Furthermore, Khiḍr mediates, he does not intercede. In lived realities of faith and in popular piety traditions, many Muslims invoke Prophet Muḥammad's name for similar reasons, seeking mediation and expressing hopes for blessings and healing. Some Muslim scholars and exegetes reject claims made by Sufis that Khiḍr's presence is real and that he was (or is) indeed a person who helped many and perhaps continues to help anyone who seeks him out as a teacher and guide. It is difficult to prove whether Khiḍr exists in the space-time continuum, however, it is equally difficult to deny his influence and its effects on people who believe in his mission. Jalāl al-Dīn Rūmī suggested a reasonable way to understand this phenomenon. He stated that even if Khiḍr as a person is no more, he has through the method of delegation appointed many individuals who have become *like* Khiḍr, and who draw their legitimacy from having taught by him. This may be Khiḍr's true legacy, his continuing mission, and even a claim of "immortality" of some sort.[5]

Rationalists often decry any claims of truth made on behalf of mystical traditions, calling them superstitions. However, many mystics thought of such knowledge as not only within the realm of certitude but as accompanied with a sort of "inner light" which is its own evidence.[6] No outside evidence is sought or is seen as necessary because it is a subjective and experiential truth and no amount of reasoning against it would either be able to strengthen or weaken such claims. Thus, the two forms of "knowledge"—the esoteric and the exoteric—seem to be on two different tracks, almost parallel to each other.[7] Similarly one can speak of the two parallel paths traversed by Khiḍr and Moses. Khiḍr is on the path of an *experience of being given* the knowledge instantaneously and immediately, while Moses is on the path of *witnessing to a revelatory event* which is comparable to the divine mandate received by other prophets such as Abraham, Noah, Jesus, and Muḥammad. Here too, the dialectic is invoked between the mystical splendor of the path of Khiḍr and the orthodoxy of the path of Moses. In these two figures the experience and the law, the *bāṭin* and the *ẓāhir*, the hidden and the manifest are differentiated—or, as one might argue, differentiated only in order to reveal a deeper course of their convergence. This is indeed what Sufis believe; they see mysticism and piety as integral to the orthodox forms of practice. In Islamic legalistic writings much has been made of the contrast between "law" and "experience" or the *shar'īah* and the *ṭarīqah,* when in fact, they should be seen as two sides of the same coin. Law requires one to practice the faith diligently, but the final aim remains the attainment of the love of God and the certainty (*al-yaqīn*) of eternal life with God in the hereafter (*al-ākhirah*) while still in this world. Both aspects of faith are necessary for an honest accounting with God.

Khiḍr's story is a powerful testament to the connection and the vital link between religion and service to others, faith and action, and spirituality and the concern for the marginalized. As we have seen, Khiḍr symbolism is used in various ways; some see in him a friend and helper who approaches strangers with kindness, compassion, and wisdom. Others regard him as their *shaykh*, spiritual teacher and *guide* par excellence; and yet others put him on the pedestal as some sort of *savior* figure who will come to rescue them from their travails. Placing blind faith in a healer with little self-effort has become part of the way in which Khiḍr is received in some circles. Muḥammad Iqbāl suggested a more a nuanced picture; for him Khiḍr is the ultimate symbol of critique of "other worldly" theologies that seek to promote resignation from the world. Forms of mysticism where help is sought without effort and toil are prevalent in many cultures. Iqbal considers them not only as antithetical to the spirit of Khiḍr's story in the Qur'ān but also an anathema to Sufism in general. Over reliance on the "savior" undermines the role of individual effort and inner striving. Spiritual acts are relevant and efficacious only when carried out through self-effort and by doing one's utmost to bring about change for the betterment of all. Saint Theresa (formerly, of Calcutta) was right on the mark when she said: "I used to believe that prayer changes things, but now I know that prayer changes us and we change things."[8]

Khiḍr is a teacher of Sufis deep in *dhikr*, but he has also guided and helped countless others—fishermen in search of their lighthouse, women seeking healing for their sick child, and many others who call on him in distress. Whether seen as a guide or a savior figure, Khiḍr occupies the landscape of thought and practice in much of the Muslim world and beyond. He is, as Carl Jung notes, truly an archetype and a figure who fits into every imaginable category of human engagement whether it is lay or sacred, prophetic or folk, theological or spiritual. In short, Khiḍr is a perfect saint, guide, mediator, and protector.[9] Khiḍr is the symbol of continued hope for many and in that he is truly immortal. Those who argue that God created human beings and other members of creation just to worship and remember God, they would not be wrong since it is indeed noted in the Qur'ān (Surat al-Dhāriyāt, 51:56). However, they should also consider broadening their understanding of "worship" for if the Khiḍr model as outlined in the quranic narrative of the Khiḍr-Moses episode has taught us anything it is that worshipping God through ritual prayer and *dhikr* is but only part of the what is required of a true believer. As one of the *ḥadīth* plainly states: "No one of you is a true believer until he loves for his brother what he loves for himself."[10] In the final analysis, the example of Khiḍr is a testament to the fact that faith and service are two sides of the same coin; indeed, they must go together. In closing it is fitting to remember the prayer Khiḍr taught to ʻAlī ibn Abī Ṭālib, the fourth caliph for Sunnis, and the first Imam in the Shiʻī tradition. It is said that while ʻAlī was doing his circumambulation (*ṭawāf*) at the Kaʻba,' Khiḍr appeared to him and recited the following prayer (also known as "duʻā' al-Khiḍr"): "O God, you are not distracted and you do not commit error and you are not made convoluted by persistent questions; give me the taste of your forgiveness and sweet memory." Khiḍr, addressing ʻAlī, said: anyone who prays this way will be forgiven even if their sins were equal to the number of stars in the sky.[11]

NOTES

1. Ahmed, *What is Islam?*, 444–45.
2. Ibid., 101.
3. Ibid., 445–46.
4. Ibid., 450.
5. Renard, *All the King's Falcons*, 85.
6. It must be added that the proponents of this idea would acknowledge the need for necessary prerequisites for one to be able to perceive this inner experience or "light." William James would call this conditioning of the self, a realization of trust in God's presence resulting in an "unaccountable feeling of safety." William James, *The Varieties of Religious Experience: A Study in Human Nature* (London: Longmans, 1905), 285.
7. This idea is drawn from Nicholson, *The Mystics of Islam*, 114.
8. Raymond Wells, *Mother Teresa in Her Own Words* (N.p.: Amazon Digital Services LLC-KDP Print US, 2021), 17.
9. Elboudrari, "Entre le symbolique et l'historique Khadir immemorial," 38–39.
10. Cited in Yaḥyā ibn Ṣaraf al-Nawawī, *An-Nawawi's Forty Hadith*, ed. Ezzedin Ibrahim (Beirut: Holy Koran Publication House, 1979), *ḥadīth* no. 13.
11. Ḥusaynī, *Ḥayāt al-Khiḍr*, 154–55.

Works Cited

'Abd al-Muqtadar, Ibrāhīm ibn Fathī. *Kashf al-ilbās: 'amma ṣaḥḥa wa-mā lam yaṣiḥḥu min qiṣṣat al-Khiḍr Abī al-'Abbās*. Jeddah: Dār al-Muḥammadī, 1997.

Abel, Armand. *Le roman d'Alexandre: légendaire medieval*. Bruxelles: Office de Publicité, 1955.

Abdel Haleem, M. A. S. *The Qur'an*. New York: Oxford University Press, 2004.

Addas, Claude. *Ibn 'Arabī ou la quête du Soufre rouge*. Paris: Gallimard, 1989.

Addas, Claude. *Quest for the Red Sulphur: The Life of Ibn 'Arabī.* Cambridge: Islamic Texts Society, 1993.

Ahmad, Irfan. *Religion as Critique: Islamic Critical Thinking from Mecca to the Marketplace*. Chapel Hill: The University of North Carolina Press, 2017.

Ahmed, Shahab. *What is Islam? The Importance of Being Islamic*. Princeton: Princeton University Press, 2015.

Albayrak, Ismail "The Classical Exegetes' Analysis of the Qur'ānic Narrative 18: 60–82." *Islamic Studies* 42, no. 2 (Summer 2003): 289–315.

'Alī Nadwī, Abu'l Ḥasan. *Nuqūsh-i Iqbāl*. Lucknow: Majlis Taḥqīqāt-o Nashrīyāt-i Islām, 1994.

Amir-Ali, Hashim. *The Message of the Qur'ān: Presented in Perspective*. Rutland, VT: Charles E. Tuttle Company, 1974.

Ammerman, Nancy Tatom. *Studying Lived Religion: Contexts and Practices*. New York: New York University Press, 2021.

Anderson, George K. *The Legend of the Wandering Jew*. Providence: Brown University Press, 1965.

Anderson, William. *Green Man: The Archetype of Our Oneness with the Earth.* London: HarperCollins, 1990.

Annan, Barbara. "Subjectivity and the Other: Khidr and Transformation in Liminal Encounters." In *Ethics and Subjectivity in Literary and Cultural Studies*, edited by William S. Haney and Nicholas Pagan, 101–115. New York: Peter Lang, Bern, 2002.

Arberry, A. J. *Sufism: An Account of the Mystics of Islam*. Mineola, NY: Dover Publications, 2002.

Arkoun, Mohammed. *Lectures du Coran*. Paris: Albin Michel, 2016.

Armstrong, Karen. *Muhammad: A Biography of the Prophet*. San Francisco: Harper Collins, 1993.

Arnaboldi, Giacomo. "Élie Le Verdoyant." *Aurora*, Supplement aux *Cahiers d'Orient et d'Occident*, no. 3. (n.d.), http://edition.moncelon.fr/index.htm.

Asad, Muhammad. *The Message of The Qur'ān*. Gibraltar: Dār al-Andalus, 1980.

Asín Palacios, Miguel. *El-Islam cristianizado*. 2nd ed. Madrid: Plutarco, 1931.

Asín Palacios, Miguel. *La espiritualidad de Algazel y su sentido christiano*. Madrid & Granada: Imprenta de Estanislao Maestre, 1934–41.

'Attar, Farid ud-Din. *The Conference of the Birds. Mantiq ut-Tair*. Translated by C. S. Nott. London: The Janus Press, 1954.

Aubaile-Sallenave, Françoise. "Al-Khiḍr, 'L'homme au manteau vert' en pays musulmans: ses fonctions, ses caractères, sa diffusion." *Res Orientales* 14 (2002): 11–35.

Augustinovic, A. *"El-Khadr" and the Prophet Elijah*. Jerusalem: Francescan Printing Press, 1972.

Ayoub, Mahmoud. "Cult and Culture: Common Saints and Shrines in Middle Eastern Popular Piety." In *Religion and Culture in Medieval Islam*, edited by Richard G. Hovannisian and Georges Sabbagh, 103–115. Cambridge: Cambridge University Press, 1999.

Ayoub, Mahmoud M. *Islam: Faith and Practice*. Markham, Ontario: The Open Press Limited, 1989.

al-Baghdādī (al-Khāzin), 'Ala al-Dīn 'Alī ibn Muḥammad. *Tafsīr al-Khāzin: al-musamma' lubāb al-ta'wīl fī ma'ānī al-tanzīl*. Bayrūt: Dār al-Ma'rifah, n.d.

Baldick, Julian. *Imaginary Muslims: The Uwaysi Sufis of Central Asia*. London: I.B. Tauris, 1993.

Bashir, Shahzad. *Sufi Bodies: Religion and Society in Medieval Islam*. New York: Columbia University Press, 2013.

Beg, A. Anwar. *The Poet of the East*. Lahore: Khawar Publishing Cooperative Society, 1961.

Boratav, P. N. "Khiḍr-Ilyās." In *The Encyclopaedia of Islam*. New ed. Vol. 5. Leiden: E. J. Brill, 1979. 5.

Brinner, William. "Prophets and Prophecy in the Islamic and Jewish Traditions." In *Studies in Islamic and Judaic Traditions II*, edited by William M. Brinner and Stephen D. Ricks, 63–82. Atlanta: Scholars Press, 1989.

Brown, Norman. "The Apocalypse of Islam." In *The Apocalypse and/or Metamorphosis*, 69–94. Berkeley: University of California Press, 1991.

de Bruijn, J. T. P. *Persian Sufi Poetry: An Introduction to the Mystical Use of Classical Persian Poems*. Surrey: Curzon Press, 1997.

de Bruijn, J. T. P., et al. "Mat͟hnawī." In *The Encyclopaedia of Islam*, edited by P. Bearman, et al. 2nd ed. http://dx.doi.org/10.1163/1573-3912_islam_COM_0709.

du Buisson, R. Du Mesnil. "Le lieu du combat de Saint Georges à Beyrouth." *Mélanges de l'Université Saint-Joseph* XII (1927): 251–65.

al-Bukhārī, Muḥammad bin Ismā'īl. *Mukhtaṣar ṣaḥīḥ al-Bukhārī*. Riyādh: Maktabah Dār al-Salām, 1994.

Carlyle, Thomas. *On Heroes, Hero-Worship and the Heroic in History*. Lincoln: University of Nebraska Press, 1966.

Canaan, Taufik. *Mohammadan Saints and Sanctuaries in Palestine.* London: Luzac, 1927.

Chishti, Yusuf S. *Sharh-i asrār-i khudī*. Lahore: Ishrat Publishing House, n.d.

Chittick, William C. *The Sufi Path of Love*. Albany: State University of New York Press, 1985.

Chodkiewicz, Michel. *Seal of the Saints: Prophethood and Sainthood in the Doctrine of Ibn 'Arabī.* Cambridge: The Islamic Texts Society, 1993.

Coates, Peter. *Ibn 'Arabi and Modern Thought: The History of Taking Metaphysics Seriously*. Oxford: Anqa, 2002.

Coomaraswamy, A. K. "Khwājā Khadir and the Fountain of Life in the Tradition of Persian and Mughal Art." *Ars Islamica* 1, no. 2 (1934): 172–82.

Corbin, Henri. *Histoire de la philosophie islamique*. Paris: Gallimard, 1964.

Corbin, Henry. *Creative Imagination in the Sufism of Ibn 'Arabi*. Translated by Ralph Manheim. Princeton: Princeton University Press, 1969.

Corbin, Henry. *En Islam iranien: Aspects spirituels et philosophiques*. 4 vols. Paris: Gallimard, 1972.

Corbin, Henry. *Spiritual Body and Celestial Earth: From Mazdean Iran to Shī'ite Iran*. Translated by Nancy Pearson. Princeton: Princeton University Press, 1977.

Crooke, William. *Religion and Folklore of Northern India.* London: Oxford University Press, 1926.

Culler, Jonathan. *Literary Theory: A Very Short Introduction*. Oxford: Oxford University Press, 2011.

Currie, P. M. *The Shrine and Cult of Mu'īn al-dīn Chishtī of Ajmer.* Delhi: Oxford University Press, 1989.

Delpech, François. "De David Reubeni au Juif Errant: dans les pas du 'Juif au soulier.'" *Revue de l'histoire des religions* 229 (2012): 53–84.

Denffer, Ahmad von. *'Ulūm al-Qur'ān: An Introduction to the Sciences of the Qur'ān*. Markfield: The Islamic Foundation, 1994.

Douglas, Elmer H. *The Mystical Teachings of al-Shādhilī*. Edited by Ibrahim M. Abu-Rabi'. Albany: State University of New York Press, 1993.

Dupre, Adam & Peter Young. "The Life and Influence of Muhyiddin Ibn 'Arabi." In *Union and Ibn 'Arabi: Proceedings of the First Annual Symposium of the Muhyiddin Ibn 'Arabi Society*, 1–10. Durham: Durham University, 1984.

Dyroff, Karl. "Wer is Chadir?" *Zeitschrift für Assyriologie* 7 (1892): 319–27.

Elboudrari, Hassan. "Entre le symbolique et l'historique Khadir immémorial." *Studia Islamica* 76 (1992): 25–39.

Elad, Amikam. *Medieval Jerusalem and Islamic Worship: Holy Places, Ceremonies, Pilgrimage.* Leiden: E. J. Brill, 1995.

Eickelman, Dale F. and James Piscatori, eds. *Muslim Travellers: Pilgrimage, Migration, and the Religious Imagination*. Berkeley: University of California Press, 1990.

Eliade, Mircea. *The Sacred and the Profane: The Nature of Religion*. Translated by Willard R. Trask. New York: Harcourt, 1959.

Encyclopedia Britannica, s.v. "Hermes," accessed February 9, 2022, https://www.britannica.com/topic/Hermes-Greek-mythology.

Engineer, Asghar Ali. "Iqbal's 'Reconstruction of Religious Thought in Islam': A Critical Appraisal." *Social Scientist* 8, no. 8 (1980): 52–63.

Etudes Carmélitaines: Elie le Prophète. Vol. 2, *Au Carmel, dans le Judaïsme et l'Islam*. Paris: Desclée, 1956.

Fiey, J. M., OP. *Assyrie chrétienne. Contribution à l'étude de l'histoire et de la géographie ecclésiastiques et monastiques du Nord de l'Iraq*. Vol. 2. Beirut: Librairie Orientale, 1965.

Florida, Nancy K. *Javanese Literature in Surakarta Manuscripts, Vol. 1: Introduction and Manuscripts of the Karaton Surakarta.* Ithaca: Cornell Southeast Asia Program Publications, 1993.

Fowden, Elizabeth Key. *The Barbarian Plain: Saint Sergius between Rome and Iran.* Berkeley: University of California Press, 1999.

Fowden, Elizabeth Key. "Saint Serge chez les Arabes." *Les Dossiers d'archéologie* 309 (2005): 54–59.

Fowden, Garth. *The Egyptian Hermes: A Historical Approach to the Late Pagan Mind.* Princeton: Princeton University Press, 1986.

Franke, Patrick. *Begegnung mit Khidr: Quellenstudien zum Imaginären im Traditionellen Islam.* Beirut and Stuttgart: Franz Steiner Verlag, 2000.

Franke, Patrick. "Khidr in Istanbul: Observations on the Symbolic Construction of Sacred Spaces in Traditional Islam." In *On Archeology of Sainthood and Local Spirituality in Islam: Past and Present Crossroads of Events and Ideas*, edited by Georg Stauth, 37–58. Yearbook of the Sociology of Islam 5. Bielefeld: Transcript Verlag, 2004.

Friedlaender, Israel. "Khidr." In *The Encyclopaedia of Religion and Ethics*, edited by James Hastings, 693–95. Vol. 7. New York: Charles Scribner's Sons, 1915.

Gardner, John. *The Sunlight Dialogues*. New York: Alfred A. Knopf, 1973.

Gardener, John and John Maier. *Gilgamesh: Translated from the Sin-Legi-Unnini Version.* New York: Alfred A Knopf, 1984.

Geertz, Clifford. *Islam Observed: Religious Development in Morocco and Indonesia.* New Haven: Yale University Press, 1968.

al-Ghazālī, Abū Ḥāmid Muḥammad. *Iḥyā' 'ulūm al-dīn*. Delhi: Kitāb Bhawan, 1933.

al-Ghazālī, Abū Ḥāmid Muḥammad. *Kīmiyā-e sa'ādat*. Tehran: Markazi Publications, 1954.

al-Ghazālī, Abū Ḥāmid Muḥammad. *Mishkāt al-anwār: The Niche for Lights.* Translated by W.H.T. Gairdner. London: Royal Asiatic Society, 1924.

al-Ghazālī, Abū Ḥāmid Muḥammad. *The Remembrance of Death and the Afterlife.* Translated by T. J. Winter. Cambridge: Islamic Texts Society, 1989.

al-Ghirnāṭī, Abū Ḥayyān. *Al-Baḥr al-muḥīṭ fī al-tafsīr*. Cairo: Dār al-Kitāb al-Islāmī, 1992.

Gibson, Helen. "St. George the Ubiquitous." *Saudi Aramco World* 22, no. 6 (November–December 1971): 4–7.

Gillot, Claude. "Mythe, récit, histoire du salut dans le Commentaire coranique de Tabari." *Journal Asiatique* 282 (1994): 237–70.

Glasse, Cyril. *The Concise Encyclopedia of Islam*. San Francisco: Harper and Row, 1989.

Goethe, Johann Wolfgang. *Goethe's Reineke Fox, West-Eastern Divan, and Achilleid.* Translated by A. Rogers. London: G. Bell & Sons, 1890.

Grossato, Alessandro. *Elia e al Khidr: L'archetipo del maestro invisible.* Venise: Fondazione Giorgio Cini; Milan: Edizioni Medusa, 2004.

Guénon, René. *Symbolism of the Cross.* London: Luzac, 1975.

Guénon, René. *Traditional Forms and Cosmic Cycles.* Translated by Henry D. Fohr. Hillsdale, NY: Sophia Perennis, 2003.

Hafez, Mounir. *Khidr: Le Bon Génie.* N.p.: Bibliothèque d'Orient et d'Occident, 2008. http://www.moncelon.fr/mounirhafez.htm.

Ḥakīm, Khalifa A. *Fikr-i Iqbāl.* Lahore: Bazm-i Iqbāl, 1957.

Halman, Hugh Talat. *Where the Two Seas Meet: Al-Khidr and Moses—The Qur'anic Story of Al-Khidr and Moses in Sufi Commentaries as a Model for Spiritual Guidance.* Louisville: Fons Vitae, 2013.

Ḥasan, Sultān. *'Irfān al-Qur'ān.* Agra: Maktaba 'Irfān, n.d.

Hasluck, F. W. *Christianity and Islam Under the Sultans.* Oxford: Clarendon Press, 1929.

Heller, Bernhard. "Yusha' bin Nūn." In *The Encyclopaedia of Islam.* Vol. 4, pt. 2. Leiden: E. J. Brill, 1933. 1117.

Hirtenstein, Stephen. "The Mantle of Khadir: Mystery, Myth and Meaning." In *Symbolisme et herméneutique dans la pensée d'Ibn 'Arabī*, edited by Bakri Aladdin, 83–97. Damascus: Institut Français du Proche-Orient, 2007.

Hirtenstein, Stephen & Michael Tiernan, eds. *Muhyiddin Ibn 'Arabi: A Commemorative Volume.* Brisbane: Element, 1993.

Hodgson, Marshall G. S. *The Venture of Islam: Conscience and History in World Civilization.* 3 vols. Chicago: University of Chicago Press, 1974.

al-Hujwirī, 'Alī ibn Uthmān. *The Kashf al-mahjūb: The Oldest Persian Treatise on Sufism by al-Hujwiri.* Translated by Reynold A. Nicholson. Gibb Memorial Lecture Series, no. 17. London: Luzac, 1959.

Ḥusaynī, Hāshim Fayyād. *Ḥayāt al-Khiḍr: 'ard wa-dirāsah.* 1st ed. [Iran]: Dār al-Kitāb al-Islāmī, 2004.

Ibn 'al-'Arabi [Muḥyiddīn]. *The Bezels of Wisdom.* Translated by R. W. J. Austin. New York: Paulist Press, 1980.

Ibn 'Arabī, Muḥyīddīn. *Divine Sayings: 101 Ḥadīth Qudsī. The Mishkāt al-Anwār of Ibn 'Arabī.* Translated by Stephen Hirtenstein and Martin Notcutt. Oxford: Anqa, 2004.

Ibn 'Arabī, Muḥyīddīn. *Al-Futūḥāt al-makkīyah.* 4 vols. Beirut: Dār Ṣādir, 1968.

Ibn 'Arabī, Muḥyiddīn. *La vie merveilleuse de Dhū-l-Nūn l'Égyptien.* Translated by Roger Deladrière. Paris: Sindbad, 1988.

Ibn 'Arabī, Muḥyīddīn. *Sufis of Andalusia: 'Rūḥ al-quds' and 'al-durrah al-fākhirah' of Ibn 'Arabī.* Translated by R. W. J. Austin. London: Allen & Unwin, 1971.

Ibn Ḥajar al-'Asqalānī, Shihāb al-Dīn Aḥmad bin 'Alī. *Al-Zahr al-naḍir fī nabā' al-Khaḍir.* Beirut: Dār al-Kutub al 'Ilmīyah, 1988.

Ibn Kathīr al-Damishqī, Abū al-Fidā' Ismā'īl. *Qiṣaṣ al-anbiyā': Qur'āno ahādith-i saḥiḥa kī roshnī mēṅ*, extracted from *al-Bidāya wa'l nihāya.* Edited and translated by 'Aṭāullah Sājid. Lahore: Dār al-Salām, n. d.

Iqbāl, Muḥammad. *Asrār-i Khudī—The Secrets of the Self.* Translated by R. A. Nicholson. Lahore: Farhan Publishers, 1977.

Iqbāl, Muḥammad. *Bāng-i darā*. Lahore: Shaikh Muḥammad Ashraf, 1924.

Iqbal, Muhammad. *The Development of Metaphysics in Persia: A Contribution to the History of Muslim Philosophy*. Whitefish, MT: Kessinger Publishing, 2005.

Iqbāl, Muḥammad. *Kulliyāt-i Iqbāl: Fārsī*. Lahore: Shaikh Ghulām Alī, 1973.

Iqbāl, Muḥammad. *Kulliyāt-i Iqbāl: Urdu*. Lahore: Shaikh Ghulām Alī, 1984.

Iqbal, Mohammad. *The Reconstruction of Religious Thought in Islam*. New Delhi: Kitāb Bhavan, 1998.

Iqbāl, Muḥammad. *Sarôd-i raftā*. Edited by Ghulām Rasool Mehr & Sādiq Alī Dilāwarī. Lahore: Shaikh Ghulām Alī, 1959.

Jackson, Paul, S.J. *A Jesuit Among Sufis*. Gujarat, India: Gujarat Sahitya Prakash, 2017.

James, William. *The Varieties of Religious Experience: A Study in Human Nature*. London: Longmans, 1905.

Jarvis, James Paul. "Al-Khaḍir: Origins and Interpretations. A Phenomenological Study." M. A. thesis, McGill University, 1993.

Johns, A. H. "Moses in the Qur'ān: Finite and Infinite Dimensions of Prophecy." In *The Charles Strong Lectures, 1972–1984*, edited by Robert B. Crotty, 123–38. Leiden: E. J. Brill, 1987.

Jung, Carl Gustav. *Four Archetypes: Mother, Rebirth, Spirit, Trickster*. Translated by R. F. F. Hull. London: Routledge, 2003.

Jwaideh, Wadie. *The Introductory Chapters of Yāqūt's Mu'jam al-Buldān*. Leiden: E. J. Brill, 1959.

Kamali, A. H. "The Heritage of Islamic Thought." In *Iqbal: Poet-Philosopher of Pakistan*, edited by Hafeez Malik, 211–42. New York: Columbia University Press, 1971.

Kerr, David A. "Muhammad Iqbal's Thoughts on Religion: Reflections in the Spirit of Christian—Muslim Dialogue." *Islamochristiana* 15 (1989): 25–55.

al-Khālidī, Ṣalāḥ. *Ma 'qiṣaṣ al-sābiqīn fī al-Qur'ān*. Vol. 2. Damascus: Dār al-Qalam, 1989.

Khundmiri, S. Alam. "Conception of Time." In *Iqbal: Poet-Philosopher of Pakistan*, edited by Hafeez Malik, 243–63. New York: Columbia University Press, 1971.

Knappert, Jan. *Islamic Legends: Histories of the Heroes, Saints, and Prophets of Islam*. Vol. 1. Leiden: E. J. Brill, 1985.

Kriss, Rudolf and Hubert Kriss-Heinrich. *Volksglaube im Bereich des Islam*. Vol. I. Wiesbaden: Otto Harrassowitz, 1960.

Küry, Ernst. "Monothéisme abrahamique et tradition primordiale." *Etudes Traditionnelles* 84, no. 481 (1983): 102–111.

Laksana, Albertus Bagus. *Muslim and Catholic Pilgrimage Practices: Explorations Through Java*. Burlington: Ashgate, 2014.

Lane, Edward W. *Manners and Customs of the Modern Egyptians*. London: J. M. Dent, 1914.

Latif, Jibril. "The Green Man: What Reading Al-Khiḍr as Trickster Evinces about the Canon." *Ilahiyat Studies* 11, no. 1 (2020): 9–46.

Laude, Patrick. *Divine Play, Sacred Laughter*. New York: Palgrave Macmillan, 2005.

Laude, Patrick. *Louis Massignon: The Vow and the Oath.* London: Matheson Trust, 2011.

Laude, Patrick. *Massignon intérieur.* Lausanne: Editions L'Age d'Homme, 2001.

Leroy, Jules. *Monks and Monasteries of the Near East.* Translated by Peter Collin. Piscataway: Gorgias Press, 2004.

Levi della Vida, Giorgio. "al-Khaḍir." In *Enciclopedia Italiana,* Vol. 20. Roma: Instituto della Enciclopedia Italiana, 1950. 177.

Lindholm, Charles. *The Islamic Middle East: An Historical Anthropology.* Oxford: Blackwell Publishers, 1996.

Lings, Martin. *Symbol and Archetype: A Study of the Meaning of Existence.* Cambridge: Quinta Essentia, 1991.

Lory, Pierre. "Hermès/Idris, prophète et sage dans la tradition islamique." In *Présence d'Hermès Trismégiste*, edited by A. Faivre, 100–109. Paris: Albin Michel, 1988.

Mahmood, Fayyaz. "Iqbal's Attitude Towards God." In *Iqbal as a Thinker*, edited by Raziuddin, et al. Lahore: Shaikh Muḥammad Ashraf, 1973.

Maneri, Sharafuddin. *The Hundred Letters.* Translated and edited by Paul Jackson. New York: Paulist Press, 1980.

al-Marākibī, Maḥmūd. *Musā wa'l-Khiḍr: 'ilmī al-ẓāhir wa'l-bāṭin.* Cairo: Dār al-Ṭibā'a wa'l Nashr wa'l Islāmīyah, 1996.

Martin, Richard. "Structural Analysis and the Qur'an: Newer Approaches to the Study of Islamic Texts." *Journal of the American Academy of Religion, Thematic Issue* 47 (1979): 665–84.

Maruf, Muhammad. "Allama Iqbal on Immortality." *Religious Studies* 18 (1982): 373–78.

Massignon, Louis. "Elie et son rôle transhistorique, *Khadiriya*, en Islam." In *Élie le prophète*, edited by Gustave Bardy, 269–90. Vol. 2 of *Au Carmel dans le Judaïsme et l'Islam*. Bruges: Desclée de Brouwer, 1956.

Massignon, Louis. *La Passion de Husayn Ibn Mansūr Hallāj.* 4 vols. Paris: Gallimard, 2010.

Massignon, Louis. *The Passion of al-Hallaj: Mystic and Martyr of Islam.* Translated by Herbert Mason. 4 vols. Princeton: Princeton University Press, 1982.

McGinn, Bernard. *The Presence of God: A History of Western Christian Mysticism*, vol. 1. *The Foundations of Mysticism.* New York: Crossroad, 1991.

Meri, Josef W. "Re-Appropriating Sacred Space: Medieval Jews and Muslims Seeking Elijah and Al-Khaḍir." *Medieval Encounters* 5, no. 3 (1999): 237–64.

Miller, Robert D., II. *Baal, St. George, and Khidr: A Study of the Historical Geography of the Levant.* University Park: The Pennsylvania State University Press, 2019.

al-Muqaddasī, Shams al-Dīn. *Aḥsān al-taqāsīm fī ma'rifat al-aqālīm.* Leiden: E. J. Brill, 1877.

Murata, Sachiko. *The Tao of Islam.* Albany: State University of New York Press, 1992.

Nasr, Seyyed Hossein. *The Garden of Truth.* New York: Harper One, 2007.

Nasr, Seyyed Hossein. *Islamic Life and Thought.* London: Routledge, 1981.

Nasr, Seyyed Hossein. *Knowledge and the Sacred.* Albany: State University of New York Press, 1989.

Nasr, Seyyed Hossein. *Sufi Essays.* Albany: State University of New York Press, 1991.

al-Nishabūrī, Isḥāq ibn Ibrāhīm. *Qeṣaṣ ol-anbiyā.*' Edited by Ḥabīb Yaghmāyī. Tehran: Intishārāt-e Bungāh-e Tarjumah va Nashr-e Kitāb, 1961.

al-Nawawī, Yaḥyā ibn Ṣaraf. *An-Nawawi's Forty Hadith*. Edited by Ezzedin Ibrahim. Beirut: Holy Koran Publication House, 1979.

Netton, Ian Richard. *Allāh Transcendant: Studies in the Structure and Semiotics of Islamic Philosophy, Theology and Cosmology*. London: Routledge, 1989.

Netton, Ian Richard. "Theophany as Paradox: Ibn 'Arabī's Account of al-Khiḍr in his *Fusūs al-Ḥikam.*" *Journal of the Muhiyiddīn Ibn 'Arabī Society* 11 (1992): 11–22.

Newby, Gordon D. *The Making of the Last Prophet: A Reconstruction of the Earliest Biography of Muhammad*. Columbia: University of South Carolina Press, 1989.

Ng, Su Fang. *Alexander the Great from Britain to Southeast Asia: Peripheral Empires in the Global Resistance*. Oxford: Oxford University Press, 2019.

Ng, Su Fang & Kenneth Hodges. "Saint George, Islam, and Regional Audiences in *Sir Gawain and the Green Knight*." In *Studies in the Age of Chaucer* 32 (2010): 257–94.

Nicholson, Reynold A. Introduction to *Asrār-i Khudī, The Secrets of the Self*, by Muhammad Iqbal, vii to xxxi. Translated by Reynold A. Nicholson. Lahore: Farhan Publishers, 1977.

Nicholson, Reynold A. *The Mystics of Islam*. London: Arkana-Penguin Books, 1989.

Nicholson, Reynold A. *Studies in Islamic Mysticism*. Cambridge: The University Press, 1921.

Noegel, Scott B. and Brannon M. Wheeler. *The A to Z of Prophets in Islam and Judaism*. Lanham, MD: Scarecrow Press, 2002.

Nu'aysah, Haydar. *Al-Khiḍr*. Damascus: Dār al-Dhulfiqār, 2006.

Nursi, Bediuzzaman Said. *Letters*. Istanbul: Sözler Publications, 2001.

Obermann, Julian. "Two Elijah Stories in Judeo-Arabic Transmission." *Hebrew Union College Annual* 23 (1950–1951): 387–404.

Omar, Irfan A. "Khiḍr in the Islamic Tradition." *The Muslim World* 83 (July–October 1993): 279–94.

Papas, Alexandre. "Soufisme, pouvoir et saintete en Asie central: Le cas des Khwajas de Kashgarie (XVIe-XVIIIe siecles)." *Studia Islamica* 100/101 (2005): 161–82.

Pigeaud, Theodore G. Th. *Literature of Java*. 3 vols. Dordrecht, Netherlands: Springer, 1970.

Polignac, François de. "Une 'dualité' du pouvoir? Empire terrestre et inspiration divine dans la légende arabe d'Alexandre et de Khidr." In *Representing Power in Ancient Inner Asia: Legitimacy, Transmission, and the Sacred*, edited by Isabelle Charleux, et al., 343–56. Bellingham: Western Washington University, 2010.

Pringle, Denys. *The Churches of the Crusader Kingdom of Jerusalem: A Corpus*. Vol. 2. Cambridge: Cambridge University Press, 1998.

Pritchett, Frances W., ed. and trans. *The Romance Tradition in Urdu: Adventures from the Dāstān of Amīr Ḥamzah*. New York: Columbia University Press, 1991.

al-Qārī al-Harawī, 'Alī bin Sulṭān Muḥammad. *Al-Ḥadhar fī 'amr al-Khaḍir*. Damascus: Dār al-Qalam, 1991.

al-Qāshānī, 'Abd al-Razzāq. *A Glossary of Sufi Technical Terms*. Translated by Nabil Safwat. London: The Octagon Press, 1991.

Quṭb, Sayyid. *In the Shade of the Qur'an, Fī Ẓilāl al-Qur'ān*. Translated by Adil Salahi. Vol. 11. London: The Islamic Foundation, 2007.

Rahman, Fazlur. "Muhammad Iqbāl and Atatürk's Reforms." *Journal of Near Eastern Studies* 43, no. 2 (1984): 157–62.

Raḥmān, Ḥifzur. *Qiṣaṣ al-Qur'ān*. Delhi: Nadwatul Musannifīn, 1975.

Ramaḍān Yūsuf, Muḥammad Khayr. *Al-Khiḍr baynā al-wāqi' wa'l-tahwīl*. Damascus: Dār al-Musḥaf, 1984.

Renard, John. *All the King's Falcons: Rumi on Prophets and Revelation*. Albany: State University of New York Press, 1994.

Renard, John. *Friends of God: Islamic Images of Piety, Commitment, and Servanthood*. Berkeley: University of California Press, 2008.

Renard, John. "Khaḍir/Khiḍr." In *Encyclopaedia of the Qur'ān*, edited by Jane Dammen McAuliffe. Washington, DC: Georgetown University. http://dx.doi.org/10.1163/1875-3922_q3_EQSIM_00248.

Renard, John. *Windows on the House of Islam: Muslims Sources on Spirituality and Religious Life*. Berkeley: University of California Press, 1998.

Reynolds, Gabriel Said. *The Qur'ān and the Bible: Text and Commentary*. New Haven: Yale University Press, 2018.

Ries, Julien. "Immortality." Translated by David M. Weeks. In *The Encyclopedia of Religion*, edited by Mircea Eliade. Vol. 7. New York: McMillan Publishing Company, 1987. 123–45.

Rios, M. Fathor. *Menyimak Kisah Dan Hikmah Kehidupan Nabi Khidir.* Jakarta: Zaman, 2015.

Roberts, Nancy N. "A Parable of Blessing: The Significance and Message of the Quranic Account of 'The Companion of the Cave.'" *The Muslim World* 83, nos. 3–4 (1993): 295–317.

Rodwell, J. M. *The Koran*. London: J. M. Dent Everyman, 1994.

Rūmī, Jalāl al-Dīn. "A Great Wagon." In *Essential Rumi*, translated by Coleman Barks, 35–37. New York: HarperOne, 2004.

Rūmī, Jalāl al-Dīn. *Discourses of Rūmī [Fīhi mā fīhi]*. Translated by A. J. Arberry. New York: Samuel Weiser, 1972.

Rūmī, Jalāl al-Dīn. *Mathnavī-e ma'navī*. Book 1. Tehran: Rozaneh Publishing, 1999.

Sale, George. *The Koran*. London: William Tegg, 1961.

Sands, Kristin Zahra. *Ṣūfī Commentaries on the Qur'ān in Classical Islam*. Abingdon: Routledge, 2006.

Schimmel, Annemarie. *And Muhammad is His Messenger: The Veneration of the Prophet in Islamic Piety*. Chapel Hill: The University of North Carolina Press, 1985.

Schimmel, Annemarie *Classical Urdu Literature from the Beginning to Iqbāl*. Wiesbaden: Harrassowitz, 1975.

Schimmel, Annemarie. *Deciphering the Signs of God: A Phenomenological Approach to Islam*. Albany: State University of New York Press, 1994.

Schimmel, Annemarie. *Gabriel's Wing: A Study into the Religious Ideas of Sir Muhammad Iqbal*. Leiden: E. J. Brill, 1963.

Schimmel, Annemarie. *Mystical Dimensions of Islam*. Chapel Hill: The University of North Carolina Press, 1975.

Schimmel, Annemarie. *The Triumphal Sun: A Study of the Works of Jalāloddin Rumi*. Albany: State University of New York Press, 1993.

Schwarzbaum, Haim. *Biblical and Extra-Biblical Legends in Islamic Folk-Literature*. Waldorf-Hessen: Verlag fur Orientkunde, 1982.

Shafī‘, Muḥammad. *Ma‘ārif al-Qur’ān*. Vol. 5. Karachi: Dār al-Ma‘ārif, 1978.

Shah, Idries. *The Sufis*. New York: Anchor Books, 1990.

Shallan, Mohammed. "Some Parallels Between Sufi Practices and the Path of Individuation." In *Sufism, Islam and Jungian Psychology*, edited by J. Marvin Spiegelman, et al., 79–103. Scottsdale: New Falcon Publications, 1991.

Sharif, M. M. *About Iqbal and His Thought*. Lahore: Institute of Islamic Culture, 1964.

al-Shawkānī, Muḥammad ibn ‘Alī. *Fatḥ al-qadīr*. Vol. 3. Riyādh: Dār ‘Ālam al-Kutub, 2003.

Sidersky, David *Les Origines des Legends Musulmanes dans le Coran et dans les vies des Prophetes*. Paris: P. Geuthner, 1933.

Singh, David Emmanuel. "Qur’ānic Moses and his Mysterious Companion: Developmental Revelation as an Approach to Christian Discourse with Muslims?" *Transformation* 22, no. 4 (2005): 210–24.

Smith, William. *A New Classical Dictionary of Greek and Roman Biography, Mythology and Geography*. New York: Harper & Brothers, 1878.

Soeratno, Siti Chamamah. "Khidlir est Proche, Dieu est Loin." *Archipel* 15 (1978): 85–94.

Stoddart, William. *Sufism: The Mystical Doctrines and Methods of Islam*. New York: Paragon House, 1985.

Subhan, John A. *Sufism, Its Saints and Shrines: An Introduction to the Study of Sufism with Special Reference to India and Pakistan*. Lucknow: Lucknow Publishing House, 1960.

al-Ṭabarī, Abū Ja‘far Muḥammad ibn Jarīr. *The History of al-Ṭabarī (Ta’rīkh al-rusul wa’l mulūk)* vol. 3 *The Children of Israel*, trans. & annotated by William M. Brinner. Albany: State University of New York Press, 1991.

Thackston, Wheeler M. "The Khidr Legend in the Islamic Tradition." A. B. thesis, Princeton University 1967.

Thackston, Wheeler M., trans. *The Tales of the Prophets of al-Kisā’ī*. Boston: Twayne Publishers, 1978.

al-Tha‘labī, Abū Iṣḥāq Aḥmad ibn Muḥammad. *Qiṣaṣ al-‘anbiyā’ al-musammā ‘Arā’is al-majālis*. Beirut: al-Matba‘ah al-Thaqāfīyah, n.d.

Toorawa, Shawkat. "The Modern Literary (After)Lives of al-Khiḍr." *Journal of Qur’anic Studies* 16 (2014): 174–95.

Trimingham, J. Spencer. *The Sufi Orders in Islam*. New York: Oxford University Press, 1998.

Ullmann, M. "al-Iksīr." In *The Encyclopaedia of Islam*. Vol 3. Leiden: E.J. Brill, 1971.

Upton, Charles. *Doorkeeper of the Heart: Versions of Rabi‘a*. Putney, VT: Threshold Books, 1988.

Vacca, Virginia. "Social and Political Aspects of Egyptian and Yamani Sufism." *Journal of the Pakistan Historical Society* 8 (October 1960): 233–59.

Van Bladel, Kevin. "The *Alexander Legend* in the Qur'ān 18:83–102." In *The Qur'ān and its Historical Context*, edited by Gabriel Said Reynolds, 175–203. London: Routledge, 2008.

Vollers, K. "Chidher." *Archiv für Religionswissenschaft* 12 (1909): 234–50.

Walī Allāh, Shāh. *A Mystical Interpretation of Prophetic Tales by an Indian Muslim: Shāh Walī Allāh's Ta'wīl al-Aḥādīth. Translated by J. M. S. Baljon. Leiden*: E. J. Brill, 1973.

Wells, Raymond. *Mother Teresa in Her Own Words.* N.p.: Amazon Digital Services LLC—KDP Print US, 2021.

Wensinck, Arent Jan. "al-Khaḍir." *The Encyclopaedia of Islam*. New ed. Vol. 4. Leiden: E.J. Brill, 1973. 902–5.

Wheeler, Brannon M. "Moses." In *Blackwell Companion to the Qur'ān*, edited by Andrew Rippin, 248–65. Oxford: Blackwell, 2006.

Wheeler, Brannon M. *Moses in the Quran and Islamic Exegesis*. Abingdon: Routledge, 2002.

Wolper, Ethel Sara. *Cities and Saints: Sufism and the Transformation of Urban Space in Medieval Anatolia.* University Park: The Pennsylvania State University Press, 2003.

Wolper, Ethel Sara. "Khidr and the Changing Frontiers of the Medieval World." *Medieval Encounters* 17, nos. 1–2 (2011): 120–46.

Wolper, Ethel Sara. "Khiḍr, Elwan Çelebi and the Conversion of the Sacred Sanctuaries in Anatolia." *The Muslim World* 90 (Fall 2000): 309–22.

Wolper, Ethel Sara. "Khiḍr and the Politics of Place: Creating Landscapes of Continuity." In *Muslims and Others in Sacred Space,* edited by Margaret Cormack, 147–63. New York: Oxford University Press, 2013.

Yāqūt al-Ḥamawī, Shihāb al-Dīn Abī 'Abdullāh. *Mu'jam al-buldān*. Vol. 1. Beirut: Dār al-Kutub al-'Ilmīyah, 1990.

Yusuf, Hamza. "Buddha in the Qur'an?" In *Common Ground between Islam & Buddhism*, edited by Reza Shah-Kazemi, 110–13. Louisville: Fons Vitae, 2010.

Yūsuf 'Alī, 'Abdullah. *The Holy Qur'ān: Text, Translation and Commentary*. 2 vols. Lahore: Shaikh Muhammad Ashraf, n.d.

Yūsuf 'Alī, 'Abdullah. *The Meaning of the Holy Qur'ān*. Brentwood, MD: Amana Corporation, 1992.

al-Zamakhsharī, Abu'l Qāsim Maḥmūd bin 'Umar. *Al-Kashshāf 'an ḥaqā'iq ghwāmiḍ al-tanzīl wa 'uyūn al-aqāwīl fī wujūh al-ta'wīl.* Beirut: Dār al-Kutub al-'Ilmīyah, 1995.

Zart, Gustav. *Chidher in Sage und Dichtung*. Hamburg: Verlagsanstalt und Druckerei Aktien-Gesellschaft, 1897.

al-Zuhaylī, Wahbah. *Tafsīr al-munīr.* Vols. 15 & 16. Beirut: Dār al-Fikr al-Mu'āsir, 1991.

Index

abdāl, 60, 74 n18
'Abd al-Muqtadar, Ibrāhīm ibn Fathī, 36
Ahmad, Irfan, 95
Ahmed, Shahab, 3–4, 13n4, 14n9, 80, 117
al-'Asqalānī, Ibn Ḥajar, 27, 41
Albayrak, Ismail, 31n53
Alexander the Great, 92, 106
'Aṭṭār, Farīd al-Dīn, 48, 95
awliyā' (or saint/saints), 5, 11, 16, 23, 41, 45, 59–60, 70, 72, 80, 85–86
Ayoub, Mahmoud, 86
al-Baghdādī (Khāzin), 'Alī Ibn Muḥammad, 19, 35

Bashir, Shahzad, 17
bāṭin (esoteric), 1, 36, 47, 50n10, 73, 119
    See also esoteric and exoteric

Corbin, Henry, 64, 68–69

Dāstān, 65–66, 84
divine law, 61, 63

esoteric and exoteric, 17, 39, 44–45, 50n10, 63, 73, 83, 119

faith, 2, 4–5, 12, 36, 48–49, 60–63, 66, 71, 75n36, 82, 118–21
    expressions of, 5, 60
    mystical dimension of, 1, 10, 57, 63
    pillars of, 36, 63
    rituals of, 62
    service's connection to, 120–21
fatā,' 44
fish, symbol of. *See* Khiḍr, symbolism of
folklore, 20–21, 26, 80–82
    South and Southeast Asian, 91–93
    West Asian (Middle Eastern), 86–91
Franke, Patrick, 21, 51n17, 71–72

George, Saint, 4, 22–24, 86–91

al-Ghazālī, Abū Ḥāmid Muḥammad, 62, 70, 84–85

Gilgamesh
    character of, 25–26, 32n57, 105, 107–8
    epic of, 10, 24–25, 104–5, 107
Goethe, 103, 108

the Green One, 1–2, 17, 43, 82, 86

See also Khiḍr, symbolism of

Guénon, René, 26, 47
ḥadīth, 2, 4–5, 7–8, 12, 20, 22, 35–36, 39, 44, 47, 57, 60, 82, 120
See also Khiḍr story, sources of the

Hermes, 26, 83
Hodgson, Marshall, 13n4, 80, 117
humility, 36, 48, 61–63

Ibn Adham, Ibrāhīm, 18
Ibn 'Arabī (or Ibn al-'Arabi), Muḥyiddīn, 38, 41, 59–60, 66, 69–71
Ibn Kathīr al-Damishqī, Abū al-Fidā' Ismā'īl, 16, 47
Idrīs (or Enoch), 26, 60, 93, 96n9
ijtihād (independent reasoning, as in exegesis), 5
ilhām (inspiration), 37, 39, 49
illumination, spiritual (inward), 5
metaphorical, 19
Ilyās (or Elijah):
meeting with Khiḍr, 45, 83
relationship to Khiḍr, 17, 22–24, 26, 28n11, 45–47, 60, 83–87, 91, 96n9, 103
interpretation, 10, 19, 23, 73
allegorical, 19, 22, 42, 44, 69, 73
literal, 19, 79
mystical, 5, 19
Iqbāl, Muḥammad (or Muhammad Iqbal), 104–113, 114n8, 116nn50, 59, 120
Islamicate, 3, 13n4, 19–22, 57, 80, 89, 95, 103
Islamic, and, 80–81

Jerusalem, 61, 84, 88, 99n62
Jesus (or 'Īsā), 16, 24, 31n39, 46, 60, 61, 84, 96n9, 109, 112, 118–19
jihād (striving), 45, 62
Joshua (Yūsha' bin Nūn), 8, 25–26, 35, 44–45
meaning of name, 44
Moses' attendant (*fatā'*), as, 35, 44
Jung, Carl G., 54n89, 77n78, 120

Kerr, David, 110

al-Khālidī, Ṣalāḥ al- 47, 51n22

Khiḍr, appearances of, 83, 87–95
Khiḍr
agency, as having, 23
clothing, 18, 43, 53n57, 91
disciples of, 59, 64–68, 104
immortality (*see* Khiḍr, immortality of)
lineage, 24, 27
location, 19 (*see also* Khiḍr, dwelling places of)
name (*see* Khiḍr, names of)
obedience of, 16, 61, 109
roles (*see* Khiḍr, roles of)
symbolism (*see* Khiḍr, symbolism of)
Khiḍr, immortality of, 22, 24, 46–50, 59, 65, 91, 104
against the, 47–48
See also Khiḍr, symbolism of
Khiḍr in literature, 2, 19
Khiḍr, names of:
Abu'l Abbās, 17, 19, 27
Khwājā Khizr, 17, 20, 84, 91
origin, 24
other names, 17, 19–20, 27, 91
spellings, 2, 28n1
Khiḍr, popular views of, 2, 4, 11, 17–24, 41, 50, 59, 73, 79–95, 103, 118–20
Khiḍr, roles of, 17, 22–23, 36
angel, 37
cup-bearer (*sāqi*), 72
eschatological, 46, 61, 88
healer, 41, 49, 89, 120
guide, 36, 80, 83–84, 91, 104, 106, 112–13, 120
illuminator of souls, 73

initiator, spiritual, 59–63, 73, 93
interpreter, 16–17
mediator, 40
prophet (*nabī*), 23, 36, 39, 41–42, 47, 54n81, 59, 73, 79, 103
saint (*walī*), 36, 41–42, 45, 59–60, 79, 85, 88, 92, 103, 118
saint, shared, 11
savior figure, 27
servant of God, 2, 38, 60–61, 103
teacher of Moses, 36, 39
wanderer, 17, 23, 82, 84, 106
Khiḍr, symbolism of
fish and water, 8, 44–45
green, 43–44, 53n51, 104
immortality, 45–50, 82–58, 104, 106
light, 57
mercy (*see raḥmah*)
renewal, 104–5
travel, 45–46
Khiḍr story, sources of the, 2, 19–27
Alexander Romance, 10, 20, 24–25
Christian parallels, 24–25
Epic of Gilgamesh (*see* Gilgamesh)
ḥadīth about Khiḍr, 4–5, 7–10, 15, 18–19, 23, 35, 43, 46
hagiographic literature (*Qiṣaṣ al-ʻanbiyāʼ*), 3, 13n2, 19, 22, 27, 57
Jewish parallels, 24–25
multiple traditions, 18, 24
other legends, 3, 13n5, 20–27, 66
Qur'ān, Khiḍr in the, 1–2, 4–8, 23, 36–39, 64
Sufi biographies, 19
See also tradition(s)
Khiḍr, transcendence of, 64–65, 83, 88–90, 118
khirqah, 59, 60
Khizr-i rāh (poem), 105–6, 113
khudī (self-hood), 12, 107–10
Khiḍr as helping to achieve, 108–9
knowledge, 17, 46
difference between Moses' and Khiḍr's, 36–42, 52n30, 57–58, 78n89, 83, 119
divine, Khiḍr as repository of, 39–41, 73; limitations, 10, 16; relationship between human and divine, 9, 49; seeking, 35; self, 58, 61; spiritual, 8, 39, 44 64; worldly, 39
divine (*ma'rifah*), 9, 16–17, 36, 38, 40–42, 46, 48–50, 51n27, 64, 66, 68, 70, 73, 104, 118 (*see also ma'rifah*)
esoteric, 17, 39, 44–45, 50n10, 63, 73, 83, 119
exoteric, 17, 39, 44–45, 50n10, 63, 83, 119
forms of, 1
given by God, 16, 17, 64, 104
individuals who possess, 16

lamp, mystical (inner), 69–70, 76n63
See also light
Latif, Jabril, 29n24, 80
Laude, Patrick, 61, 93–94
light:
allegory, as, 69
divine (*al-Nūr*), 41, 68–69, 73
Khiḍr, reflecting divine, 73
relationship to knowledge, 68, 70
spiritual, 57, 68–70, 71, 73
Lindholm, Charles, 79–80

majma' al-baḥrayn, 15, 26, 43, 45, 83
Maneri, Sharafuddin, 66–67, 72

al-Marākibī, Maḥmūd, 36

ma'rifah, 9, 16–17, 36, 38, 40–42, 46, 48–50, 51n27, 64, 66, 68, 70, 73, 104, 118
Massignon, Louis, 61

McGinn, Bernard, 57
Metatron, 93–94
Miller, Robert D., II, 86–87
mishkāt, 69
Moses:
  Khiḍr, relationship to, 17, 24, 37–41, 48–49, 116n50, 119
  knowledge (*see* knowledge)
  lawgiver, 9, 36, 37, 48
  meeting Khiḍr, 8–10, 15, 35–26, 44–45, 48, 83
  messenger (*rasūl*), as, 11, 38–39, 41–42
  prophet (*nabī*) as, 11, 38–39, 42, 104
  Qur'an, in, 6
  role, 37
Muḥammad, Prophet, 40, 63, 65, 69, 79, 85, 117, 119
mysticism, 4, 57, 95, 119–20

Nasr, Seyyed Hossein, 26, 58, 62

al-Nawawī, Abū Zakariyyā, 19, 46

Nicholson, Reynold, 37, 42–43
Noah, 38, 119
nubūwwah (prophethood), 38, 60
  See also prophets
Nursi, Said, 46, 72

Obermann, Julian, 24, 31n50, 32n53

patience, 9–10, 48, 97n30
pilgrimage (*ḥajj*), 46
prophets, 16, 23–24, 27, 31n39, 36–42, 48, 65, 68, 79, 84, 89, 94, 104, 118–19
  immortal, 24, 47, 60
  role of, 23–24, 40, 79
  stories of, 2
providence, 36, 62, 84–85

qalb (heart, spiritual center), 69, 73

Qur'ān, 1–8, 12, 15–27, 37–40, 46, 48, 58, 60, 82–83, 93–94, 118, 120
  commentaries (and commentators) on the, 2, 10, 13n2, 17 27, 36, 40, 41, 49, 60, 69
  Khiḍr in the (*see* Khiḍr story, sources of the)

al-Qurtubī, Abū 'Abdullah, 49

Qutb, Sayyid, 36, 51n1

raḥmah, 37–42
  Khiḍr as symbol of, 36, 38, 40–41, 60, 73
  knowledge's relationship to, 41, 49
  prophets, relationship to, 37–38, 40, 60
Renard, John, 42, 44
revelation, 16–17, 36, 38–39
Rūmī, Jalāl al-Dīn, 67–68, 85, 95, 103–4, 108, 110, 113, 116n59, 119

sacred space, creation of, 71–72
saints. *See awliyā'*

al-Sarrāj, Abū Nasr, 42

Satan, 8, 40, 44
Schimmel, Annemarie, 59
Schwarzbaum, Haim, 25
Sergius, Saint, 89–90
service, 60, 73, 120–21

al-Shādhilī, Abu'l Ḥasan 'Alī, 47

sharī'ah, 3, 5, 17, 36, 41, 62–63, 75n36, 78n89, 79, 104, 119
shaykh (spiritual teacher), 59, 65–67, 112, 120
spiritual illumination, 57
spiritual path (*ṭarīqah*), 16, 18, 62, 72, 103
  Sufism, in, 61–65, 71–72, 103

See also ṭarīqah
Sufism (*taṣawwuf*), 2, 11, 21, 41–42, 57–63, 68, 73, 83, 85, 103, 105, 109–12, 118–19
encountering Khiḍr in, 71–72, 118
goal of, 58, 62
Khiḍr as guide in, 18, 60, 63–65, 103
masters in, 67–68
Suhrawardī, Shihābuddīn, 68–69

al-Ṭabarī, Abū Ja'far Muḥammad Ibn Jarīr, 19, 23, 57

tafsīr literature, 2, 19, 49, 57, 85, 95
ṭarīqah, 16, 59, 63, 72, 73, 119

ta'wīl, 5
tradition(s)
Christian, 13n5, 27, 90–91
folk, 2, 11–12, 13n5, 18–20, 27, 28n11, 50, 57, 79–95
Hindu, 91
Islamic, 15, 17, 24, 50
Islamicate, 3, 17, 19–20, 50, 80–81, 103, 117
Jewish, 13n5, 27, 93–95
Persian, 25
pre-Islamic, 2, 13n2, 19–21, 24–25, 27, 32n53, 83, 85, 117
'ubūdiyyah, 60–62

Uwaysī Sufi order, 29n22, 59, 65, 74n12, 118

waḥy, 16, 37, 39
water of life, 59, 81, 82, 85, 87, 91, 104
Wensinck, Arent Jan, 24, 31n50
Wheeler, Brannon, 24–25, 27, 32n53
wilāyah (or *walāyah*) (sainthood), 58–60
Wolper, Ethel Sara, 87, 89–91
world:
images, of (*'ālam al-amthāl*), 18
material (*'ālam al-khalq*), 18, 43, 53n69
spiritual (*'ālam al-rūḥ*), 18, 53n69, 60

Yūsuf Alī, Abdullah, 48
ẓāhir (exoteric), 1, 36, 50n10, 119

al-Zamakhsharī, Abu'l Qāsim Maḥmūd bin 'Umar, 49
al-Zuhaylī, Wahbah, 49

About the Author

Irfan A. Omar is associate professor of theology at Marquette University in Milwaukee where he teaches courses in peace studies, Islamic theology, and interfaith dialogue. His research areas include Sufism and South Asian studies. He is also an affiliated faculty member with the Center for South Asia at the University of Wisconsin–Madison. Previously he was a visiting Fulbright lecturer at Muhammadiyah University in Malang, Indonesia. He is the author of *El-Khaḍir/El-Khiḍr: Le Prophète-Sage dans la tradition Musulmane* (2021). He has edited several volumes including *Interfaith Engagement in Milwaukee: A Brief History of Christian—Muslim Dialogue* (2020, co-edited with Kaitlyn C. Daly), *Peacemaking and the Challenge of Violence in World Religions* (2015, co-edited with Michael Duffey), *The Judeo-Christian-Islamic Heritage: Philosophical and Theological Perspectives* (2012, co-edited with Richard C. Taylor), and *A Christian View of Islam: Essays on Dialogue by Thomas F. Michel, S.J.* (2010). He currently serves on the editorial/advisory boards of the *Journal of Ecumenical Studies*, the *Journal of Race, Ethnicity, and Religion*, and *İslāmī Araştirmalar/Journal of Islamic Research*. From 2010 to 2014 he served on the steering committee of the Ethics Section of the American Academy of Religion (AAR).

www.ingramcontent.com/pod-product-compliance
Lightning Source LLC
Chambersburg PA
CBHW020126010526
44115CB00008B/985